# A House Divided

Slavery and
Emancipation
in Delaware
*1638–1865*

## Patience Essah

UNIVERSITY PRESS OF VIRGINIA

Charlottesville and London

T

THE UNIVERSITY PRESS OF VIRGINIA
Copyright © 1996 by the Rector and Visitors
of the University of Virginia

*First published 1996*

♾ The paper used in this publication meets the minimum
requirements of the American National Standard for
Information Sciences—Permanence of Paper for Printed
Library Materials, ANSI Z39.48-1984.

Library of Congress Cataloging-in-Publication Data
Essah, Patience.
    A house divided : slavery and emancipation in Delaware, 1638–1865
/ Patience Essah.
        p.   cm.—(Carter G. Woodson Institute series in Black
studies)
    Includes index.
    ISBN 0-8139-1681-X (cloth : alk. paper)
    1. Slaves—Emancipation—Delaware.   2. Slavery—Delaware—History.
3. United States.   Constitution.   13th Amendment.   4. Delaware—
Constitutional law—Amendments—Ratification.   I. Title.
II. Series.
E445.D3E87   1996
975.1'00496—dc20                                        96-15045
                                                            CIP

Printed in the United States of America

*Dedicated to the memory of my teacher, editor, and friend*
ARMSTEAD L. ROBINSON

# Contents

# Tables

# Foreword

IN A PROVOCATIVE analysis of emancipation in Delaware, Patience Essah peels away layers of mystery surrounding one of the most enigmatic paradoxes in the history of New World slavery: why did tiny Delaware wait until 1901 (longer than any of the other nonseceded states) formally to abolish an institution known to be economically moribund decades before the American Revolution? To unravel this paradox Essah took the bold step of examining the Delaware slavery experience whole, that is, through a multidimensional analysis of slavery from its early colonial origins in the 1630s through 1901, when Delaware finally signaled, by an act of its legislature, formal acquiescence in the Thirteenth Amendment to the Constitution. Essah insightfully locates the site where cultural contestation and political interest combined to frustrate both antebellum reform and also Civil War–era constitutionalism. And in so doing, Patience Essah breaks important new ground in the study of the rise and the demise of racial slavery.

Perhaps no set of issues bear more centrally on the Afro-American experience than questions about how slavery arose, how it died, and how cultural domination begun during slavery shaped the contours of postslavery race relations. Because the Essah study covers such an extensive time period, it represents an exhaustively researched and thoughtfully analyzed microcosm of Afro-American experience. Focusing on the coming of freedom in Delaware enables Essah to shed important new light on the history of slavery, race, and racialism in America. Tiny Delaware's experience with emancipation has much to tell us.

Since the publication in 1979 of Leon Litwack's Pulitzer Prize winner *Been in the Storm So Long: The Aftermath of Slavery,* emancipation has remained one of the most productive areas of scholarship in American history. At the heart of this scholarly project lie two basic facts: slavery existed throughout the New World, from Chile to Canada; and the distinctive aftermaths of slavery framed the social and cultural discourse on race throughout the New World. Contestation over matters of race and the stubborn persistence of racialized cultural domination represent the varied trajectories of failed experiences with slave emancipation in various New World societies.

Delaware occupies a paradoxical position, seemingly outside the two primary patterns of New World emancipation. New World slavery either died suddenly, by the application of armed force, or it ebbed away after losing economic viability. Thus, the revolution in Haiti led to the first New World emancipation when sugar slavery imploded as a consequence of mass violence. Slavery in the Spanish colonies suffered an analogous fate; the Bolívarian revolutions precipitated the rapid demise of slavery in most of central and South America. In Brazil, Canada, and the northern United States, slavery died more peacefully as a consequence of legislative initiatives recognizing that slavery contradicted the spirit of the Enlightenment at the same time that it no longer paid its way. Independent state action in the New England and Middle Atlantic states brought slavery to an end in the wake of the American Revolution. However, in the more southern states, the slaveholders clung tenaciously to their beloved "peculiar institution" until defeat in the American Civil War imposed general emancipation. All this while Delaware meandered along its own path.

In many ways Delaware is the great paradox, the missing link in the history of American slavery and American freedom. How and why tiny Delaware resisted the wave of northern state-mandated abolition after the American Revolution, abstained from state secession during the secession crisis, resisted the movement toward border state abolition during the Civil War, and stubbornly opposed ratification of the Thirteenth Amendment until 1901, these enigmas form the primary subjects of a study which presents a clear and convincing analytic narration of the Delaware experience with slavery and freedom.

Economic logic suggests that the fate of Delaware slavery should have followed the pattern established in its neighbors, Pennsylvania and New Jersey, both of which moved toward gradual emancipation when the proportion of slaves freed by individual slaveholders exceeded 25 percent of the black population. Delaware reached this tipping point by 1790, and the state debated abolition on an annual basis until the eve of the American Civil War. But rather than deciding to abolish a moribund institution, Delaware remained stalemated for decades. State statutes mandating abolition repeatedly failed because of tie votes in one or both house of the legislature. Even though by 1860 more than 90 percent of the black population was free, Delaware could not find the political will to resolve its emancipation stalemate.

Why did Delaware stand outside the primary streams of New World emancipation? Essah unravels the Delaware enigma to reveal that the state remained divided against itself because the political culture, whose origins lay in colonial settlement patterns, lacked the moral dynamism to resolve the prolonged emancipation stalemate. In order to make this case, Essah breaks new ground in emancipation studies; she treats Delaware slavery from its earliest inception to its final demise. She shows that Delaware slavery developed along lines quite similar to those of Virginia and Maryland with a crucial distinction; tiny Delaware had neither a western frontier nor a major metropolis. Like its Chesapeake neighbors, Delaware slavery flourished in concert with the fortunes of tobacco. But when Chesapeake tobacco entered its post–1750 decline, Delaware's diminutive size robbed it of the options available to its neighbors. Virginia slavery expanded toward its piedmont, while prosperity in Maryland depended increasingly on the port of Baltimore. Locked in a situation where it could neither grow nor develop, the Delaware economy stagnated. And slavery became less and less profitable in the aftermath of the American Revolution.

Why did the state fail to enact gradual abolition, adopted by its Delaware River valley neighbors Pennsylvania and New Jersey? Had slavery become such a marginal institution that its fate seemed too insignificant to warrant attention? Did Delaware deal with this moribund institution by simply ignoring it? Or did contestation over abolition of legal slavery provide an instrumental metaphor in highly partisan debates about the racial boundaries of Delaware citizenship?

Essah approaches this subject on two levels; she traces changes over time in slavery and race relations while carefully analyzing the history of legislative debate on abolition. She finds a paradox, an enormous gulf separating private actions by slaveholders shedding the unprofitable burdens of slavery by manumitting their slaves side by side with obstinate resistance in the legislature to acknowledging by statute what had already occurred in practice. The legislature enacted a number of statutes to facilitate and regulate manumission. But it could not summon the will to mandate final abolition. Those arguing against final abolition expressed fears that this step might inadvertently alter the delicate balance of political power in the state by granting the black 20 percent of the population a moral claim to the franchise. What Essah has found, at the base of the Delaware paradox, is a political discourse stalemated by instrumental appeals to racialism.

Essah grounds her explanation for this stalemate in the bipolar cultural heritage of the state. Delaware is a hybrid of oppositional influences from Pennsylvania and Maryland. The influence of Quaker and abolitionist Pennsylvania was felt most strongly in the northernmost of Delaware's three counties, while the influence of proslavery Maryland manifested itself most in the southernmost county. Because Delaware's central county received virtually equal influence from both directions, the balance of political power in the state as a whole remained so precarious that elections often turned on margins of fewer than one hundred votes. Slaveholders could not breathe life into a moribund institution, but neither could the Quaker abolitionists produce a legislative majority for abolishing slavery. Abolition soon became the definitive marker of political differentiation in antebellum Delaware due to fears in southern Delaware that freed blacks would vote with the Quaker north. Thus did racialist appeals to preserve Delaware as a white man's country become the staple of those who opposed abolition. Precisely because abolition became such an important issue to rival political parties, retaining the status quo through annual stalemates became the default option. Much as Sisyphus labored mightily but in vain to escape his torture, so too did Delaware politicians endlessly debate the wisdom and expediency of abolition without ever resolving their differences.

This stalemate persisted well past the end of the Civil War. In the spring of 1862, Lincoln offered federal compensation to slaveholders in nonseceded border slave states in exchange for final abolition. Partisan interest in preserving the balance of power placed many Delaware slaveholders in a difficult position; they fought against their own Democratic party over the expediency of accepting Lincoln's final offer of compensated emancipation. Democratic politicians enmeshed in the ideology that legal slavery made Delaware a white man's country led the successful fight to reject an offer that many of the few remaining slaveholders desperately wanted to accept. Seven decades of futile debate over abolishing a moribund institution had so reified popular belief that the Republicans could not carry the day against deeply mythologized racial concepts of citizenship. Delaware's wartime debate over emancipation bears a striking resemblance to the discourse three decades later between elite conservatives and the Populists over Jim Crow laws. This was why it was not until 1901, when Republicans gained control of Delaware politics, that the legislature finally found the votes to ratify a thirteenth amendment which had earlier abolished slavery by federal action thirty-six years earlier.

Patience Essah has produced what will surely be the standard monograph on tiny Delaware's struggle to grapple with the intertwined American paradoxes of slavery, freedom, and racialism. Unraveling this tangled skein enables Essah to present the Delaware experience in full historical context. Hers is a study which merits wide reading. It frames the discourse on racialism by showing the limits of economic forces in the demise of a social institution, suggesting that strong cultural beliefs may well be more decisive than the fabled profit motive. The Delaware emancipation stalemate also suggests the narrowness of the time band available during windows of cultural change. The failure to consummate cultural change at an opportune moment may leave a stubborn residue of unresolved contradictions (slavery existing simultaneously with 90 percent voluntary emancipation) that persists until the next window of change comes open. By showing us how and why Delaware drew so near to the brink of abolition without cresting it, the Essah book facilitates discourse on the cultural limits on social reform. Thus, this book not only provides authentic context for the Delaware experience with emancipation, but it locates as well the canonical source of cultural silence about persistent American racialism.

ARMSTEAD L. ROBINSON

# Acknowledgments

THE DEBTS I have incurred in the preparation of this book are many. I take this opportunity to thank my colleagues Tawiah Ankumah, Michael Conniff, and Daniel Szechi for their many useful suggestions. I would also like to thank Allan Kulikoff of Northern Illinois University, who read an earlier draft of the manuscript and was generous with his time, encouragement, and suggestions. I am deeply indebted to my editor and good friend Armstead L. Robinson of the University of Virginia; his help was simply invaluable.

I am very grateful for the encouragement and the financial support that the Department of History and the College of Liberal Arts at Auburn University have provided toward the research and publication of this book.

My deepest appreciation goes to my family. Their support, freely given, sustained me throughout.

# A House Divided

*Slavery and Emancipation*
*in Delaware, 1635–1865*

# Introduction

THE TORTUOUS coming of freedom to Delaware blacks may well be the most enigmatic such episode in the history of emancipation in the Americas. From North America to South America, freedom came to slaves either through violent revolutions and wars, as for example in Santo Domingo and the southern United States, or through peaceful legislative action as exemplified by the experience of Colombia and the northern United States. Delaware remained the exception to this New World experience with emancipation. Here, neither warfare (the American Revolution and the Civil War) nor peace exerted sufficient pressure to induce Delaware to legislate the abolition of chattel slavery.

Within the context of emancipation in the United States, Delaware's experience remained unique. During the two decades after the American Revolution, Delaware, like its southern sister states, resisted the wave of manumission by state action that swept slavery into oblivion in New England, Pennsylvania, New York, and New Jersey. Indeed, not during the early national period when it seemed most likely, or during the first half of the nineteenth century when slavery lost all pretense of profitability in the Delaware economy, not even during the Civil War when the survival of legal slavery seemed very much in doubt, did the state of Delaware mandate abolition. But at the same time Delaware refused to follow the South in entrenching or defending the economic viability of the institution of slavery.

Presented here is a causal narration of the prolonged debate in Dela-

ware over de jure emancipation. The central problem is this: Why did
the economic devolution that carried slavery in Delaware to the edge of
oblivion fail to lead to the abolition of de jure slavery? Why did Delaware
cling to a lifeless institution with an intensity that seems overwhelmingly
out of proportion with the economic importance of slavery in the state?
Why did it require the force of the Thirteenth Amendment to the
United States Constitution—ratified over Delaware's strenuous objections—to end legal slavery in the state? Not until 1901, thirty-six years
after the end of the Civil War and the effective date of national universal
emancipation, did Delaware, then under Republican control, belatedly
ratify the Thirteenth Amendment.[1]

Unraveling the paradox of slavery and abolition in Delaware requires
consideration of the state's prolonged record of contradictory public
and private responses to the rise and demise of the institution of slavery.
Colonial Delaware turned to slavery by default: slavery did not come to
the colony after years of experimentation as it did in the Virginia colony,
nor did it ensue from a definite commitment to the institution as occurred with the proprietors of the Carolina colony. Rather, slavery in
Delaware began by accident. An unsuccessful privateering expedition
returning with a single slave marked the birth of an institution which at
its peak comprised 20 percent of the total state population. Delaware's
default institution was spawned out of the Dutch West India Company's
bungling attempts to secure its commercial empire against financial
ruin. However, once having taken root, slavery in Delaware proved resis-
tant to all attempts to uproot it legally.

For most of the century before the Civil War, the public and private
spheres in Delaware remained perpetually at loggerheads over the issue
of slave emancipation. At the same time that individual slaveholders voluntarily freed the vast majority of Delaware slaves, the state's legislature
narrowly but persistently refused to demolish the statutory edifice
that kept de jure slavery in place. From the mid-eighteenth century on,
Delaware slaveholders privately freed their slaves for reasons ranging
from Enlightenment and religious principles to economic necessity, the
same forces that fostered peaceful, legislated gradual abolition in the
northern states.

In the absence of state-mandated abolition, Delaware slave owners
voluntarily fashioned a successful gradual abolition system, taking care
to ease both conscience and economic burdens. Slaveholders escaped
from manumission-related economic ills by retaining the rights to the
labor of their slaves during their most productive age, thus offering complete freedom only after prolonged indentures. As for the conscience
instilled by Enlightenment or religious principles, voluntary gradual

manumission allowed owners to soothe both; technically they became a class of nonslaveholders, legally entitled to benefit from the temporary labor of their "indentured servants."

By contrast, the state legislature remained so deeply divided over the political consequences of emancipation that it repeatedly failed to mandate abolition despite numerous attempts to enact the necessary legislation. From the era of the American Revolution, the balance of political power between proslavery and antislavery forces remained stalemated, with final resolution seemingly beyond the reach of public Delaware. Antislavery advocates could not cobble together the majority needed to dismantle the legal basis of slavery, but they succeeded in persuading the state to sanction private and voluntary manumissions. Proslavery legislators could not revive a slave system already destroyed by the economic misfortunes of tobacco culture in a diminutive state without a frontier, but by maintaining the slavery stalemate, they succeeded in keeping de jure slavery in place.

Thus, the answer to the Delaware slavery and emancipation enigma lay not in a decision by the state to ignore the slavery question but rather in its inability to break the stubborn and persistent stalemate over slavery. However, unlike the battle over emancipation in the remaining slave states, the debates in Delaware revolved not around the economic ramifications—both sides agreed that there were none—but rather on its political consequences.

For well over a century the Delaware legislature struggled in vain to break the slavery impasse. The line of division within the legislature correlated closely with a stubbornly persistent cultural boundary. Much as was the case with the Mason-Dixon Line, Delaware's "line of discrimination" divided north and south Delaware into rival domains with antagonistic religious, cultural, and political interests. On one side of this line stood the northernmost of Delaware's three counties plus one-half of the central county. Reflecting the influence of colonial settlement patterns, "North" Delaware encompassed the area of greatest Quaker influence, the home of the Republican party, and the center of support for de jure emancipation. On the other side of the line stood the southernmost of the three counties, which effected an alliance with the other half of the central county. "South" Delaware encompassed the area of greatest Methodist influence but was also the home of the Democratic party and the center of rigid opposition to the abolition of de jure slavery.

This division over emancipation reflected a keen awareness of the partisan implications of freeing and granting citizenship to blacks who made up 20 percent of Delaware's population. Delaware Republicans, themselves believers in white supremacy, supported freedom and the franchise for blacks with the expectation that free blacks would most certainly vote for the party of emancipation. Delaware Democrats opposed emancipation, for blacks seemed unlikely to find Democratic party principles and constituencies very attractive. Thus did religion, slavery, emancipation, and racism define the contested issues that oriented political competition between rival groups of white Delawareans for more than a century.

So long as de jure slavery remained intact, Democrats could delay or evade discussing the moral and legal enfranchisement of a group which would hold the balance of power in a state whose elections often turned on margins of less than a hundred votes. The existence of legal slavery seemed to justify the exclusion of blacks from "political rights and privileges" and excused the Democratic party ideology of preserving Delaware as "a government of white men for the benefit of white men."[2] Consequently, until 1901 these noneconomic but potentially explosive ramifications of emancipation blocked and delayed final legislative action on abolition.

The Delaware emancipation stalemate offers a vehicle for reevaluating our understanding of the development of political racism in nineteenth-century America. It appears that Democrats in pre–Civil War Delaware had begun to develop the ideology that eventually became the basis for the emergence of the Jim Crow system in the late nineteenth-century South. When faced with the rise of black and white Populists of the 1890s—an alliance with the potential to upset the political balance—conservative southern Democrats employed racial politics to deter this biracial farmers' alliance from coming into fruition and further precluded a future occurrence by enshrining the racial divide through Jim Crow legislation, laws that effectively reserved the franchise and political power for white men by disfranchising black men.[3] Because antebellum Delawareans linked opposition to emancipation to the preservation of Delaware as "a government of white men for the benefit of white men," it may well be that the roots of Jim Crow ideology existed decades earlier than previously thought.

The prolonged stalemate over de jure emancipation in a de facto free Delaware poses a challenge to Abraham Lincoln's "house divided" dictum that the "government cannot endure, permanently half slave and half free." The analytic narrative presented here suggests that had the Civil War amendments not destroyed the constitutional basis for chattel slavery, a "half slave and half free" public Delaware might have continued its long stalemate over the efficacy of de jure emancipation until well into the twentieth century.

In light of Delaware's slavery impasse, it is not surprising that contemporaries often experienced great difficulty deciding how to classify the state that anchored the eastern terminus of the Mason-Dixon Line. In July 1787, as the delegates to the Constitutional Convention pondered the intricate structures of government, a Virginia delegate, James Madison, commented on what he saw as the most potent conflict facing the nation they were creating. "The real difference of interests lay, not between the large & small" states, he said, "but between the N & Southn. States." "The institution of slavery & its consequences," Madison continued, had "formed the line of discrimination" between North and South, free and slave states. On the side of slavery, he counted "5 States on the South," while free states numbered "8 on the Northn. side of the line" of demarcation.[4]

Madison's sectional mathematics curiously failed to include Delaware in his southern five of Maryland, Virginia, North and South Carolina, and Georgia. Although puzzling in hindsight, portraying tiny Delaware as aligned permanently with the free states was far from illogical. Indeed, by 1787 all indications pointed to de jure abolition in the immediate future. Delaware during the 1780s permanently banned the international slave trade, severely restricted the domestic slave trade, repealed antimanumission codes, and engaged in a serious debate on a bill for the gradual abolition of slavery. Thus, when in July 1787 Madison identified Delaware as a free northern state, he did so as an astute politician assessing the likely direction of future policy in a state that appeared headed inexorably toward de jure abolition.

Three-quarters of a century after Madison's generation created the American Republic, the United States found itself embroiled in a bitter dispute over slavery during the political crisis of the 1850s. At stake was the future of the nation. Should the Union be saved or destroyed? And if preserved, should the Union condone or disavow slavery? Amid the brewing controversy, in 1859 another Virginian, the "fire-eating" southern nationalist Edmund Ruffin, drew attention to Delaware's peculiar position. "There are now thirty-three States in the Union, of whom fifteen only, if including Delaware, are slaveholding," Ruffin remarked, "or but fourteen, if excluding Delaware, which holds very few slaves, and is already, in sentiment and political action, almost identified with the more northern States."[5] Echoing Madison's sectional mathematics, Ruffin apparently saw little reason to include Delaware within the "sacred circle" of slaveholding states deemed ready to disrupt the Union in order to preserve the "peculiar institution" and the southern way of life.

As the Civil War drew to a close, the northern Congress debated several measures to consolidate its impending victory; one was an amend-

ment to abolish slavery in the nation, the thirteenth amendment to the
United States Constitution. The response of the nonseceding states to
the amendment was generally favorable with the exception of a few
states, Delaware included. Even though Delaware refused to join the
Confederacy in 1861, the legislature assumed a stridently antiemanci-
pation stance when called upon in February 1865 to ratify this amendment. While the majority of the nonseceding states approved the
amendment that would forever abolish slavery and involuntary servitude
in the nation, the legislature of Delaware declared its "unqualified disapproval of said proposed amendment to the Constitution of the United
States, and . . . refuse[d] to adopt and ratify the same," a rejection the
state carried into the twentieth century.[6] The tone of the legislative debate revealed that not even the impending victory of a Union cause
pledged to emancipation could break the slavery stalemate in Delaware.

The attitude of the Delaware legislature in February 1865 seems peculiar. By the Civil War slavery in Delaware was a totally defunct institution. Even without the coercion of an abolition law, the overwhelming
majority of slaveholders had freed their slaves privately, with the result
that by 1860 only 1,798 of the Delaware blacks were still listed as slaves
(table 1). Even this negligible figure was an overstatement; since passage
of an 1810 state law, all Delaware blacks serving premanumission indentures were counted as slaves. A conservative estimate would place nearly
50 percent of the slaves counted in the 1860 census in the class of half-
free, indentured blacks, scheduled to be fully emancipated in the very
near future.

The surprising actions of public Delaware in the aftermath of four
years of bitter warfare once again led Ruffin to comment on the Delaware slavery enigma. He found it "strange that the little state of Delaware, alone, should have voted against the constitutional amendment to
abolish slavery."[7] Why, indeed, did Delaware refuse to give its sanction
to an amendment ratifying the fait accompli of de jure emancipation at a
time when even the Confederacy was considering limited emancipation?
Only when viewed against the backdrop of Democratic "South" Delaware's determination to preserve the state as "a government of white
men for the benefit of white men" does the state's prolonged slavery
impasse become rational.

When Secretary of State William H. Seward announced on 18 December 1865 that the Thirteenth Amendment had been ratified by the
required number of states (through a coalition of nonseceded states
and former Confederate states), the nonseceded states of Delaware, New
Jersey, and Kentucky were conspicuously absent from the list. However,
New Jersey in 1866 and Kentucky in 1891 finally ratified the amend-

Table 1. Population of Delaware, 1790–1860

| | | Black | | | |
|---|---|---|---|---|---|
| Year | County | Slave | Free | White | Total |
| 1790 | New Castle | 2,562 | 639 | 16,487 | 19,688 |
| | Kent | 2,300 | 2,570 | 14,050 | 18,920 |
| | Sussex | 4,025 | 690 | 15,773 | 20,488 |
| | Subtotal | 8,887 | 3,899 | 46,310 | 59,096 |
| 1800 | New Castle | 1,838 | 2,754 | 20,769 | 25,361 |
| | Kent | 1,485 | 4,246 | 13,823 | 19,554 |
| | Sussex | 2,830 | 1,268 | 15,260 | 19,358 |
| | Subtotal | 6,153 | 8,268 | 49,852 | 64,273 |
| 1810 | New Castle | 1,047 | 3,919 | 19,463 | 24,429 |
| | Kent | 728 | 5,616 | 14,151 | 20,495 |
| | Sussex | 2,402 | 3,601 | 21,747 | 27,750 |
| | Subtotal | 4,177 | 13,136 | 55,361 | 72,674 |
| 1820 | New Castle | 1,195 | 4,344 | 22,360 | 27,899 |
| | Kent | 1,070 | 5,533 | 14,190 | 20,793 |
| | Sussex | 2,244 | 3,081 | 18,732 | 24,057 |
| | Subtotal | 4,509 | 12,958 | 55,282 | 72,749 |
| 1830 | New Castle | 786 | 5,708 | 23,226 | 29,720 |
| | Kent | 588 | 5,671 | 13,654 | 19,913 |
| | Sussex | 1,918 | 4,476 | 20,721 | 27,115 |
| | Subtotal | 3,292 | 15,855 | 57,601 | 76,748 |
| 1840 | New Castle | 541 | 6,773 | 25,806 | 33,120 |
| | Kent | 427 | 5,827 | 13,618 | 19,872 |
| | Sussex | 1,637 | 4,319 | 19,137 | 25,093 |
| | Subtotal | 2,605 | 16,919 | 58,561 | 78,085 |

Table 1  (*cont.*)

| Year | County | Black | | White | Total |
|------|--------|-------|------|-------|-------|
|      |        | Slave | Free |       |       |
| 1850 | New Castle | 394 | 7,621 | 34,765 | 42,780 |
|      | Kent | 347 | 6,385 | 16,084 | 22,816 |
|      | Sussex | 1,549 | 4,067 | 20,320 | 25,936 |
|      | Subtotal | 2,290 | 18,073 | 71,169 | 91,532 |
| 1860 | New Castle | 254 | 8,188 | 46,355 | 54,797 |
|      | Kent | 203 | 7,271 | 20,330 | 27,804 |
|      | Sussex | 1,341 | 4,370 | 23,904 | 29,615 |
|      | Subtotal | 1,798 | 19,829 | 90,589 | 112,216 |

*Source:* Compiled from U.S. Bureau of the Census, Manuscript Returns for Delaware, 1790-1860.

ment, thereby leaving Delaware as the only nonseceded state still in opposition to its ratification.

For more than a century, through wars and through peace, a closely divided public Delaware fought against itself over an institution already rendered economically moribund by the cumulative impact of private acts of emancipation. Not until the victorious "free states" exerted truly irresistible pressure by ratifying the thirteenth amendment, then and only then, did Democratic-controlled Delaware capitulate to the emancipation of fewer than 1,798 slaves.

# *1*

# The Dutch, Swedes, English, and Slavery

DELAWARE BECAME a "house divided" against itself over slavery during the period before the American Revolution. The origins of this division lay in the complicated history of slavery and European settlement patterns in colonial Delaware. These two independent factors, the emergence of slavery as a labor system alongside the placing of two competing streams of European settlements in Delaware, eventually linked to produce the prolonged Delaware stalemate over slavery and emancipation.

In June 1638 officials of the newly founded New Sweden colony inadvertently inaugurated the institution of slavery in Delaware when they dispatched the *Gripen* on a privateering expedition in search of gold-carrying Spanish ships. The *Gripen*'s voyage in West Indian waters failed to produce Spanish bullion but returned with the first "black gold," a "negro named Anthony," to the New Sweden colony in April 1639.[1] Anthony was possibly the first black slave or servant to serve in what would become the state of Delaware. His arrival was an ordinary beginning to an institution that grew to enslave approximately 20 percent of Delaware's population and confounded the state and society of Delaware from 1639 to 1901.

Dutch, Swedish, and later English ambitions turned Delaware slavery from an accident to an institution. While fiercely contesting for control of the Delaware Valley, these European nationals wielded slavery, the slave trade, and staple crop agriculture as weapons. From 1639 to 1664 the Dutch in particular pursued slavery, the slave trade, and agriculture in defense of their commercial interests. Relying on their slaves, a majority of whom were company-owned, Dutch officials sought to produce staple crops, populate the colony, and protect their precarious trade position against competition from the Swedes and the English.

The English conquest of Delaware in 1664 effectively ended the European contest over the Delaware Valley, only to replace it with an enduring intrastate division. When the English issued an open invitation to whites to settle the colony, they unintentionally set the stage for a divided Delaware. Two diverse groups of white settlers headed to the colony: to northern Delaware came the Quakers and the Scotch-Irish, while white migrants from the Chesapeake headed to southern Delaware. From this accidental settlement pattern emerged the stubborn cultural line of demarcation that divided the colony and state in half and nurtured the prolonged stalemate over slavery in Delaware.

The English takeover of Delaware also heightened the pace of slave imports to the colony. Because the English now firmly controlled Delaware, the focus of slavery in the colony shifted from a company-owned and defense-related institution to private ownership and profits. And the English, out of their interest in pursuing colonization, cultivating a profitable tobacco crop, and increasing their share of the Atlantic slave trade, energetically fostered the growth of the black population of Delaware.

The rapid growth of the slave population in Delaware led, inevitably perhaps, to a spate of restrictive slave codes. Responding to the growing slave population, Delaware from the 1680s through the mid-eighteenth century regularly passed, amended, and supplemented slave codes with the intention of confirming slaveholder rights to their human property and assuring white citizens of their security and privileges. On occasion, the legislature of Delaware even dared suggest that the slave codes were intended to safeguard the welfare of the slaves.

## The South River and New Sweden Colonies, 1639–64

In June 1621 a group of Dutch merchants formed the Dutch West India Company with the dual goal of duplicating the success of the earlier, eastern-based Dutch East India Company while also gaining access to the New World treasures then enriching the coffers of their rival, Spain. The company began with a twenty-four-year monopoly on trade in the New World and a license to attack and capture Spanish ships and colonies.[2] Initially neither colonization nor slavery interested the Dutch West India Company; almost exclusively the company focused on a quest for the riches of the New World through commerce.

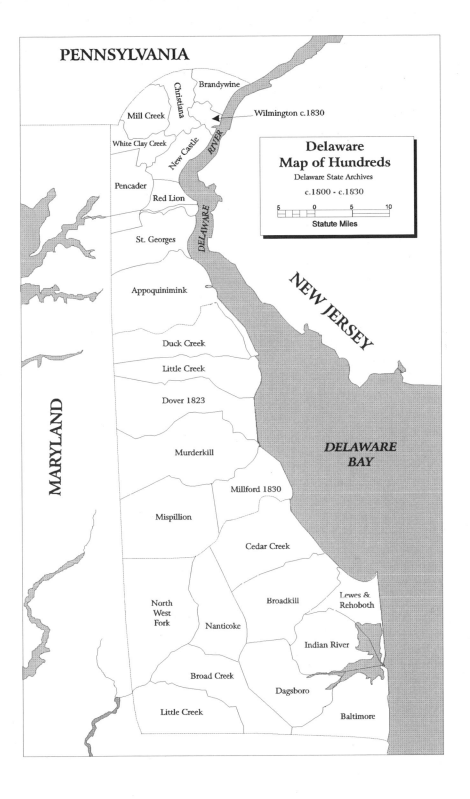

PENNSYLVANIA

Brandywine

Christiana

Mill Creek

Wilmington c.1830

White Clay Creek

New Castle

RIVER

Pencader

Red Lion

DELAWARE

St. Georges

**Delaware
Map of Hundreds**

Delaware State Archives

c.1800 - c.1830

5    0    5    10

**Statute Miles**

NEW JERSEY

Appoquinimink

Duck Creek

Little Creek

Dover 1823

MARYLAND

Murderkill

*DELAWARE
BAY*

Millford 1830

Mispillion

Cedar Creek

North
West
Fork

Broadkill

Lewes &
Rehoboth

Nanticoke

Indian River

Broad Creek

Dagsboro

Little Creek

Baltimore

All company policies, including those on slavery and colonization, were assessed by their ability to further this primary commercial goal. Dutch officials freely acknowledged their nation's preoccupation with trade, lauding the benefits that could accrue to nation, trading companies, and citizens. Pursuit of trade led the Dutch to fund the exploration of the eastern seaboard of North America. Under Dutch sponsorship Henry Hudson in April 1609 set sail in the *Half Moon* in search of a northeastern route to the Far East. Although Hudson failed to find an open way to the Orient, he explored a broad section of the eastern North American coast, and the Dutch laid claim to the territory they called New Netherland stretching from New York in the north to the South River (Delaware) in the south.[3]

Originally the company planned on generating sufficient profits from the fur trade and minerals, but it was forced to revise its goals as harsh New World reality proved its plans either illusionary or transient. A series of financial troubles plagued the company: no mineral deposits existed in the New Netherland colony to provide instant wealth, the supply of furs was depleted with time, and costs continued to escalate. As early as 1628 the company declared the New Netherland colony a financial failure.[4]

To salvage this faltering trading empire, the company from March 1628 on initiated various "Freedom and Exemptions" charters, the patroonship system, hoping at least to prevent a financial disaster and at best to reap a profit.[5] The Dutch expected the system to attract both investors and settlers, increase trade and profits, and save the company from financial ruin. However, the success of the patroonship plan mandated a fundamental change in company policy: promotion of colonization. A strictly commercial empire with only a few outlying trading posts would no longer suit. Only by promoting a substantial, permanent, settler population could the Dutch provide the patroons and company with profits from the sale of land, collection of taxes, and increased trade.

A group of Dutch investors led by Samuel Godijn in 1631 sponsored the founding of Swanendael colony in Delaware, but the next year the colony failed to survive an attack by a local group of Native Americans. Even without the attack it is doubtful that Swanendael would have endured. The liabilities of the patroonship system were many, and it soon collapsed throughout New Netherland. Disappointing returns on investments, company restrictions on the fur trade, and opposition within the company conspired against it. By the end of the 1630s the company was once again seeking the means to save its floundering commercial empire.[6]

During this period of uncertain Dutch policy in the South River, the Swedes established the New Sweden colony. Dutch disinterest in colonization pointed disgruntled former Dutch trading company employees toward Sweden in search of sponsors for their colonization dreams.[7] One former employee, Peter Minuit, led the colonization venture to New Sweden. Of French descent, Minuit had held the post of director general of New Netherland from 1626 until a dispute with his Dutch employers forced him out of office in 1632. Four years later Minuit offered his services to Sweden.

In 1637 the Swedish government commissioned Minuit to lead an expedition of two ships, the *Kalmar Nyckel* and the *Gripen,* to the Delaware Bay. His instructions called for the creation of a permanent settlement, promotion of trade, and acts of piracy against Spanish ships plying the Caribbean Islands. Landing in March 1638, Minuit purchased land from the local Native Americans and built the first permanent European settlement in Delaware, Fort Christiana, in honor of the queen of Sweden. Three months later he authorized a privateering venture in West Indian waters. It was this expedition that returned to the colony in April 1639 with its first known African slave or servant, Anthony.[8]

The founding of New Sweden served as a catalyst in the growth of slavery in the South River colony. New Sweden posed a direct challenge to Dutch authority, for the Dutch were caught unprepared as Minuit and the Swedes brazenly built Fort Christiana in an area claimed by the Dutch since the Hudson expedition. New Sweden compounded this aggravation by undermining Dutch control of the Delaware River and the fur trade. Fort Christiana and subsequent Swedish settlements were built south of the Dutch garrison at Fort Nassau, thus giving the Swedes a more favorable position on the Delaware waterway system and the ability to divert the fur trade. Furthermore, an additional challenge came from English settlers in New England, Maryland, and Virginia, all of whom seriously competed with the Dutch for both territory and the diminishing supply of furs.[9]

Clearly by the 1630s the Dutch West India trading empire in New Netherland faced a major financial crisis, one requiring immediate and effective response. Even the States General of Holland, which had so far refrained from directly meddling in company business, was alarmed by these developments. Blaming the financial crisis on inept officials and policies, as well as on the intrigues of foreign nationals, the States General in 1638 sought to save New Netherland with a new charter promoting Dutch immigration to and settlement in New Netherland.[10]

Only by changing its lukewarm attitude toward colonization could the company effectively counter the serious challenges posed by the Swedes

and the English. Trade still remained its avowed goal, but the company
finally acknowledged the importance of linking the effective control
of New Netherland to the survival of its commercial empire. It could
strengthen the colony by encouraging Dutch nationals and their slaves
or servants to settle in New Netherland. A rapid increase in the slave
population, for example, would bolster the population and defense of
New Netherland, answer the need for labor on the staple-crop farms,
and increase the Dutch share of the Atlantic slave trade while boosting
company trade prospects.

It was while attempting to stave off financial ruin that the company
fostered the growth of the African presence in Delaware. The company
seems to have taken the first step in 1639, for Dutch traders began using
the labor of servants, most likely African servants, in their trading forts
on the Delaware River. Dutch records confirm that in February 1639
company officials in Manhattan convicted one Coinclisse for wound-
ing a soldier at Fort Amsterdam; as punishment, he was condemned "to
serve the Company, along with the Blacks, to be sent by the first Ship to
the South River."[11]

Successful colonization required the creation of a viable society which
was capable of meeting most of its own agricultural needs while still turning a profit. An agriculturally self-reliant New Netherland, said company
officials, would not only strengthen the colony but also eliminate the
cost of importing food for the colonists, and possibly turn the colony
into the granary for Dutch colonies such as Brazil and Curaçao.[12] The
success of the new agricultural policy hinged on the availability of land,
labor, and market. There were relatively few obstacles to obtaining land
or market access: land could be purchased from local Native Americans,
and demand for grain exceeded supply. Labor, however, proved prob-
lematic.

Labor could come from Dutch immigrants, but the company found
itself unable to persuade enough Dutchmen to emigrate to New Netherland, certainly not those interested in agriculture and permanent
settlement. While the young, poor, indentured, and the persecuted were
fleeing other parts of Europe—particularly England—in search of instant wealth or religious toleration, the Dutch, by comparison, were relatively free of these desires and problems. There existed little internal
push for the Dutch to migrate and no pull from the colonies to attract
prospective Dutch colonists. Neither New Netherland as a place of residence nor trade with the Dutch West India Company proved attractive
to Dutchmen. Those in search of wealth found better opportunities elsewhere: the trade conducted by the Dutch East India Company more
than overshadowed that of its counterpart in the West, and Dutch ships

plying European waters provided another attractive avenue to wealth.[13]

But if the company could not attract its own nationals to New Netherland, it could solve the twin problems of labor and population by using bound labor. Slaves not only would provide much needed labor but also would quickly augment the population of New Netherland. This explains why in 1644 the Board of Accounts on New Netherland recommended that "for the advancement of the cultivation of the land" in New Netherland, "it would not be unwise to allow, at the request of the Patroons, Colonists and other farmers, the introduction, from Brazil there, as many Negroes as they would be disposed to pay for at a fair price." The board believed that these slaves "would accomplish more work for their masters, and at a less expense, than farm servants, who must be bribed to go thither by a great deal of money and promises." Notwithstanding company recommendation, only a small number of slaves were sold to the colonists during the 1640s and 1650s. A low agricultural return and continuing fiscal difficulties conspired to delay the company's plans.[14]

However, in 1656, amid renewed fears of an English takeover along with persisting financial problems, the company agreed to transfer responsibility of a section of its colony including Fort Casimir (renamed New Amstel) to the City of Amsterdam. Thus, from 1656 to 1663 Delaware had two proprietors: the City of Amsterdam controlled New Amstel while the Dutch West India Company retained possession of the remainder of the South River colony. Finally, in December 1663 the company formally transferred the entire colony to the City of Amsterdam, but the city's tenure was short-lived. In October 1664 the colony fell to the English.[15]

Acquisition of New Amstel, and later the South River colony, provided the opportunity for the City of Amsterdam to promote cultivation of agricultural products not readily available or too expensive in Holland, particularly grain, tobacco, and timber. Unlike the Dutch West India Company's earlier policy, agriculture assumed premier importance, with trade occupying a secondary role in the city's policy in New Amstel. The directors of New Amstel stressed cultivation of grain with the intention of making the colony self-sufficient and selling grain at a reduced rate to the citizens of Amsterdam. Consequently, the city not only granted liberal terms to prospective farmers but also promised to purchase all grain produced in the colony.[16]

The City of Amsterdam did not entirely eschew commerce, for it envisioned additional profit from trade with Maryland. In the past an informal but profitable business had evolved between the two colonies; now the city proposed an official development of this trade, and the directors of the South River colony gave their wholehearted approval. In exchange for tobacco, the Delaware colonists would provide the English in Maryland with barley and buckwheat. The City of Amsterdam and the company foresaw "that from both these, namely agriculture and trade, the expense will be sufficiently met." But the city's agricultural and colonization plans faced the same problems that had earlier beset the company: willing Dutch settlers and an adequate labor supply. Because the city, like the company, could not persuade the Dutch to come to the colonies, it turned to unwilling immigrants from Africa, slaves who would provide the labor for agricultural production.[17]

As far back as the late 1620s, the Dutch West India Company promised to supply its New Netherland colonists with slave labor, but not until the mid–1650s and after did the Dutch deliver on this promise. Two major events encouraged them to provide New Netherland colonists a steady supply of African slave labor: their rise in the Atlantic slave trade and the reorganization of that trade after the company lost its hold on northeastern Brazil in 1654.[18]

From its founding, the company had steadily encroached on Spanish and Portuguese possessions until it successfully captured northeastern Brazil and Curaçao from the Portuguese and Spanish in 1630 and 1634, respectively. The Dutch topped this off in 1637 with the seizure of the Elmina Fort on the coast of West Africa, thus completing their capture of key Portuguese slave- trading and slave-using centers. Consequently, from 1637 to the beginning of the eighteenth century, the Dutch controlled one of the most important centers of supply and demand for the Atlantic slave trade and had the means to supply their colonists with African slaves on a regular basis, if and when the decision was made to do so.[19]

Also helping to entrench the Dutch in this lucrative trade position was their acquisition in 1662 of their first *asiento,* the contract granted by Spain for supplying its New World colonies with slaves, followed in 1668 with an award of a twenty-year monopoly of the license. The confusion of civil war and its aftermath temporarily interfered with English interests in West Africa, thereby removing any serious European competition to Dutch domination of the Atlantic slave trade. As Philip D. Curtin has pointed out, "The Dutch carried a high proportion of the seventeenth-century slave trade and they remained an important source of supply into the eighteenth."[20]

For the colonists in New Netherland, the company's promise to supply them with slaves on a regular basis became a reality after the company lost control of Brazil in 1654. The sugar-rich northeastern sector of Brazil had served as the slave-trading headquarters of the Dutch West India Company; its loss to the Portuguese in 1654 compelled the company to search for an alternate market for its slaves.[21] In response, the company moved the center of its New World slave trade to two areas, Curaçao and New Netherland, a decision of immense benefit to the Dutch colonists of New Netherland.

In the late 1640s Peter Stuyvesant, director general of both Curaçao and New Netherland, took charge of organizing the slave trade between the two colonies. With slaves in great demand in New Netherland and the company able and willing to satisfy this demand, Stuyvesant probably found it easy to accomplish his task. As a resident of New Netherland, Stuyvesant possessed firsthand knowledge of the labor needs of the colonists; thus, he could act sympathetically on their requests. The company decision in 1646 that the director "notify the Assembly hereof every year, when further order shall be taken regarding the transport of Negroes thither" paved the way for additional slave imports.[22]

Stuyvesant went further than the original company policy. In 1659 he successfully persuaded the directors to open the slave trade to private citizens. Not willing to abandon the company's monopoly totally, the directors agreed to allow colonists limited participation in the slave trade. Two successful joint slave sales in New Netherland in 1660 convinced the directors of the potential profits in Stuyvesant's plan, and the company instructed Vice-Director Beck, stationed at Curaçao, to supply Stuyvesant with a fresh cargo of slaves at the earliest opportunity. As an additional concession, the directors "resolved not only that slaves shall be kept in New Netherland, as we have heretofore ordered, but be moreover exported to the English and other Neighbors."[23]

The demand for slaves as labor and as an item of trade to other colonists rapidly increased during the 1660s. In a letter dated 18 March 1662, William Beeckman, the vice-director of the South River colony, confessed his dependence on slave labor, pleading that Stuyvesant "accommodate [him] with a company of negroes, as [he was] very much in want of them in many respects."[24] The following year the director of New Amstel, Alexander d'Hinoyossa, made a similar plea. While relaying d'Hinoyossa's request to the burgomasters of the City of Amsterdam, the company advised the city that

> it will be necessary, according to the report of Director Alexander d'Hinojosa, to send thither immediately 50 negroes who are particularly adapted to the preparation of the valleys, which are found exceedingly fertile, . . . and for other heavy work; also for the advancement of agriculture which we, too, can apprehend; wherefore we, under correc-

tion, are of opinion that a contract ought to be entered into with the West India Company here for the delivery of such number; we think they can be obtained for 230 guilders each, or thereabout, which in such case, would be for 50 negroes fl. 11,500.[25]

Altruism played no role in the company's decision to heed d'Hinoyossa's request. It served the company's interest to encourage the use of slave labor, for a significant proportion of its financial investment lay in the Atlantic slave trade system. Not surprisingly, the company believed slave labor essential to the success of agriculture; it warned the burgomasters that failure to dispatch a sufficient number of slaves to New Amstel meant that "another entire year will have been lost, which would tend to the serious disadvantage of agriculture in that country." To show good faith the company offered "to share one-half the expense which will be incurred after this, in the advancement of the Colonie."[26]

Apparently the fifty slaves sent by the company in 1663 did not satisfy New Amstel's labor needs. Barely a year later the directors contracted with Simon Cornelissen Gilde to deliver "a lot of Negroes for Agricultural purposes." Gilde imported 290 slaves, a quarter of whom were sold to the colonists in New Amstel on "the express condition, that they shall not be exported out of our district, but specially retained therein, to be employed in the cultivation of the soil." On 17 August 1664 the Council of New Netherland delivered to Peter Alrichs, commissary of Indian cargoes and councilor of the colony of New Amstel, the largest number of slaves to reach the Dutch colony on the South River: seventy-two African slaves, consisting of thirty-eight men and thirty-four women.[27]

But before the Dutch could effectively employ these slaves in Delaware, the English attacked the colony, and in October 1664 the Delaware territory fell under the control of the duke of York. The loss of the colony spelled the end to Dutch plans to colonize and develop agriculture in the South River, but not before the Dutch adopted slavery as a solution to their defense and economic woes. In turn, once planted, slavery became firmly entrenched in the Delaware colony.

## The English Colony of Delaware

With the exception of a brief interval in 1673–74 when the Dutch reoccupied the colony, Delaware remained English. The duke of York held it from 1664 until 1682, when Charles II included Delaware in the land allocated for William Penn's Holy Experiment. In 1701 Penn granted the colony a separate assembly, and Delaware regained its identity, although it continued to share governors with Pennsylvania.

Unlike the Dutch, both the duke of York and William Penn promptly

pursued colonization, the only practical means to extract wealth from
the colony of Delaware. Without mineral deposits to provide immediate
wealth, exploitation of the land offered the only profitable avenue open
to proprietors: through the sale of land and the collection of taxes on
the land and its produce, they could accrue substantial sums. Simply
put, the economic well-being of Delaware's proprietors depended upon
bringing significant numbers of settlers to the Delaware colony. To attain
the desired density of settlement as quickly as possible, the English
needed to attract a mix of immigrants, free, indentured, and enslaved.

Free white settlers had a choice between an array of English colonies stretching from New England in the north to Virginia in the south,
and later, even farther south to the Carolinas and Georgia. Delaware
could draw a fair share of prospective white settlers if the colony's social,
religious, and political climate remained tempting; if land continued
cheap and easily accessible; and if labor—preferably cheap—could be
obtained to work the land. All these prerequisites became available to
whites interested in settling the English colony of Delaware.

Politics under the duke of York and William Penn posed no undue
burdens and did not hinder white settlement. In fact, the duke of York's
policy proved more liberal than that of the government in England and
was no more intrusive than what the colonists had experienced under
the Swedes and Dutch or that endured by white settlers in the other
North American colonies. The chief representative of the duke of York,
Sir Edmund Andros, painstakingly assured prospective settlers of Delaware of his intentions; he was there, he said, for their protection and
benefit.[28]

When compared to government in the other North American colonies, William Penn's Holy Experiment may well have been the most progressive: the white settlers participated in the running of the government and enjoyed a religious toleration unknown in England or the
other English colonies. Crowning these liberties, Penn's Native American policy encouraged peaceful relations, thus reducing the incidence
of conflict in the colony at a time when other colonies repeatedly engaged Native Americans in warfare.

A liberal land grant policy instituted under the English offered the
most compelling attraction to white settlers, new and old. Evidence of
the success of the English in attracting colonists to Delaware may be seen
in the numerous land grants recorded in this period.[29] Agents of both
the duke of York and Penn often requested land grants for white settlers.
So did the collector of quitrents, William Tom, upon whose request the
grants of the colonists already resident in Delaware were increased in
1669. In the same year Tom requested and received permission for some

settlers from Maryland "to come and settle upon the kill below Apoqui-nimy, within the government." He hoped that through such actions "the said place may be inhabited and manured, it tending likewise to the increase of the inhabitants."[30]

From August 1673 to February 1674, English rule in Delaware was interrupted by Dutch reconquest. But the returning Dutch government did not reverse the English colonization policy. In fact, the Dutch con-firmed land grants issued under the English, made additional land grants, and encouraged further immigration from other colonies, espe-cially Maryland.[31]

Early in 1674, the English regained control of the Delaware colony. The official instructions given to Andros asked that he "give all man-ner of encouragement to planters of all Nations, but especially to Eng-lishmen, to come and settle" in Delaware. The "encouragement" took the form of "lands, either of the unplanted or such planted lands as shallbe confiscated from time to time." Andros took his instructions seri-ously; as a special incentive to new settlers, he offered in 1675 to remit the quitrents for the first three years. The policy proved quite successful, for Delaware's population more than doubled between 1680 and 1700, with an increase in both black and white immigrants.[32]

William Penn, proprietor of Delaware after 1682, continued the pol-icy of liberal land grants and sales. In a letter to the justices of the peace in Kent County, Penn agreed to remove "all Obstructions to the due Improvement" of the colony and to give "Reasonable Incouragement" to persons interested in settling in Delaware. Toward this end he made an offer of land not exceeding three hundred acres, at the rate of a penny per acre or its equivalent in produce, to the heads of families. Single persons could purchase up to a hundred acres on the same terms.[33]

Access to labor remained crucial in attracting prospective settlers to Delaware. With both indentured servants and slaves available to colo-nists, personal preference and need dictated the choice of one system of labor over the other. Ultimately, many white settlers chose slave labor, as it seemed to serve them best. Like the Dutch, the English takeover of Delaware coincided with the period of England's prominence in the Atlantic slave trade, a development of great benefit to English colonists in search of slave labor.

Just as the Dutch had controlled the Atlantic slave trade during the seventeenth century, the eighteenth century belonged to the English. English dominance in the slave trade partly arose from improved orga-nization and policies. In 1672 the weak Royal Adventurers company was replaced by the better-organized Royal African Company. Protected by a monopoly, this company pursued dominance over the Atlantic slave trade and by the beginning of the eighteenth century achieved its goal. Even the English government's decision to revoke the company's monopoly boosted English participation in the slave trade; in 1698 the crown opened the Atlantic slave trade to all its citizens, colonials included, further increasing England's share of the slave trade.[34]

After 1664 the task of supplying slave labor to the Delaware colony fell to private citizens. Unlike the Dutch West India Company, neither the duke of York nor William Penn assumed responsibility for directly supplying the settlers with slaves. This was not a testament of proprietary opposition to the trade in human beings, nor did their inaction reduce slave imports to the colony. While the proprietors abstained from direct involvement, they did not prohibit the slave trade, and indeed their policies, and later those of the crown, facilitated the importation of slaves to the colonies. But these policies did mark a new departure for the white settlers of Delaware, who now had to rely on their own initiative. Without direct slave imports to the Delaware colony, previous trade patterns were reversed; rather than selling slaves to other colonies, Delaware residents now purchased slaves from nearby Maryland and Pennsylvania. In 1678 the residents of New Castle petitioned Andros "that liberty of trade may be granted us with neighbouring colony of *Maryland, for supplying us with negroes,* servants, and utensils, without which we cannot subsist."[35]

For Delaware residents in the market for slaves, Maryland offered the advantages of a growing slave market and proximity. From the 1680s Delaware residents like William Clark of Sussex County purchased their slaves from Maryland. Clark in 1682 bought from "Capt. John Osborne, of Sumersett County in the province of Mary Land An negor man Called or Knowen by the name of black Will for and during his natrill Life." Pennsylvania, the other major supplier of slaves to the state, shared close political and economic ties with Delaware even after the two colonial assemblies formally separated in 1701. Like their counterparts in Maryland, Philadelphia slave merchants sold slaves to Delaware residents.[36]

Migrating white settlers from other North American colonies also helped increase the state's slave population. Delaware's land policy encouraged white settlers to bring in their slaves or servants, rewarding those who did so with free land. This practice became the official policy under the duke of York, with the amount of land based on the number of bondsmen brought to the colony. Thus, Captain Edmund Cantwell, the high sheriff of Delaware, was instructed "to give such New Comers as desire to continue there, any reasonable Quantity of Lands, . . . according to their capacity and Number of Hands they shall bring for Clearing it."[37]

Coinciding with the evolution of slavery, white migrants unintention-ally readied the Delaware landscape for a cultural stalemate that persists today. Quite by accident two distinct white cultures were planted within the boundaries of this small colony. Southern Delaware—Sussex County and portions of Kent County—attracted white Chesapeake migrants, tobacco, and slavery. This Chesapeake influence became more pro-nounced after the boundary dispute between Delaware and Maryland was finally settled in 1775. The state, and specifically Sussex County, gained land and settlers at the expense of Maryland, for "the completion of the boundary lines meant a significant addition of territory [pre-viously part of Maryland] on the west and the south" of Delaware. To the north lay New Castle and the other half of Kent County. Attracted by William Penn's proprietorship of Pennsylvania and Delaware, Quaker migrants spilled from Pennsylvania to New Castle County and portions of Kent County. Later, Scotch-Irish migrants came to the same area and also absorbed the northern culture.[38]

Meeting in the middle of Delaware, these two significantly different white cultures, over time, hardened into a rigid sectional boundary that came to be of immense importance to Delaware slavery. Reflecting the cultural influence of its neighbor to the north—Pennsylvania—north-ern Delaware, by the mid-eighteenth century, had adopted an antislav-ery stance and a willingness, out of political expediency, to extend the vote to freed black men. Influenced by its southern origins, southern Delaware chose to resist legislated abolition and the franchise for blacks.

Unlike its slaveholding neighbors, Maryland and Virginia, the Dela-ware colony lacked the room for expansion afforded by a western fron-tier. This factor spared Delaware the friction with restive western settlers that loomed so large in the political histories of antebellum Maryland and Virginia. In place of loud complaints from western settlers about malapportionment and discriminatory taxation policies, politics in Dela-ware evolved into a "house divided" between perpetually feuding cul-tures in its northern and southern regions. Not surprisingly, a politics based on friction between two regions of equivalent size settled into a prolonged and embittered stalemate.

### The Slave Population

The actual number of slaves brought to the colony by European nation-als remains unclear. Delaware held no official census before the First Federal Census of 1790; consequently, only estimates can be provided for the earlier period. The Census Bureau estimates Delaware's black population in 1650—about a decade after Anthony's arrival—as 15; the projection suggests a total of 135 half a century later, in 1700, and an estimated high of 2,996 in 1780.[39]

Available data, though limited, clearly indicate that colonial Delaware's slave population significantly exceeded these estimates. When the Census Bureau estimate for 1780, for example, is compared to the actual census count of 1790, the flaws become patently clear. While the 1790 census counted 12,786 black residents, the 1780 estimate calculated a black population of only 2,996, implying that within a ten-year period the black population increased by 9,790. Nothing short of a massive influx of blacks could account for the implied 326.7 percent increase in Delaware's black population for these ten years. Since no evidence exists of any mass migration of blacks, free or slave, into Delaware during the intervening decade, the fault must lie with the low estimates.

A massive black migration, free or slave, into Delaware must be discounted as a possible explanation for the implied growth. Slavery was on the decline in Delaware, and owners seemed more interested in freeing or exporting their slaves than in importing new slaves. And although the closing decades of the eighteenth century coincided with the beginning of the voluntary manumission movement, Delaware had fewer attractions for free persons of color than neighboring Pennsylvania. The city of Philadelphia lay barely a day or two's journey away, even on foot, and offered greater opportunities for freedom, employment, and social relations with other free blacks.

Unquestionably, a revision of colonial Delaware's black population is indicated. The figures for the number of slaves in the South River colony can be revised by projecting backwards from the First Federal Census of 1790. However, an estimate based on this simple approach is fraught with problems. First, the slave population did not necessarily increase in a uniform fashion. The Dutch, for instance, waited until the 1660s before authorizing their agents to unload slaves at the South River colony, but within a short period of time a significant number arrived. Second, it is impossible to measure with any degree of accuracy the rate of death or the number of secondary sales of slaves out of the colony.

A convenient waterway system linking the South River to the English colony of Maryland provided Maryland colonists with an accessible and easy way to circumvent the restrictions of trade laws, such as the 1660 Navigation Act. Maryland colonists often shipped tobacco and other colonial products and received imports—mainly slaves—from Dutch ships plying the Delaware Bay, thus evading payment of duties imposed by the various Navigation Acts. Maryland colonists seemed as interested in this trade as were the Dutch and Swedes. In his report of 1661, Vice-Director

William Beeckman claimed that English settlers in Maryland "offered to transport yearly 2 or 3000 hogsheads of tobacco to our stream or Apoquenemingh, if they were supplied with Negroes and other merchandise."[40]

Data from sources such as shipping records and the eyewitness testimony of the 1664 English invasion provide a vehicle for constructing a more reasonable, if still speculative, estimate of the pre–1790 Delaware black population. Official accounts of the October 1664 invasion confirm that after the Dutch surrendered, Sir Robert Carr and the English soldiers "plundered and took everything, even the bedding from under the people's bodies, and carried away everything, except what they kept for their own needs."[41] The spoils of war taken by the English included the slaves belonging to the City of Amsterdam and its officials, as well as slaves owned by private citizens of the Dutch colony. Gerritt Van Sweringen, a Dutch sheriff, testified that the English carried off "one hundred sheep & thirty or forty horses, fifty or sixty cowes and oxen, the number of betweene sixty and seventy negroes."[42] Most likely, these were the slaves recently purchased by the City of Amsterdam, fifty slaves in 1663 and seventy-two in 1664.[43]

To the city-owned slaves seized by the English must be added those of the officers of the colony. Sir Robert Carr gave Ensign Arthur Stocke, one of his officers, certain possessions of Peter Alricks, a wealthy Dutch planter, among which were eleven slaves.[44] For himself, Carr kept the rich estate of Governor d'Hinoyossa, including several African slaves whom Carr later sold into Maryland in exchange for food and supplies. "I have already sent to Merryland," reported Carr to his superior Colonel Nicolls, "some Neegars wch did belong to the late Governor att his plantation above, for beefe, pork, corne and salt, and for some other small conveniences, wch this place affordeth not." Carr did not indicate the exact number of slaves that he sold into Maryland, but it must have been substantial, since he relied on the proceeds of this sale to feed more than a hundred soldiers under his command.[45]

If the reports of the English takeover are accurate, then the Census Bureau's estimate of Delaware's black population is extremely low. If "betweene sixty and seventy negroes" belonging to the city were seized, Ensign Stocke acquired eleven slaves previously owned by Peter Alricks, and the slaves of the d'Hinoyossa estate were sold to feed over one hundred English soldiers; then the estimate of the black population in 1664 should reflect a minimum number of eighty but most likely a figure of one hundred and above. Furthermore, except at Whorekill, no evidence exists that the English soldiers plundered the personal property, including slaves, of the private citizens.[46]

Table 2. Number and percentage of blacks in Delaware, 1790–1860

| | Population | | |
|-----|-----|-----|-----|
| Year | Total | Blacks | % Black |
| 1790 | 59,096 | 12,786 | 21.6 |
| 1800 | 64,273 | 14,421 | 22.4 |
| 1810 | 72,674 | 17,313 | 23.8 |
| 1820 | 72,749 | 17,467 | 24.0 |
| 1830 | 76,748 | 19,147 | 24.9 |
| 1840 | 78,085 | 19,524 | 25.0 |
| 1850 | 91,532 | 20,363 | 22.2 |
| 1860 | 112,216 | 21,627 | 19.2 |

Source: Compiled from U.S. Bureau of the Census, Manuscript Returns for Delaware, 1790 to 1860.

The official census from 1790 to the Civil War reveals a pattern which can serve as the basis for reconstructing the estimates for colonial Delaware. From 1790 to 1860 the black population as a proportion of the state total remained fairly consistent, peaking at a range between 19 to 25 percent (table 2). In the absence of evidence indicating any massive discontinuity in this population pattern, it seems reasonable to assume that a similar ratio prevailed in the decades preceding 1790. Thus, a suggested low median of 20 percent of the state population seems not unreasonable an estimate of the black population.

Using the 20 percent base to calculate the black population in colonial and early Delaware, the 1780 estimate would be adjusted to 9,077, giving a more likely growth from 1780 to 1790 of 29 percent, one easily explained by natural increase and imports (table 3). As the reconstructed census indicates, the Delaware black population was very visible at the time of the English takeover. And the duke of York, William Penn, and the crown continued the policy of increasing the black population.

From 1790 on, the guesswork can be eliminated from the census. The black population in that census totaled 12,786, of whom 8,887 were slaves and 3,899 free. Blacks in the state comprised 22 percent of the

Table 3. Estimated population of Delaware, 1650–1780

| | Population | | |
| --- | --- | --- | --- |
| Year | Total* | Blacks* | New estimate of blacks |
| 1650 | 185 | 15 | 37 |
| 1660 | 540 | 30 | 108 |
| 1670 | 700 | 40 | 140 |
| 1680 | 1,005 | 55 | 201 |
| 1690 | 1,482 | 82 | 296 |
| 1700 | 2,470 | 135 | 494 |
| 1710 | 3,645 | 500 | 729 |
| 1720 | 5,385 | 700 | 1,077 |
| 1730 | 9,170 | 478 | 1,834 |
| 1740 | 19,870 | 1,035 | 3,974 |
| 1750 | 28,704 | 1,496 | 5,741 |
| 1760 | 33,250 | 1,733 | 6,650 |
| 1770 | 35,496 | 1,836 | 7,099 |
| 1780 | 45,385 | 2,996 | 9,077 |

*Compiled from U.S. Bureau of the Census, *Historical Statistics* (Washington, D.C., 1975), 2:1168.

whole population, an average that prevailed with little variation between 1790 and the Civil War.

### Labor, Law, and Slavery

Repeating a practice common in many New World colonies, Delaware slaveholders purchased slaves to employ their labor primarily in staple-crop agriculture. Although successful staple-crop cultivation did not necessarily mandate slave labor, other labor options—free and indentured—became less and less available throughout the colonial period. By the closing decades of the seventeenth century, Delaware farmers viewed slave labor as the most advantageous in tobacco culture and thus made the transition to slave labor. Theirs was a choice heavily influenced

by cost, availability, and the practicality of slave labor as compared to the
other labor options.

Delaware farmers employed slave labor in the production of a variety
of grains and tobacco. Because farmers could cultivate either staple, they
generally leaned toward the crop that was favored by current market
demand and received the highest price. A close examination of the evolution of Delaware agriculture reveals its sensitivity to market demand.
In the earliest days, as the new colony struggled for survival, grain cultivated for self-sufficiency was most valued. Then in the 1680s, with the
survival of the colony no longer in doubt and amid the lure of higher
profits, Delaware farmers turned aggressively to tobacco cultivation.

Each staple crop required distinctive types and amounts of labor; first
for cultivation and then for processing. Thus, the decision to shift from
one cash crop to another led inevitably to significant changes in the
amount of labor—typically slave labor—needed on Delaware farms. Tobacco cultivation, in particular, compelled detailed repetitive attention
to each plant; a stark contrast to the plow, sow, and thresh routines used
to cultivate grain. The decision to shift to a labor-intensive market crop
like tobacco dramatically increased the demand for labor for its cultivation and processing. In turn, the task of satisfying these new labor demands led tobacco farmers toward heightened reliance on slavery, the
most readily available form of bound labor. Consequently, the numbers
of slaves grew rapidly during the period when Delaware farmers made
tobacco their primary cash crop.

New Sweden as the first permanent European settlement in Delaware
was also the first to outline its agricultural policy. The investors of New
Sweden assigned agriculture a central role in the development of the
colony, with the objective of promoting an agricultural program capable
of producing sustenance for the colonists and profit-making cash crops
for both colonists and investors. But they failed to attain this goal. Agriculture offered few incentives to Swedish settlers, certainly not when
participation in the fur trade—even with a diminishing stock—brought
better economic returns. Certain key provisions of New Sweden's charter inadvertently discouraged colonial self-sufficiency. To attract settlers
to New Sweden, article 9 of the colony's charter promised colonists free
food and supplies during the first year, thus removing a primary incentive for self-reliance, hunger.[47]

But if agriculture in New Sweden did not develop into the lucrative
plantation economy envisioned by investors and colonists, neither did it
fail completely. Before New Sweden's incorporation into the Dutch colony, its residents began limited cultivation of the two crops that affected
slavery in Delaware the most, grains (barley, wheat, corn) and tobacco.

Noticeable improvement in New Sweden's agriculture occurred following the arrival of Governor Johan Printz in 1643. Indeed, within a year of his arrival, Printz recorded the export of New Sweden–grown tobacco weighing 4,991 pounds and, in 1647, an export figure of 6,920 pounds. But the amount of tobacco grown in New Sweden could not offset investor expense, so the company often purchased tobacco from English colonists in the Chesapeake.[48]

Unlike New Sweden, the Dutch West India Company's irresolution regarding settlement had first to be conquered before any serious promotion of agriculture could be launched. Following the policy change by the company, officials promoted grain as the leading staple crop in the Dutch-controlled South River. Both wheat and corn were cultivated in significant quantities for local consumption and export.[49] Several factors combined to promote grain culture in Delaware: favorable markets in Europe and the Americas generated moderate demand and profits, while the colony's numerous rivers and creeks permitted the cheap operation of water mills for grain processing, even as they provided an easy and cost-effective mode of transporting grain to local and distant markets.

Along with grain, Dutch settlers, like New Sweden colonists, cultivated and traded tobacco. Dutch officials encouraged its growth in the hope that tobacco culture could promote trade and settlement and solve the company's financial woes. Such was the belief of Vice-Director Jean Paul Jacquet. "It is apparent that this [South] river stands to acquire a good reputation from its tobacco, and people would be motivated to settle here," he said, "if care were taken that the same be packed in as good condition as possible."[50]

Toward this goal, in December 1656 Jacquet authorized the appointment of two tobacco inspectors and instituted fines against tobacco merchants who failed to meet or comply with the inspection. And perhaps it was a testament to the importance of tobacco in the South River economy that a few high-ranking company and city officials resorted to unethical trade practices. In June 1662 William Beeckman accused d'Hinoyossa of selling a company-owned brew kettle and some millstones to the English in Maryland for a thousand pounds of tobacco.[51]

The coming of English rule to Delaware in 1664 profoundly changed the nature of agriculture and slavery in the colony. First, the volume of cash crop–oriented farming in Delaware dramatically increased under English rule. Second, from the outset of the English takeover, grain cultivation lost ground to tobacco, possibly because the English, unlike the Dutch, did not seriously pursue the idea of making Delaware a granary. Most likely, it was because higher prices and increasing demand lured farmers into the tobacco economy.[52] By raising the level of staple-crop farming and particularly that of tobacco, the English heightened the demand for labor, slave labor, to produce the tobacco staple.

The analysis of the effect of tobacco culture on Delaware slavery and its demise is severely hampered by a paucity of data. Yet similar changes transpired in the neighboring tobacco-growing Chesapeake, where they were better documented. From these sources much can be inferred regarding the changes occurring in Delaware's tobacco economy.[53]

Delaware's shift to tobacco culture occurred gradually, with farmers often combining or rotating tobacco with grain. By the 1680s the switch from grain to tobacco culture was largely complete. The inhabitants of New Castle County provided testimony to this change; in 1680 they requested permission to pay the quitrents on their lands in tobacco rather than grain because they had "no wheat, and nothing else than tobacco." Further, the importance of tobacco in the post–1680 Delaware economy is documented by its use as legal tender and the assessment of court fines in tobacco.[54]

Tobacco remained Delaware's leading staple crop until the mid eighteenth century when it was permanently replaced by grain. But even at its peak, tobacco and slavery in Delaware remained on the periphery of the tobacco and slave culture of the Chesapeake. Neither in the volume and quality of tobacco nor in the population of slaves did Delaware remotely approach the Chesapeake system. The diminutive size of Delaware and the absence of an internal and external frontier not only prevented the development of large scale tobacco plantations but also denied Delaware tobacco farmers the room to escape from tobacco-related ills.

Tobacco culture, despite its popularity in the Chesapeake and colonial Delaware, was replete with problems. Tobacco farmers repeatedly experienced a cyclical pattern of prosperity and depression. But whether boom or bust, tobacco farmers usually responded by increasing production. High tobacco prices predictably tempted tobacco farmers to increase production and profits. However, low prices and uncertain markets did not necessarily convince farmers to abandon tobacco culture; rather, they sought ways and means of survival within the tobacco economy. Farmer responses to low tobacco prices ranged from temporary crop diversification to regulation of trade and credit. Often these changes generated enough revenue to sustain farmers until the tobacco economy recovered. But low prices at times also sparked an increase in crop production as desperate farmers sought to recoup lost income by expanding the acreage under cultivation. Thus, as both high and low tobacco prices brought more land under cultivation, the demand for labor increased, and hence so did the slave population, the primary labor force employed in tobacco cultivation.[55]

Tobacco cultivation, more than grain, demanded constant labor through planting, harvesting, and curing. Labor was required to prepare the ground for seedlings, only to be followed by constant weeding and worming until harvesting, which was followed by several labor-intensive stages of curing, sorting, and packing the tobacco for sale. Each stage of tobacco cultivation demanded incessant labor; lack of adequate labor could mean a tobacco crop lost to worms, disease, inclement weather, or inferior curing.[56] Preparing quality tobacco for market required endless labor in "fallowing, hilling, cutting off hills, planting and replanting, toppings, succerings, weedings, cuttings, picking up, removing out of the ground by hand, hanging, striking, stripping, stemming, and prizing," lamented one tobacco farmer.[57]

Slave labor was by no means the only workforce capable of producing a profitable tobacco crop; indentured servants and free labor—black or white—served as well. But given the few options realistically available to tobacco farmers, slave labor seemed best suited for the ceaseless and tedious labor required in tobacco production. Native Americans were difficult to hold permanently in bondage so close to their kith and kin. Promises of high wages had failed to attract free and waged European laborers because the few who came voluntarily could aspire to farm ownership. Neither did indentured servants adequately meet the needs of Delaware tobacco farmers. Delaware's shift to a tobacco economy occurred at the same time as the number of desirable indentured servant immigrants to the colonies dropped sharply, leaving slavery as the only viable source of constant labor. As a labor system, indentured servitude had a serious drawback, for its temporary nature forced planters to seek new servants every five to seven years. Still, farmers who preferred indentured servants would have borne the inconvenience had the market guaranteed a constant flow of prime indentured servants. But as the seventeenth century drew to a close, it became increasingly difficult to get them.

Until midcentury, the supply of young Englishmen who perceived temporary indenture in the colonies as the best answer to the shrinking economic opportunities at home easily met the demand for servants. Conversely, whenever England's economy improved, as it did periodically, fewer young men willingly chose to serve indentures in the North American colonies. Although immigration of servants to the North American colonies continued during this quarter century, many of the new arrivals did not fit the profile preferred by tobacco farmers: strong, adult, English-speaking males capable of performing the arduous tasks involved in tobacco culture.[58]

The availability of Africans as part of the Atlantic slave trade made Delaware's decision to rely on slaves economically rational. Farmers trying to produce a labor-intensive cash crop like tobacco turned to bound African labor because no other source of labor was available at a price they could afford. Fresh from Africa, slaves did not speak English, but they offered so many other advantages that farmers seemed willing to forgive the language barrier. The supply of slave labor seemed unending and constant, its cost was relatively affordable, and the bondage remained permanent, while the mark of color easily set the slave apart from the rest of colonial society.

When compared to the cost of indentured servants, slaves commanded a higher initial investment, but the permanence of slave labor more than offset the higher cost. The lower mortality rate that prevailed after the 1680s almost guaranteed slaveholders a better return on their investment in slaves. Owners could reap double benefits from slaves: long and permanent bondage and, because slavery was hereditary through the mother, all the issue born to female slaves. That tobacco farmers were aware of the special demands of tobacco culture is evident in the dramatic increase in slave imports to the Chesapeake and the secondary market of Delaware.[59]

The shift to tobacco culture affected the structure of slavery in Delaware but in ways significantly different from the tobacco economies of the Chesapeake. The distribution of slaves in Delaware, even during the peak of the institution, remained less extensive than in the Chesapeake where it was possible to have large slave units working on large-scale plantations. Delaware's small size precluded the establishment of large slave plantations or medium-sized farms, both of which were common to the Chesapeake but a rarity in Delaware. The typical Delaware tobacco farmer, in need of labor but owning a relatively small farm, could profitably employ only a very limited number of slaves. From 1790 to 1860 only a handful of Delaware slaveholders recorded ownership of more than twenty slaves. In 1810 only two slaveholders owned more than twenty slaves; the largest slaveholder, Eli Covington of Kent County, owned thirty-one slaves. On the eve of the Civil War, Delaware's largest slave owner, Benjamin Burton of Sussex County, reported only sixteen slaves.[60]

In sharp contrast to the neighboring colonies, only a small minority of the state's slaves lived and worked in Wilmington, Delaware's only sizable town. Even the South with its heavily concentrated rural slavery reported a significant slave population in the major urban centers. Philadelphia, less than thirty miles away, had a higher proportion of slaves than the surrounding countryside. But in 1800 the city of Wilmington reported only 121 slaves (1.9 percent) out of a total state slave population of 6,153. Wilmington recorded 14 slaves in 1820, 15 in 1840, and 4 in the 1860 census count. It is doubtful that the slave presence in Wilmington dramatically differed in the period before 1800. The need for slave labor there was liable to be relatively small, since the main non-tobacco-related sector, light industry, for the most part excluded black labor. The Wilmington area also had a steady supply of Scotch-Irish indentured servants; often they performed the same laboring tasks as slaves.[61]

The few Wilmington slaves were employed as laborers, house servants, and occasionally as artisans. They lived and worked in white households, sometimes with free blacks. Of the 121 slaves living in Wilmington in 1800, 26 lived together with free blacks in white households. In 1840, 2 out of the 15 slaves lived with free blacks in white households.[62] For the most part these few slaves in Wilmington lived as free persons of color. The presence of a relatively large free black population in Wilmington made this possible.

The changing nature of Delaware's staple crop and labor system manifested itself in the state's slave codes. Although slavery in Delaware was not plantation based, maintaining the institution became as important to owners there as it did to the large and medium-sized tobacco planters in the Chesapeake. Slave codes evolved from the slaveholders' need and desire to ensure owner control over the labor of the slave, safeguard white society from the anger of the enslaved, and protect the special liberties reserved for those of European descent. With a high slave population and heavy dependence on slave labor, the Chesapeake and southern states deemed it necessary to control the burgeoning slave population, ensure the owners' profit, and protect white citizens through the restrictive slave codes. The northern colonies with relatively little dependence on slave labor and thus a small slave population displayed less anxiety over the institution and tended to be more lenient in their slave codes.[63]

Delaware's slave codes reflected neither of these extremes. Reliance on slavery varied greatly, and as a result the state passed slave codes that varied from lenient to severe. The state's codes reveal a clear pattern: a mild slave code prevailed during the initial phase of slavery, followed by restrictive laws at the height of the institution; but as slavery declined in importance, the Delaware slave codes grew more moderate. Delaware enacted few slave codes before the 1680s. However, during the era when tobacco became profitable, slave labor was highly valued, and the slave population continued to expand rapidly, Delaware responded with numerous and increasingly restrictive slave codes. Delaware slave codes, it seems, kept steady pace with the change from grain to tobacco and later from tobacco back to grain. Tobacco culture proved most inimical to the interests of slaves.

The Dutch and Swedes who introduced slavery to Delaware never clarified the status of blacks in the colony. However, it is doubtful if their status differed from that of the company-owned slaves serving in the North River colony (New York). It is known that the company awarded freedom to slaves in consideration of long and faithful service. And apparently New Netherland slaves were allowed rights and privileges quite similar to those "reserved for white indentured servants."[64] The same treatment was probably offered to South River colony slaves.

When the South River came under the authority of the duke of York in 1664, the laws of the colony changed. But like the Dutch, the duke of York enacted few slave codes, preferring, it seems, to allow custom to prevail. Only indirectly did one of the duke's laws authorize slavery. The issue concerned slavery versus Christianity, and whether baptism should free a slave from bondage. The resulting law assumed the legality and permanence of slavery, for it prohibited blacks or Indians from gaining their freedom as a result of conversion to Christianity.[65]

William Penn, the next proprietor of Delaware, began as the Dutch and duke of York had, by only indirectly sanctioning slavery. Penn's acceptance of the bylaws of the Free Society of Traders in 1682 implied his support of the institution of slavery. The law allowed the society to manumit any of its slaves on condition that the former slaves turn over to the society two-thirds of the crops grown on the land provided them. While the law did not expressly define the legal status of slaves, it conceded that slaves were being held for life and that masters had the right to free them. Penn seemed to accept that slaves were held for life; he confessed to his steward that he preferred to have the labor on his farms done by blacks because "a man has them while they live."[66]

Not until 1700 did William Penn and the legislature of Pennsylvania—of which Delaware was a part—pass the colony's first comprehensive slave code. Perhaps the relatively small number of slaves found in early Delaware and Pennsylvania society did not justify a comprehensive slave code. But in 1700, in reaction to the growing black population, two separate slave codes were enacted, "An Act for the better Regulation of Servants" and "An Act for the Trial of Negroes."[67] The preamble of the second act explained that it was intended to remedy the difficulties that had "arisen within this province and territories about the manner of trial and punishment of negroes committing murder, manslaughter, burglary, buggery, rapes, attempts of rapes and other high and heinous enormities and capital offenses." The crimes selected for special review in 1700 and the punishments specified testify to the society's obsession with controlling slaves, displaying its anxiety over slave resistance and revolts. First, the act established a special court for the trial of all blacks, slave and free, comprised of two justices of the peace and six respectable white citizens. Death was prescribed as the punishment for murder and rape, with castration as the penalty for any black male convicted of the attempted rape of a white female. To prevent slaves from acquiring the means for vengeance or revolt, slaves caught with weapons faced twenty-one lashes, while those meeting in groups of more than four were to receive a public whipping not exceeding thirty-nine lashes. Because slaves, unlike indentured servants, could not be threatened or punished with additional servitude or fines, slaves convicted of lesser crimes paid with time in the pillory and with public whipping.

Even after the Delaware colony formally separated from the legislative authority of Pennsylvania, it continued to model its slave codes after Pennsylvania's. Delaware's 1726 revision of the 1700 slave code, for example, was an almost verbatim reproduction of a law passed by Pennsylvania in 1725.[68] The revised code contained a mixed bag of lenient penalties without sacrificing the desire to assure the safety of white society. It commuted the penalty for attempted rape of a white female by a black male from castration to four hours in the pillory, and the number of blacks who could meet without fear of punishment was increased from four to six, with the penalty reduced from thirty-nine to twenty-one lashes. The code continued to protect the interests of white society by providing inducements for masters to report criminal activity by their slaves. The revision provided for the reimbursement of slave owners, amounting to two-thirds of the value of any slave who was executed.

A second 1726 act introduced a new element into Delaware's slave codes, proscriptions on interracial liaisons. The preamble stated that it was needed to ensure the "preservation of virtue and chastity among the people of this government, and to prevent the heinous sins of adultery and fornication." But this noble intent was neither universally nor fairly applied; the legislature reserved its harshest penalties for incidents of adultery and cohabitation involving interracial couples, specifically between white females and black males. The penalties assessed against others who committed adultery, proved less exacting. White males, in particular, received less severe punishment and often could satisfy the court with payment of a fine. The act remained silent on the question of children born out of liaisons between white males and black females.

Possibly the legislature merely refrained from stating the obvious—that the child followed the status of the mother into slavery. The act made no mention of adultery committed by slaves, presumably because slave marriages were not recognized by law and possibly because it was in the interest of slave owners to encourage slave women to bear children. The brunt of the 1726 law fell heavily on white females bearing illegitimate children, particularly children of mixed race. Punishment for the white mother ranged from fines, lashes, and time in the pillory to servitude. The mulatto children born of these unions were punished with indentures lasting until they reached the age of thirty-one.[69]

Until the mid-eighteenth century tobacco and slavery continued to flourish in Delaware. Amid this success of the tobacco culture, Delaware farmers and slaveholders failed to foresee the imminent economic destruction of both tobacco and slavery. Yet within the triumph of Delaware's tobacco culture lay the seeds for its destruction, for its success without room for expansion and growth soon doomed the cultivation of tobacco to extinction, while the intense intrastate rivalry destined de jure slavery to prolonged torpor.

# 2

## The Making of Voluntary Emancipation, 1740–1865

DELAWARE slaveholders made a way to freedom for a variety of reasons, all of which tended to work toward undermining the integrity of slavery in the state. Voluntary emancipation of Delaware slaves began long before the mid-eighteenth century. However, the most dramatic rise in manumissions did not occur until around the time of the American Revolution. Although Delaware never legislated the abolition of slavery, by the First Federal Census of 1790, 30 percent of Delaware blacks were already free. From its peak of 70 percent of the black population in 1790, slavery in Delaware rapidly and permanently declined. Within two decades of the first census, by 1810, the proportion of slaves among Delaware blacks had declined to 24 percent; by 1850 the percentage had decreased to 11 percent, and by 1860, to 8 percent. In reverse order, the proportion of free persons among blacks in Delaware steadily increased until ratification of the thirteenth amendment to the United States Constitution freed the remaining slaves.

Although not bound by any coercive abolition laws, Delaware slaveholders voluntarily freed a high proportion of their slaves in response to a fateful combination of complex religious, ideological, and economic forces. Religion took precedence as the initial factor inspiring most Delaware slaveholders. The Society of Friends inaugurated this trend by exhorting members to free their souls from the bonds of sin and their slaves from physical bondage. Next, they launched a crusade aimed at the citizens and state of Delaware, seeking to convince both of the religious and moral imperative of emancipation. The Methodists soon added their voice to Quaker protests. From their base in rural Delaware, Methodists persuaded many slaveholders to practice Christian charity by manumitting their slaves.

The ideology and events of the American Revolution provided advocates of abolition with a powerful instrument for change. The fundamental principle behind the Revolution, the natural rights of mankind, stood starkly as the antithesis of slavery. Natural rights ideology rested on the assertion of equality and liberty for all. In turn, this exposed the contradiction between a nation fighting for its liberty yet depriving people of color of the same freedom. Although the Revolutionary rhetoric did not specifically declare slaves to be entitled to these rights, the logical implication seemed obvious. For slaveholders unable to reconcile slavery and the rights of mankind, manumission of slaves seemed the only rational option.

As important as religion and the Enlightenment were to abolition, these ideologies alone cannot sufficiently explain the extensive emancipation that swept through the state of Delaware. At the core of the voluntary manumission movement lay secular changes in the state's economy, a final shift from tobacco to grain culture. Along with other Chesapeake agricultural areas, Delaware switched back to grain during the mid-eighteenth century when profits from tobacco declined precipitously. The decision to return to less labor-intensive grain cultivation set the stage for the demise of slavery in Delaware.

The change a century earlier from grain to tobacco ignited a surge in the demand for slave labor. Inevitably, therefore, the late eighteenth-century switch back to grain sharply reduced the need for slave labor, creating a chronic labor surplus from which slavery in Delaware would never recover. However, because of religious and ideological concerns, the state legislature chose to interfere with market mechanisms that under ordinary circumstances would have drawn Delaware's surplus slaves toward the booming demand sectors in the Deep South slave states. A religiously and ideologically motivated decision to ban sales of slaves to buyers in other states ensured that for the next century Delaware would struggle constantly to reduce the number of surplus slave laborers without becoming a slave exporter. Lacking the political will to enact abolition, the state saddled itself with an unexportable population of slaves whose labor could not be profitably employed in cultivating grain. Individual Delaware slaveholders coped as best they could; they manumitted slaves whom they could neither use nor legally export.

Thus, voluntary manumission in Delaware represented a compromise or a second-best option to the principal parties: slaves, abolitionists, slaveholders. No group possessed the power fully to have its way. Delaware slaveholders discovered they could neither will tobacco and slavery back to economic viability nor persuade the legislature to allow out-of-state sales of surplus slave laborers. Antislavery proponents could not cobble together a majority in the legislature to impose mandatory abolition, so they settled for incremental reforms that enabled economically desperate slaveholders to rid themselves of surplus slaves. The slaves, lacking the political power to achieve mandatory emancipation, often found in this complex set of circumstances opportunities they did not miss to gain their freedom.

### Delaware Laws and Voluntary Emancipation

Although Delaware never legislated abolition, the pace of manumission within its borders compared favorably with that of the northern states that mandated abolition by statute. Delaware easily surpassed the rate of manumission in New York and New Jersey. Not until the 1830s did those two states, both with gradual abolition laws, exceed Delaware's pace of emancipation. In 1810, eleven years after New York passed its gradual abolition law, only 63 percent of the state's black population was counted free. Delaware during the same period, but without the force of an abolition mandate, could point to a black population that was 76 percent free. New Jersey, even with its 1804 gradual abolition law, trailed Delaware in its proportion of free blacks until the 1830s.

Delaware's actions appear even more exceptional when compared to the states where slavery remained legal until the Civil War. The proportion of blacks who were free was dramatically higher in Delaware than in any slave state. By 1860 approximately 92 percent of Delaware blacks were free; by comparison, in nearby Maryland—the slave state with the next highest proportion of free blacks—only 49 percent of the black population had attained freedom (table 4).

Although the rate of voluntary emancipation peaked at the beginning of the nineteenth century, the progression toward voluntary manumission in Delaware began far earlier and became visible as early as the 1740s. From the mid-eighteenth century, additions to Delaware's slave codes shifted the focus of attention to the related issues of manumission and free blacks. The first of these acts, passed in 1740, revealed a colony struggling to cope with the growing incidence of manumissions.

The preamble to section 10 of the 1740 act rationalized the code by claiming that "it is found by experience, that free Negroes and Mulattoes are idle and slothful," "often prove burthensome to the neighbourhood wherein they live," and, "are of evil example to slaves." Thus, the law sought to relieve white society from the burden of supporting "lazy" free

Table 4.  Percentage of free blacks in black population, 1790–1860

|            | 1790 | 1800 | 1810 | 1820 | 1830 | 1840 | 1850 | 1860 |
|------------|------|------|------|------|------|------|------|------|
| New York   | 18.0 | 33.2 | 62.7 | 74.3 | 99.8 | 99.9 | 100  | 100  |
| New Jersey | 19.4 | 26.1 | 41.9 | 62.2 | 89.0 | 96.8 | 99.0 | 99.9 |
| Delaware   | 30.4 | 57.3 | 75.8 | 74.1 | 82.8 | 86.6 | 88.7 | 91.6 |
| Maryland   | 7.2  | 15.6 | 23.3 | 27.0 | 33.9 | 40.8 | 45.2 | 49.0 |
| Virginia   | 4.2  | 5.4  | 7.2  | 7.9  | 9.1  | 9.9  | 10.3 | 10.5 |
| N. Carolina| 4.7  | 5.0  | 5.7  | 6.6  | 7.3  | 8.4  | 8.6  | 8.4  |
| S. Carolina| 1.6  | 2.1  | 2.2  | 2.5  | 2.4  | 2.4  | 2.2  | 2.4  |

*Source:* Compiled from U.S. Bureau of the Census, *Negro Population, 1790–1915* (Washington, D.C., 1969), 57.

blacks and also hoped to prevent slaves from emulating the "corrupt" practices of free blacks. The 1740 act copied almost verbatim the provisions of a slave code passed by Pennsylvania in 1726. Perhaps Delaware waited until 1740 before enacting this law because the free black population before then was too insignificant to warrant special legislation.

Oddly, to counter the alleged lazy behavior of free blacks, the 1740 law targeted not adult free blacks but their children. The law required children of "indigent" free blacks to serve indentures, males until age twenty-one and females until they turned eighteen. To curb the "evil" influence of free blacks on slaves, the law prohibited free blacks from harboring or trading with any slave or servant without the owner's permission. Free blacks found guilty of violating the provisions of the law faced fines and a public whipping (not exceeding twenty-one lashes); those unable to pay the assessed fines were expected to compensate with servitude.

An increase in manumissions, especially of old and infirm slaves, seemed of particular concern, though the preamble was less candid about this reason. The code did not restrict owners willing to free healthy and young slaves, but it mandated the posting of a bond of £30 before freeing unhealthy slaves or those past the age of thirty-five. Ostensibly, the bond covered state costs in supporting sick and indigent ex-slaves.[1]

The question of manumission was again debated by the state in 1767. Once again the preamble portrayed free blacks as "idle and slothful" and followed with the state's acknowledgment that its previous laws had "not been found to answer all the good purposes thereby intended," that is, the attempt to restrict manumission. Convinced that manumission in the colony had gone awry, the legislature replaced the 1740 act with a more restrictive law. The 1767 act deleted the age limit and imposed double the bond, £60, for setting "free any Mulatto or Negro slave or slaves."[2]

The additional restrictions indicate a significant increase in the practice of manumission. The doubling of the manumission bond expressed the state's awareness of its failure to stem the tide of manumission and its hope that the new and higher bond would deter slaveholders. Too, the provisions of the act stood as an admission that slaveholders were freeing not only old and sick slaves but also younger and healthy slaves, and in such significant numbers as to compel deterrence, if not an end to manumission.

The legislature's attempts to impede manumissions failed. Instead, the rate of emancipation reached epic proportions by the closing decades of the eighteenth century, and the rapid pace continued during the early years of the nineteenth century. Finally, in response to intense pressure mounted by Quakers, abolitionists, and northern Delaware, the state abandoned its opposition to voluntary manumissions. By the end of the eighteenth century, the legislature had cleared the path to voluntary manumission. It had eased manumission laws, restricted the import and export of slaves, granted freedom to slaves whose owners sought to circumvent the import and export of slave laws, and firmly committed slaveholders to manumission contracts that could no longer be easily disputed or invalidated. But at the same time and in response to an equally powerful campaign by the proslavery and southern section of the state, the legislature continued to uphold the constitutional basis of slavery.

The legislature enacted the first of the promanumission laws in February 1787. It legalized all past manumissions of healthy slaves aged twenty-one to thirty-five and permitted slaveholders to free healthy slaves aged eighteen to thirty-five without posting a bond. The code banned sale of slaves and indentured blacks out of state except upon grant of permission by three justices of the peace. A violation of the law did not free the slave victim, but the state punished the guilty slaveholder with a fine of £100 for each slave in question. The act outlawed the domestic slave trade to Delaware; slaves brought to the state for sale were "declared free to all intents and purposes," while the offender, in addition to losing the slave, faced a fine of £20.[3] The law did exclude migrants intending to settle permanently in Delaware; such persons were allowed to bring in their slaves. It was unlikely, however, that migrating slaveholders would take advantage of this provision with the fertile western frontier beckoning.

Two years later the state passed a supplement and through its provisions further proscribed the import and export of slaves.[4] The supplement subjected vessels equipping for the "iniquitous traffic" in slaves to seizure, while persons manning the ships could be fined up to £500. Bowing to pressure from the Quakers and the abolition societies and because the 1787 law had not effectively curbed the export of slaves from Delaware, the state now decreed that permission to export slaves should be obtained from five, instead of three, justices of the peace. The penalty for illegal exporting of slaves remained at £100, but the supplement now imposed a fine of £20 on persons convicted of attempted export of slaves. The supplement ended by granting jury trials to slaves convicted of capital offenses.

A code enacted in 1793 further restricted slave exports by mandating that persons charged under the 1787 and 1789 laws post bail or remain in custody until the adjudication of their case. Unlike the earlier laws, which refrained from offering freedom to slave victims, the 1793 act penalized and restrained illegal slave exports by granting immediate and unconditional freedom to any slave whose owner had attempted to sell or had sold him or her out of state.[5]

In 1797 the state capped its voluntary manumission laws with an act that made freedom contracts binding and enforceable. The state found it "necessary for the security of Negro and Mulatto slaves, whose masters or mistresses may intend to manumit them, and also for the safety of persons holding such property," that manumission contracts "be rendered certain, and not depend upon verbal contracts or manumissions, which are often misunderstood and forgotten."[6] Consequently, the legislature declared all verbal manumissions null and void and decreed that all freedom contracts should be written, witnessed by a competent white citizen, attested to, and recorded by the state. These steps legally bound the slaveholder to honor the contract; in the event of a failure to do so, the slave could seek redress through the courts.

## Delaware Quakers and Abolition

The Society of Friends and the Methodists led the religious crusade against slavery in Delaware. Whether they were Quakers, Methodists, or of other denominations, many Delaware slave owners confessed their uneasiness over slavery, particularly in light of such Christian principles as universal brotherhood and the "golden rule." However, salvation for the troubled Christian conscience could be found, as many slaveholders apparently did, through the emancipation of the slave.

As in all the other North American colonies, the Society of Friends was the first religious group in Delaware to espouse abolition of slavery. A pacifist group, Quakers fled persecution in England for a more tolerant religious climate in North America. The founding of Pennsylvania by the Quaker William Penn furnished the Society of Friends with the religious haven they sought. From its founding, Pennsylvania and nearby colonies, especially Delaware, which was granted to Penn in 1682, drew settlers of the Quaker persuasion. Of Delaware's three counties, Quakers were particularly attracted to the northernmost and middle counties, New Castle and Kent, while southernmost Sussex County appealed to fewer Friends.

The road to Quaker antislavery was long; not until 1776 did the society mandate abolition for all members. Early Quaker proponents of abolition faced two obstacles: convincing fellow Friends to support the antislavery crusade and promoting emancipation in the society at large. First, reformers had to rid their society of slavery before taking the battle to non-Quakers. It was an uphill battle, for Quakers in colonial North America, and in particular in the city of Philadelphia, were heavily involved in the external and domestic slave trade. Because the economic interests of these Quaker merchants conflicted with the goals of the antislavery advocates, it would require extraordinary time and effort to convince them to renounce the practice of slavery and the profits of the slave trade.[7]

Notwithstanding Quaker belief in an inner light of conscience and spiritual guidance, it took a century of prolonged soul-searching before the Quakers permanently lit the torch of abolition. Quaker antislavery activism began with individual and small group protests before ballooning into a societywide movement. During the 1670s William Edmundson, an Irish Quaker, led the fight for abolition in the North American colonies when he called on Friends to live by the "golden rule." Who among them, he asked his fellow Quakers, "would have the blacks or others to make you their Slaves with out hope or expectation of freedom or liberty?" Rather, a policy promoting abolition, Edmundson reasoned, would demonstrate the worthiness of Quakers to the world.[8] While Edmundson's campaign did not immediately stir the conscience of Quakers in colonial America, his voice set the pattern for Quaker antislavery thinking.

Among Delaware Valley Friends the first official protest against slavery was a 1688 Germantown petition. These petitioners also based their argument on Christ's admonition to the world—the golden rule—and called on fellow Quakers to shine their inner light on their conscience by doing unto others as they hoped would be done to them. Though the Philadelphia Yearly Meeting did not grant their request, it did not silence critics of slavery. Throughout the late seventeenth century, Quaker reformers continuously protested against slavery. Finally, in 1696 opponents of slavery scored a significant victory when the Philadelphia Yearly Meeting took a first, albeit a hesitant, step toward antislavery: it advised Friends to refrain from importing slaves.[9]

As the eighteenth century opened, there came a flood of Quaker antislavery reformers. Through the work of such Friends as William Southeby, Ralph Sandiford, and Benjamin Lay, Quakers in colonial North America gradually moved toward an antislavery stance. But the reformers did not win their struggle until the 1770s. Until then, they were often disciplined by their fellow Quakers for creating dissension and occasionally were disowned. Their antislavery message directly challenged the financial interests of many of Philadelphia's prominent Quaker families who still made their living through slavery and the slave trade and therefore were not favorably disposed to curtailing their activities. Rather, they used their influence to keep the society from committing itself to an antislavery stance.[10]

By the mid-eighteenth century, the Quaker proslavery old guard had gradually given way to a new generation of Friends, younger and antislavery, who now controlled the meetinghouse. More receptive to critics of slavery than the earlier generation, the new Quaker leadership allowed antislavery reformers like John Woolman and Anthony Benezet to be heard. But even with the change in the climate of opinion, Friends still approached abolition with extreme caution.

A series of resolutions passed at the Philadelphia Yearly Meetings from the 1750s to the American Revolution gradually prohibited Friends from importing, owning, or selling slaves. In 1755 the Yearly Meeting issued an advisory against the slave trade but imposed no sanctions. Three years later in 1758, the Yearly Meeting moved halfway to mandated abolition: visiting committees would bring societal pressure to bear on slaveholding Friends while those who persisted in slaveholding would be denied full participation in society business. The Yearly Meeting in 1774 reiterated the appointment of committees to visit slaveholding Friends: recalcitrant members would be censured, and if they persisted in holding slaves, disownment was prescribed. Finally in 1776, amid the opening round of the American Revolution, the Yearly Meeting removed the restraints from the 1774 directive by formally sanctioning disownment for slaveholding Friends.[11]

Delaware Quakers were very familiar with these antislavery sentiments and directives. Their state shared political and economic ties with Pennsylvania, and their meetinghouses fell under the authority of the Philadelphia Yearly Meeting. Like Quakers elsewhere, Friends in Delaware went through an ambivalent period before adopting a strong antislavery stand. By the mid-eighteenth century, several of Delaware's prominent Quakers had realized that their inner light was at odds with the practice of slavery; thus, they began to question the morality of slavery. The monthly meetings at Wilmington in New Castle County and Duck Creek in Kent County became the nerve centers of the Delaware Quaker antislavery crusade. Both had influential persons leading the antislavery campaign: David Ferris in Wilmington and Warner Mifflin at Duck Creek.

Ferris expressed little sympathy for Friend slaveholders. In 1766 he described them as a "hindrance to Israels march" and predicted that "such Leprous persons" would soon be removed from the society. Ten years later his prediction came true when the Yearly Meeting mandated abolition and penalized slaveholders with disownment. Ferris seemed unimpressed with Quakers who excused slaveholding as a necessary means to bring civilization and salvation to the "inferior" African race. It was no more than grandiose missionary talk; their real missionary duty, said Ferris, lay in the freeing of their slaves. Additionally, Ferris recommended a duty beyond manumission: helping the ex-slaves into their new lives as free persons. For as Moses cautioned the people of Israel, Ferris continued, ex-slaves should not be sent away empty-handed; rather, they should be rewarded for their years of service.[12] Thus, healthy ex-slaves should be provided with a start in life as free persons, or if they were too old to work, such free persons should be cared for until the end of their days.

Friends who rejected the appeals of the visiting committee faced the censure of Ferris and the Wilmington monthly meeting. Often the Wilmington society approved penalties in excess of those prescribed by the Yearly Meeting. When the 1758 Yearly Meeting directive recommended committee visitations and loss of leadership for slaveholders, the Ferris-led Wilmington monthly meeting went further by prescribing disownment for any member found guilty of buying and selling slaves. The monthly meeting reported thirteen disciplinary cases between 1760 and 1776. A majority of the offenders acknowledged and made reparation for their error—including manumission, education, training, and monetary awards to the ex-slaves—but approximately 40 percent were hardcore offenders who refused to abide by the antislavery policy and were disowned.[13]

Delaware's other monthly meeting, Duck Creek, had an equally strong abolitionist at helm: Warner Mifflin. Born of Quaker parents in 1745, he moved with his wife to Delaware in 1767 and died there in October 1798. Apparently at age fourteen, an encounter with one of his father's slaves led Mifflin to question the morality of enslaving others. However, not until after his marriage and the Quaker resolutions of the 1770s prohibiting members from enslaving others did Mifflin put his convictions into practice. In 1774 and 1775 he manumitted the thirty slaves he had inherited. Having made the commitment, Mifflin went further and made "restitution on to those I had held in a state of bondage, for the time so held," and for slaves he had sold in the past, he fell "under an obligation to release them; which I did to a considerable amount, on my own account, my then Wife's, and some who belonged to her Father and Grandfather."[14]

With the ardent abolitionist Mifflin leading the Duck Creek monthly meeting, his meetinghouse, and indeed the county of Kent, led the state in manumissions. Like fellow Friends in Wilmington, the Duck Creek monthly meeting employed committee visits to pressure slaveholding Friends to free their slaves. Those they failed to persuade were often disciplined in excess of the 1758 Quaker directive. Also like their coreligionists in Wilmington, Duck Creek Friends imposed disownment even before the main Quaker body made it obligatory. In August 1771 the Duck Creek meetinghouse censured William Corbit for buying a slave, and in March 1772 it disowned him for refusing to free the slave. Nine years passed before Corbit experienced a change of heart; in November 1781 he freed the slave and appealed for readmission to the society. The society readmitted Corbit in December 1782, after he complied with all the prerequisites, including paying the assessed fine plus reasonable compensation to the slave in question.[15]

Under the authority of the 1758 directive, the Duck Creek Friends voted in 1772 to exclude Jonathan Hunn, a Quaker slave buyer, "from having any right to sit in . . . meetings for Discipline or contribute in any manner to the affairs of the Church." Four years later, after freeing the slave, Hunn expressed interest in returning to the Quaker fold. A committee in August 1781 tracked down the ex-slave, ascertained the amount due for the time served, and assessed the sum against Hunn. Only after payment of the fine and compensation to the ex-slave plus his agreement to serve as benefactor did Hunn in 1781 receive permission to return to fellowship.[16]

Although lack of data prevents an accurate tally of Wilmington manumissions, in Duck Creek the meetinghouse reported 620 slaves freed by 138 slave owners between 1774 and 1792. Not all the reported cases of manumissions involved Delaware slaves, for a few of the slaveholders were not residents of Delaware; neither did all the manumitters claim membership in the Quaker faith. For example, when Daniel Mifflin of Virginia freed 109 slaves in 1777, the Duck Creek society deservedly took credit for this and similar manumissions, for they were accomplished through the effort of the society. Also included in the Duck Creek record of manumissions were freedom deeds executed by non-Quaker slaveholders from Kent County.

Excluding non-Delaware freed slaves and slaveholders, approximately 123 Duck Creek Quaker or Quaker-influenced slaveholders freed 460 slaves from 1774 to 1792. Because of the Quaker influence, Kent County led the state in manumissions; in 1790, 52.7 percent of Kent County blacks were counted as free persons as opposed to 19.9 percent in New Castle County and 14.6 percent in Sussex County.

Within three years of mandated Quaker abolition, the Duck Creek visiting committee reported that "only one member of the meeting-house, James Morris, still held slaves."[17] Perhaps the statement was a bit premature, as the Duck Creek manumission records reveal an additional 107 slaves freed by forty-three slaveholders between 1780 and 1792. But the freeing of these additional 107 slaves does not necessarily negate the claim of the visiting committee. Many of the post–1780 manumissions reflected some extenuating circumstance that had prevented an earlier manumission date, for example, slaves acquired through recent inheritance or the freeing of slaves who had completed their premanumission indentures.

John Dickinson, the Quaker-influenced president of Delaware from 1782 to 1783, freed all his slaves between 1772 and 1777. However, in 1779 he freed two additional slaves, who "lately fell to [him] by a Redivision of [his] Wife's Father's Estate." Similarly, Mary Turley, who freed six slaves in 1792, was simply disposing of her brother's estate. And so was Elizabeth Molleston, who in 1781 inherited a slave from her brother's estate but "being convinced that it is contrary to the royal Law of doing unto all Men as we would be willing to be done by, to hold him as a slave . . . [did] manumit and set absolutely free the said Negro."[18]

The majority of the slaves freed after 1780 were released by non-Quakers influenced by Quaker antislavery and natural rights ideology. They recorded their deeds of manumission with the Quakers as an additional precaution. These non-Quakers, knowing many in the state opposed abolition, wanted to defend the freedom of the ex-slaves by having the Society of Friends register their manumission deeds.

Not all Friends willingly abided by the directives of 1774 and 1776.

Some did so after extensive societal pressure, and others adamantly refused to free their slaves. James Morris of Duck Creek monthly meeting absolutely refused to free his six slaves, "alleging he dont see it to be his duty to do it yet."[19] Even with Duck Creek's early start on the campaign to abolish slavery, it was still complaining about the unyielding resistance of Friend slaveholders toward abolition on the eve of the American Revolution. The visiting committee reported in January 1775 that it had

> attended to the service and a visit has been made to all or nearly all in
> that circumstance and altho it was attended with exercising close labour
> of mind, yet a good degree of satisfaction attends our minds on account
> thereof and more so in that we found in many places the minds of
> Friends engaged under an exercise to their duty to the poor slaves in
> their possession many of whom still need the encouragement and assis-
> tance of Friends—But on the contrary too many appear to be too un-
> thoughtful of their duty herein and divers painful circumstances there
> are which require the time, care and faithful labour of Friends.

In October 1775 the committee reported further progress but requested additional time since several members still held slaves. The committee sounded hopeful in its June 1776 report; it announced "that the minds of several have inclined toward setting them at Liberty . . . and others it is expressed will soon comply herein." Three years later, in 1779, the committee gladly reported that "James Morris is the only one in membership now remaining who holds slaves within the verge of this meeting who has the entire disposing power."[20] Morris still did not see manumission as his duty.

Some Friends cited lack of authority or shared ownership as reasons for their failure to free their slaves. Such was the case of Mary Jones, who declared she had no power to free her slaves for she had already willed them to her daughter. To this excuse the visiting committee replied that "it appeared her desire was to have the labour of the Negro." Others offering excuses, more genuine than Mary Jones's, were female Friends married to non-Quakers. These women found themselves in an awkward position: their faith required that they free their slaves, but their non-Quaker spouses were not bound by the same directive. From August 1777 on, the visiting committee pressured these women into persuading their husbands to manumit their slaves. Two years later the committee sadly admitted that it had experienced limited success among this group.[21] Yet the situation was not so gloomy as reported. In April 1778, Charles Hilliard and his wife Elizabeth recorded the manumission of twenty-two slaves, because Elizabeth claimed membership in the society.[22] Similarly, Henry and Margaret Newell freed five slaves in January 1779 because she was a Friend.[23]

Duck Creek Friends, convinced of the sin of slavery, at times took extraordinary steps to correct their past mistakes. It was not unknown for Quakers who had sold personal slaves in the past to search for the slaves, buy them back, and promptly free them. Although Quakers Thomas and Elizabeth Bowman had "time back manumitted and set free all the Negroes" they owned, they remained troubled about previous slave sales. Recalling that Elizabeth's mother, Sarah Draper, "did in her lifetime sell and dispose of a negro Woman named Dinah" and that Elizabeth before her marriage "did also sell a negro man named Isaac Miller," and "finding uneasiness to remain in our minds for and on account of the said Negroes," the Bowmans purchased and freed the slaves. Jonathan Neal, a Friend from Kent County, made two trips to the Carolinas before he could locate a slave he had sold in the past. Neal purchased the slave for £100 and immediately freed her.[24]

The 1776 Yearly Meeting directive mandated manumission but remained vague on method. The directive left unanswered questions such as whether the freeing of slaves should be immediate and unconditional or preceded by a period of indenture. Failure to clarify these procedural issues left the local meetinghouses to resolve them in their own fashion.

David Ferris anticipated this problem as far back as 1766 when he commented that at "what age they [slaves] ought to be discharged, is a matter, that all are not agreed about." According to Ferris his fellow Friends recommended a manumission age ranging from twenty-one to forty years of age, but he argued that slaves should serve no longer than white servants. Ferris did not think much of those who freed their slaves past age twenty-one; to him it was only "half Justice" reminiscent of "Ananias Selling his Estate, but bringing part of the price into the Treasury."[25]

In instances where Quaker slaveholders explained their actions, they typically cited religious duty as the primary force behind the emancipation. When John Flynn freed his slaves in 1781, it was because he found slavery "incompatible with the royal Law of our Blessed Lord, as well as the General Scope, Tenor and Spirit of the Gospel which breathes Mercy and Justice in the most extensive Manner to all Creatures universally and indiscriminately." Similarly, in 1774 Warner Mifflin offered freedom to his slaves because he was "fully persuaded in my Conscience that it is a Sin of a deep Dye to make Slaves of fellow Creatures or to continue them in Slavery." He believed it would be "impossible to obtain that Peace my Soul desires" until he freed from "Bondage those that have as just

& equitable Right to their Freedom and Liberty of their Persons" as he did."[26]

As the eighteenth century drew to a close, the Quaker rationale for manumission changed. Although religion remained the primary motive, the ideals of the American Revolution provided an equally powerful stimulus. From the late 1770s onward, Quakers began to cite both religion and the natural rights ideology as grounds for freeing slaves. The Manlove family's decision in 1779 to free the slaves inherited from their father's estate illustrates this point. Because they believed "that Liberty is the natural Birthright of all Men" and that to deny freedom to slaves would be a "manifest Breach of the royal Injunction of our blessed Lord to do unto all Men as we would they should do unto us," the Manloves emancipated all eleven slaves. Catherine Ennals grappled with the contradiction between her faith as a Quaker, the rights of all mankind, and her right to own property, before freeing her slave. Ennals strongly believed in the right of all free persons to own property, a right which citizens "cannot in Justice and Equity be deprived of." But she confessed that although "entitled by the oppressive Custom" prevalent in the nation to own slaves, she could not "do it with a good Conscience for which Reason" in May 1779 she freed her slave.[27]

Quaker slaveholder Joshua Fisher freed his slaves because of his belief in both Christian charity and the principles of natural rights. Fisher, who in the past had sold some of his personal slaves—as allowed under the law—now questioned the basis of such power; he concluded that "one human Creature cannot and ought not to have" such authority "over another." Therefore, out of his "Duty as a Christian," Fisher bought back the slaves and promptly freed them, but not before assigning the ex-slaves new surnames that confirmed Fisher's new consuming passion for the ideology of natural rights and liberty. As a condition of freedom, his ex-slave James was renamed James Freeman; James's son Cato became Cato Freeman; another Cato was to be known as Cato Freeset, while his ex-slaves Paris and Sabrina became Paris and Sabrina Freedom.[28]

Quaker antislavery campaigning transcended the bounds of the society. After manumitting their slaves, they set out to convince non-Quaker Delaware slaveholders of the moral necessity of doing the same. The Quakers launched their crusade against slavery at a propitious time. It occurred in an age when many citizens, Quaker and non-Quaker alike, believed it possible to legislate abolition. Throughout the new nation, particularly in the North and upper South, legislatures debated abolition, proposing plans ranging from an end to slavery and the slave trade to the colonization of the freed men and women. From the Continental

Congress to the new state legislatures, elected representatives vigorously debated the incompatibility of slavery and natural rights principles, deciding in some states to pass gradual abolition laws.

Basing their argument for emancipation on Christian duty and natural rights ideology, Delaware Quakers repeatedly petitioned the state legislature for an end to the slave trade, external and domestic, and an end to slavery. The society did not realize its goal of legislated abolition, but it successfully sponsored laws that made it easier for Delaware slaveholders privately and voluntarily to free their slaves.

The first of several Quaker petitions was presented to the state legislature in 1786. It applauded the abolition of slavery by neighboring states and called on the legislature of Delaware to emulate this example by repealing the state-mandated manumission bond. In February 1787 the society relieved the committee appointed to present the memorial to the legislature of its duty because "the subject [had] been attended to and Relief granted to that People in many of their grievances."[29]

The "relief" was the passage of the February 1787 promanumission law that severely checked the domestic slave trade while easing restrictions on private manumissions. But the act did not address the major issue raised in the Quaker petition of 1786; it failed to legislate the abolition of slavery. Nonetheless, Quakers and advocates of abolition had good reason to celebrate, for the act proved extremely damaging to the survival of slavery.

Delaware blacks immediately took advantage of the law, for it provided a legitimate avenue for slaves seeking freedom. As was to be expected, it became a special mission of abolition advocates and Delaware slaves to monitor slaveholder observance of the 1787 law. The ability to sue and invariably win freedom should the owner attempt to skirt the intent of the law provided an opportunity too tempting for abolitionists in Delaware to ignore. Abolitionist scrutiny possibly prevented many slaveholders from openly flouting the law. What is certain is that with the help of the abolition societies and Quakers, many Delaware slaves sued and won their freedom. Warner Mifflin, in particular, was frequently named as the "next best friend" or adviser on many freedom suits, which often resulted in freedom for the slave.

"Negro Boy Levi" wasted little time in suing for his freedom. On 18 August 1787, only six months after passage of the manumission law, he petitioned for his freedom on the grounds that "your petitioner by the Laws and Customs of the Delaware State is justly intitled to his freedom, and is now illegally held in servitude by Watson Wharton—against justice and the rights of freemen." Negro Boy Levi's petition served notice on Delaware slaveholders. In 1788 "Negro Robert" appealed for relief under the law because his owner, Daniel Dawson, was "about to remove to Caroline"; thus, Robert believed he was "justly intitled to his Liberty and Freedom."[30]

In an undated petition Mariah Cole argued for her freedom, pleading "equity, good conscience and the Laws of the Country." She requested that the legislature summon her "pretended master" to "shew cause if any he hath why your Petitioner may not enjoy her Liberty which she apprehend, herself legally intitled to in common with others of her kind." Cole expressed fear of being illegally sold out of state and thus requested a speedy adjudication of her case. But should the court rule against her, she was prepared, she said, to "return to her alotment, contentedly till it shall be the will of God to dispose of her [in] other ways." In May 1795 the court not only ruled in her favor but ordered her former owner Sylvia Sipple to pay court costs.[31]

There is no accurate record of the total number of slaves who won their freedom by appealing to the provisions of the 1787 law. However, it appears that the number was substantial enough to aggravate slaveholders. By 1801 the impact of the law had provoked Sussex County representative Outerbridge Horsey to introduce a bill "compelling negroes petitioning for their freedom, to give surety for the payment of the costs in case the prayer of their petition be rejected." The bill failed. White Delawareans continued to protest against the provisions of the 1787 law. Some in 1810 complained to the legislature "that they have long considered certain parts of the law relative to the petitioning of Negroes for their freedom as unjust and oppressive to their Masters," particularly because until the court's final decision, "no Master however just his claim can take possession or have the service of his slave, or any security for his forthcoming or payment of wages." The petitioners found equally irritating the requirement making slaveholders liable for court costs regardless of the outcome of the freedom suits. Thus, they implored the legislature to amend the law by requiring that future petitions for freedom be sponsored by a leading resident of the county. Such sponsors, they continued, must be held liable for any loss of wages and court costs, if the court ruled against the slave. Their petition was not granted.[32]

Delaware Quakers never lost sight of their original goal of mandated abolition, not even after the partial victory in 1787. In a petition submitted to the 1788 legislature, the Quakers asked not only for the abolition of slavery but also the suppression of the slave trade, a strong enforcement of the law against the importation of slaves, and an end to the unnatural separation of slave families through sale. The state failed to act on the petition; therefore, on 20 January 1789 the Quakers reminded the legislature of their petition the previous year. This time the legislative committee formed to study the petition recommended "in the most earnest manner, a revision of the now existing laws relative to those unfortunate sufferers," because the "good purposes for which the act of the 3rd of February 1787, was passed, have not been effectively answered, nor the general benefit expected therefrom produced." Twelve days later the 1789 supplement to the 1787 act became law.[33]

Repeating the pattern of 1787, the state in the 1789 act neglected some of the major goals of the petitioners. It ignored the issue of abolition of slavery, failed to prevent the breakup of immediate slave families by sale, and chose not to prohibit excessive punishment of slaves. But in providing jury trials for slaves convicted of capital offenses, the law granted part of what the Quakers had requested in 1786. The combined effect of the 1787 act and the supplement of 1789 virtually brought the slave trade to and from Delaware to a halt.

Just before the turn of the century, Quakers again petitioned the legislature for a gradual abolition law. The bill answering the petition went through several readings only to have the legislature resolve in January 1797 that it "appears imperfect in its provisions" and would adversely affect the state, without being more specific. It came up with the most diplomatic way of eliciting "mature deliberation" on the abolition bill, deciding to publish it in the newspapers—from 1 August until the next election—so that white citizens could comment and convey their wishes to the next legislature.[34] The legislature of 1798, however, took no further action on the abolition bill.

The nineteenth century began with Delaware Quakers still trying to obtain an abolition law. In an 1801 petition they again called for abolition on the basis of religious and natural rights principles. However, this petition was tendered in a new century; no longer did the Quaker petitioners deem it necessary to prove that slavery was against the unalienable rights of mankind. Had not the nation, they asked, "long declared them to be 'self-evident truth'?" Rather, the petition stressed the issues of morality and pecuniary gain. It implored slaveholders to "deal justly, and to love mercy," and show gratitude for God's blessings by freeing their slaves. The petitioners asked the legislature to abolish slavery, for only then would Delaware be able to "redeem the solemn pledge" of freedom that it "gave to the world and to God" during the American Revolution. Certainly, abolition would not only save Delawareans from their sins but "destroy the odious inconsistency with which, both as politicians and christians, we stand justly charged; and . . . discourage effectually that most detestable of all crimes, so common among us, the crime of man-stealing."[35]

With less than a thirtieth part of the Delaware population still enslaved, Quakers claimed that the financial loss would be minimal. Also, by the 1790s Quakers could cite real cases to support their contention that emancipation would prove beneficial to all, black and white. The success of emancipation in nearby Pennsylvania was often mentioned; its benefits, including "a more rapid increase of the white population," "improvements of every kind," and "a permanent rise in the value of real property," were held up as attractions.

The Society of Friends continued to appeal for abolition through the new century, carrying on the campaign up to the Civil War. But from the early nineteenth century, they operated in an age that viewed abolition differently; no longer did the society consider state-mandated abolition a certainty. The changing nature of abolitionism and the Quaker role in it are best illustrated by a comparison between the careers and actions of the earlier Quaker abolitionist Warner Mifflin and the nineteenth-century antislavery proponent Thomas Garrett.

Mifflin began his abolition crusade during the Revolutionary era when the new nation sought to shed its colonial past and to embark upon an idealistic future based on republican principles of natural rights. Many living in a nation founded on these ideals believed that the next logical step was to extend this natural liberty to the most shackled element in society, slaves. States north of Delaware legislated abolition and achieved the desired goal in a peaceful fashion. When Mifflin looked at his nation and neighboring states, he confidently concluded that through appeals to conscience and the law abolition in Delaware could be attained.

Mifflin began his antislavery fight among his fellow Quakers and soon extended it well beyond the confines of his society to include other slaveholders and the state legislature. On several occasions Mifflin, sometimes in conjunction with others and at times on his own, petitioned the legislature for the abolition of slavery.[36] His 1791 petition, for example, called for an end to slavery and the slave trade and a ban on the kidnapping of free blacks and slaves for sale south. Mifflin's repeated fight for legislated abolition failed, but he successfully persuaded the state to impose stiffer penalties for the crimes of kidnapping and the illegal importing and exporting of slaves.

Mifflin convinced slave owners to free their slaves and diligently fought for slaves entitled to their freedom, but stopped short of openly encouraging slaves to escape from their bondage. Mifflin was known occasionally to bend the law in the interest of helping slaves escape from their bondage. In one instance he was charged with harboring and concealing a runaway slave; he confessed his guilt and willingly accepted the consequence.[37] Such behavior was atypical for Mifflin but not in the case of Thomas Garrett.

Thomas Garrett was born in Pennsylvania in 1789, only a few years before the death of Mifflin. From 1820 when he moved to Wilmington, he earned a reputation as an ardent abolitionist and a key operator on the Underground Railroad. Garrett also joined the Delaware Abolition Society and worked with its members to improve the condition of blacks, both free and slave.

Garrett's antislavery crusade opened amid the abatement of the optimism of the Revolutionary period about the antislavery effects of the natural rights ideology. Abolition no longer seemed a simple moral crusade. Now in the wake of the Missouri admission crisis, antislavery emerged as a divisive political issue, one which threatened to disrupt national harmony by pitting the sectional interests of the free and slave states against each other. National political leadership seemed unable or unwilling to find the means to achieve a lasting compromise on the slavery question. This is the context that led fiery abolitionists like William Lloyd Garrison and Thomas Garrett to conclude that politics constituted the root cause of the cancer of slavery.

Garrett's strong antislavery convictions and consequent disregard for the law often got him in trouble with the authorities. The most serious brush came in 1848, when he was convicted of aiding a family of slaves to escape along the Underground Railroad. The fine imposed apparently wiped out his personal fortune. If Delaware authorities hoped this rebuke would curb his antislavery crusade, Garrett soon proved them wrong. On the day he was fined, Garrett promised Judge Roger B. Taney and all in "the Court House that [he] would double [his] diligence, in aiding all in [his] power at whatever cost." It was a promise he kept. Garrett continued his quest, except he now refrained from having his name publicly associated with the Underground Railroad. He took the new precaution, he insisted, not from personal concern but because "the hard-hearted and unjust" Judge Taney might "feel uncomfortable" over such revelations.[38]

Passage of the 1850 Compromise did not daunt Garrett. The law, he admitted, could alarm runaways, but he doubted whether the new fugitive bill would prove any more effective in curtailing his antislavery activities. He insisted that there remained "so many more who feel an interest in affording them [slaves] shelter, and protection" as to assure survival of the Underground Railroad. He ended his reflections on the compromise on a note of prayer: he wished the current feeling of Christian charity would "increase till not a soul can be found in the free states mean enough to assist the master in reclaiming them."[39]

Unlike Mifflin, Garrett chose not to rely principally on appeals to conscience, for he believed that both the state and society lacked reverence for that noble sentiment. He held an unflattering view of government; he refused to vote or "take part further than cannot be avoided in such a tyrannical government." It seemed perfectly reasonable to him to disobey the law, especially if it helped in challenging an institution he deemed morally indefensible. When many in the 1850s called for compromise and salvation of the Union, Garrett prayed for disunion. In his opinion it was "the only certain & effectual remedy for abolishing slavery" for "should that take place, the slaves will soon be free."[40]

But Garrett did not so oppose the political system as to reject legislated abolition. Rather, he remained skeptical of the ability of the state to pass such a law. He had more faith in the citizens of Delaware, particularly residents of New Castle County, whom he claimed favored abolition and indeed would rejoice were the legislature "induced to pass laws abolishing slavery in this State, immediately." Believing the legislature too corrupt to pass an abolition law, Garrett proposed a compromise: a "law that no child born after . . . (1856) could be held till more than 21 years of age."[41]

Garrett was best known for the role he played in the Underground Railroad. Unlike Mifflin, who targeted the government, Garrett's antislavery sense of mission led him to encourage and provide safe passage for slaves escaping to freedom. He derived much satisfaction from depriving slave owners of their property, for he believed it was his duty "to aid all of God's poor in their flight from their cruel Task masters." He even complained when the Civil War interrupted his Underground Railroad activities; he had "wanted to help off three thousand" escaping slaves but "only got up to twenty-seven hundred," for the "war came too soon for [his] business."[42]

Garrett did not physically remove slaves from their place of enslavement, but he actively encouraged and indeed prayed for all slaves to escape from their masters. He wanted slaves to take the initial step, after which he would help by directing the runaways through the Underground Railroad to safety, and usually to a job at the end of the journey. He expressed this wish in one of several letters to William Lloyd Garrison. "My list of slaves," he wrote in 1854, "has now got to 1,874, having passed seven this day week, and the one day previous, and the best of it is, for our little State they were all natives of Delaware. Would to God that all of the remaining slaves would run off before this time next year, so that we might take rank with the nominally Free States." By October 1856 Garrett had assisted 2,028 slaves to escape to freedom. On the eve of the Civil War, in 1860, his total stood at 2,246 escaped slaves. By 1863, which was also Garrett's thirty-eighth year in the Underground Railroad, the total reached 2,322. What proportion of the slave escapees were from the state of Delaware is unknown, but it was likely substantial. Even so, Garrett expressed extreme dissatisfaction with this achievement; he complained to his friend Samuel May, Jr., that "since the first of the year I have had it in my power to aid so few it is hardly worth stating."[43]

The outbreak of the Civil War provided Garrett with new opportunities for promoting the cause of abolition. Garrett was ambivalent about the war; he viewed it as necessary, predicting that slavery would not survive the war. Yet as a Quaker his avowed pacifism conflicted with his desire to excuse, if not support, a war that he believed would end slavery. Garrett revealed this dilemma in the case involving escaped slave Winlock Clark. Claiming the slave had "been unrighteously sold for seven years," Garrett helped Clark escape from slavery. Subsequently, Clark expressed interest in the Union army and was helped by Garrett to enlist. Aware of how contradictory his actions were, Garrett concluded a letter to William Still by asking, "Am I naughty, being a professed nonresistant, to advise this poor fellow to serve Father Abraham?"[44]

The most fitting commentary on Garrett's work with the Underground Railroad came from himself. "No labor has given me so much real happiness as what I have done for the slave," he wrote in April 1870, "and I now rejoice most heartily that African Slavery is forever ended in this country."[45] His fellow Quakers and abolitionists who worked just as hard to bring an end to slavery in Delaware most likely shared his sentiment.

### The Methodists and Abolition in Delaware

Joining the Quakers, the Methodists of Delaware also sought the abolition of slavery. But unlike the Quakers, the Methodist antislavery stand did not long endure. Methodist antislavery sentiment peaked while the nation examined its soul over slavery and liberty. By early nineteenth century, however, the Methodist church had experienced a fundamental policy change, in the process reversing itself on the slavery issue.

A Methodist stand against slavery at some point was almost a certainty since John Wesley, founder of the Methodist faith strongly opposed slavery and the slave trade. Influenced by his own religious beliefs and by Quaker success in promoting abolition, Wesley came to regard slavery and the slave trade as impediments to the ultimate goal of Christian perfection. As early as 1743 Wesley used the Methodist General Rules to counsel against the purchase and sale of human beings as slaves, an admonition he repeated in his 1774 *Thoughts upon Slavery*. Wesley's writings did not explicitly ban slavery among Methodists. Rather, like the early

Quakers, the leader of the Methodist faith only cautioned against slavery and the slave trade.[46]

Wesley's representatives, in particular Francis Asbury and Thomas Coke, carried his opposition to slavery to North America, and his views were further expounded by American converts like Freeborn Garretson. From 1771 Asbury not only spearheaded the spread of Methodism in America, he also encouraged Methodists to emulate Quaker antislavery. Asbury began in 1780 with a cautious policy on slavery. Like the Quakers, he did not immediately preach abolition, but he urged owners to instruct slaves in the Christian faith and to offer freedom at some future date. Under Asbury's leadership Methodist circuit riders in 1784 voted to expel members who sold or bought slaves with the exception of sales conducted out of humanitarian consideration. Further, itinerant preachers who lived in states where manumission remained legal but did not free their slaves could face suspension.[47]

In 1784 Thomas Coke, a supporter of Wesley and a strong opponent of slavery, came to the United States to head the Methodist church in North America. Unlike Asbury, caution was not the strong forte of Coke; he recommended exclusion from the Lord's Supper and expulsion of members who failed to free their slaves. Coke's more radical approach to antislavery disturbed many devout Methodists, particularly in slavery's stronghold, Virginia. When slaveholders responded by threatening to discontinue their membership and by withholding the gospel from their slaves, church leaders felt compelled to seek a middle ground, one that would not alienate the influential slaveholding class but would still foster freedom for the slave and salvation of souls in the hereafter. By 1796 the church had reached what seemed to be an acceptable compromise; it backed down from Coke's radical position and instead recommended emancipation as soon as possible, local law permitting. Yearly and local conferences could, however, adopt a stricter antislavery stand.[48]

Delaware remained one of those Methodist strongholds where a more radical antislavery policy continued to operate. After the introduction of Methodism into the state in the 1770s, the church experienced a rapid growth, particularly in rural Delaware. Largely untouched by the earlier churches—Anglicans and the Society of Friends—rural Delaware provided fertile ground for the Methodist church. The Anglican church had confined its ministry to the more populous areas of Delaware, possibly because of poor finances and an insufficient number of ministers. The Society of Friends, the state's other significant religious group, did not proselytize; fellowship was restricted to persons born into the society or those who on their own sought membership.

The nature of early Methodism seemed well suited to rural Delaware.

Unlike the other churches, the Methodists determinedly ventured out into the most rural areas. The early Methodists did not rely on an established church-associated clergy to spread the gospel. Instead, they employed itinerant preachers and circuit riders like Freeborn Garrettson, who swept through rural Delaware not only winning converts for the church but also spreading the antislavery message. More than the Quakers, these Methodist circuit riders took the antislavery message directly to the heart of slaveholding rural Delaware.

Until the 1790s rural Delaware with its insignificant Quaker population lagged far behind the statewide pace of manumission. But the spread of Methodism coincided with a changing economy and with the Revolutionary era's popular belief in the obligations under the principles of natural rights to make emancipation more than a religious duty. A rush of manumissions quickly followed, spreading through rural Kent and Sussex counties.[49] The changing pace of emancipation was particularly noticeable in Sussex County; from a low of 14.6 percent in 1790, Methodist antislavery helped push the proportion of the county's black population who were free to 30.9 percent in 1800 and 76.5 percent by the Civil War.

Methodist antislavery influence in the counties of Kent and Sussex was acknowledged by the Wilmington-based abolition society. A committee formed by the society to examine ways to promote abolition suggested capitalizing on Methodist influence in those two counties. It recommended the founding of abolition societies in Duck Creek, Dover, and Milford that would be "composed chiefly of the people called Methodists." "If the leading members" of Kent and Sussex County Methodist groups "could be engaged in the establishment of such Institutions, they would be eminently serviceable not only in the protection of free people of colour and the relief of slaves; but they would contribute largely towards producing a change in public opinion favourable to the abolition of slavery."[50] The Methodists and Quakers thus joined forces to form the backbone of the abolition societies.

How successful were Delaware Methodists in persuading slaveholders to free their slaves? Delaware Methodists did not keep a record of member manumissions, thus making it impossible to give a precise count of the number of slaves freed because of Methodist-inspired Christian conscience. Nevertheless there is no doubting the effect of religion on owners who freed their slaves or that in rural Delaware the Methodists were the force behind these manumissions.

Non-Quaker slaveholders were also known to cite Christian charity as rationale for manumitting their slaves. In 1787 Joseph Emmall of Kent County unconditionally freed his ten slaves because he believed it was

"contrary to the will of God as well as directly opposite to the true principles of Christian charity to hold any of our fellow creatures in slavery."
William Armor, who freed his slave in 1800, found it necessary to address the manumission document "to all Christian People, to whom
these presents may concern."[51] Both slaveholders were non-Quaker residents of rural Delaware, and their religious convictions were most likely
Methodist in origin.

### The Abolition Societies

While Delaware Quakers and Methodists continued freeing their slaves,
some among them formed abolition societies to speed up the pace of
manumission and to help the newly freed men and women make the
transition to a new life of freedom. They took up the cause of antislavery
out of a sense of humanitarianism and a belief in natural rights and
religion. It was not enough to free their slaves (if they held any); they
felt compelled to take their message to the society at large. Members
of these societies described themselves to the state legislature as "the
guardians of the public welfare—as the friends of justice and humanity
. . . [seeking] the preservation of the principles of political and moral
justice."[52] They fought for abolition because it was "a duty which they
owed to their country, & to the unhappy black people held in slavery in
this State."[53]

Those imbued with these feelings were behind the work of four abolition societies in the state: the Delaware Society for Promoting the Abolition of Slavery, for Superintending the Cultivation of Young Free
Negroes, and for the Relief of Those Who May Be Unlawfully Held in
Bondage; the Delaware Society for the Gradual Abolition of Slavery; and
the Delaware Society for Promoting the Abolition of Slavery and for the
Relief and Protection of Free Blacks and People of Colour Unlawfully
Held in Bondage or Otherwise Oppressed, as well as a fourth society,
founded in Sussex County, which left little record of its activities.

Quakers and Methodists dominated membership in all the abolition
societies, although some members were affiliated with other religious
groups, while others claimed no particular affiliation. Among Methodist
members of the abolition societies were Richard Bassett, a prominent
Dover lawyer and a founding member of the state's first abolition society,
and John Thelwell, founder of the free black school in Wilmington.
However, from their inception Quakers dominated the three best-known
Delaware abolition societies. Warner Mifflin, his fellow Quakers, and
Methodists from Kent County founded the Dover-based society, the
state's first; the second and third abolition societies, both based in Wilmington, were also heavily dominated by Quakers.[54] The fourth, based

in Sussex County, presumably was Methodist in origin and membership.

Founded in 1788, Delaware's first abolition society was closely modeled after the Pennsylvania Abolition Society and maintained close ties with its parent. Within a few months after its founding, the society petitioned the Delaware legislature for the abolition of slavery, termination of the slave trade, an end to the disparate punishment of slaves, and a toughening of the laws prohibiting the export of slaves out of state. Its petition together with others sent by Mifflin and the Quakers led to the enactment of the 1789 supplement. The society, however, was short-lived. The delegation it sent to the American Convention for Promoting the Abolition of Slavery and Improving the Condition of the African Race (ACPA) in Philadelphia in 1795 was its last; it disbanded shortly thereafter, probably for financial reasons.[55]

Founded in the same year and of an equally short duration was the Delaware Society for the Gradual Abolition of Slavery. From its base in Wilmington, members of this society joined the Dover-based abolition society and Quakers in petitioning the legislature in 1788, and the result of the combined effort was the passage of the 1789 law. In 1795, and again in 1796, the society sent delegates to the ACPA meeting in Philadelphia. The delegation of 1796 reported the society near dissolution, primarily because of the "lukewarmness or the dereliction of principle in some, and the death or removal of many others of the original promoters of the Institution." Equally important, however, was "the opposition experienced from the Country in general and some of those in office upon whom success in a great measure must depend." The report acknowledged that membership in the society had never exceeded sixty and on average no more than fifteen members attended regular meetings.[56]

By the end of 1800, the Wilmington society no longer operated; financial problems hastened its demise. Appeals for financial aid in 1794 were answered when the society received support from the Pennsylvania Abolition Society, but this infusion was not enough to sustain operations. Still bemoaning its desperate fiscal situation as the eighteenth century drew to a close, the society described its finances in 1799 as so "deranged as to prevent their answering the end of their institution"; all attempts to raise more money proved unsuccessful. Despite the weakness and problems that plagued the society, it achieved impressive results. Its report to the ACPA convention of 1797 proudly noted that notwithstanding its dire financial state, the society, from 1788 to 1796, helped free eighty Delaware slaves.[57]

Even as the earlier Wilmington abolition society disbanded, another took its place on 12 December 1800: the Delaware Society for Promoting the Abolition of Slavery and for the Relief and Protection of Free Blacks and People of Colour, Unlawfully Held in Bondage or Otherwise Oppressed.[58] As its name suggests, the society had two basic aims: the abolition of slavery and the protection of free blacks. This second Wilmington abolition society, unlike the first, lived a long time, surviving into the 1830s.

It sought to achieve abolition through a two-pronged attack on slavery: persuading slaveholders to free their slaves and then convincing the state to dismantle the legal basis of slavery. The new society submitted its first petition to the legislature in 1801. Recalling that the preamble to the state constitution guaranteed that "through divine goodness all men have by nature the rights of enjoying and defending life and liberty," how in good conscience, it asked, could the state continue to deny blacks these rights. Subsequent petitions to the legislature repeated the demand for abolition on the grounds that slavery violated the laws of God and the principles behind the federal and state constitutions.[59]

The new society proposed a change in strategy for exposing the ills of slavery: through education it hoped to enlighten both the citizens and the state of Delaware.[60] As part of this plan, the society commissioned a series of antislavery essays for state and public perusal. The first essay was approved at the 23 May 1801 meeting; three hundred copies were distributed to the public, and it was reprinted in the Delaware *Mirror.*

To discredit assertions of black inferiority, members were asked to record incidents or examples that would help "prove the mental equality of blacks and whites under similar conditions." For the enlightenment of the society and the public, members agreed to keep a library collection of documents on slavery and the slave trade. And to rebut arguments that slave labor was essential to a successful agricultural economy, the society presented Pennsylvania and the free northern states as examples of successful free-labor economies.

Next, the society devised plans to ensure that slave owners who contracted to free their slaves fulfilled the agreement, and by the time specified in the manumission deed. In July 1801 the society decided to monitor closely all pending manumissions by keeping track of these half-free slaves, making sure that such persons received the freedom due them. The members planned to keep a detailed record of the names of the prospective free blacks and their owners as well as their dates of emancipation. To remind or perhaps to pressure slaveholders into honoring the contracts of manumission, the society decided to publish in the local newspapers each month the names of slaves due to be freed in that month.[61]

Several slaves were freed through the services of the society, and re-

ports to the ACPA always mentioned such manumissions. At the end of
its first year of operation, the Delaware society proudly reported to the
ACPA that it had submitted to the state legislature a petition for the gradual abolition of slavery, and six cases relating to manumission were under the active care of the acting committee. In 1804 the society reported
that "twelve slaves have been liberated since last report, through the
agency of the society." Subsequent annual reports listed similar numbers
of manumissions.[62]

The case of the ex-slave Lydia demonstrate how diligently the society
tracked slaveholders suspected of withholding or delaying the freedom
of Delaware slaves. Asserting that Lydia should have been freed six
months earlier, the society paid a visit to her owner, Joshua Carter. Carter
successfully convinced the society that he had indeed freed Lydia, but
that she voluntarily, and as a free person, chose to continue in his employment at the salary of three dollars a month.[63]

Slaveholder Catherine Collyer was not so fortunate, for she failed to
convince the abolition society of her innocence. The society suspected
her of planning to defy state laws on slave exports. Collyer's claim that
she was a permanent resident of Worcester County, Maryland, and was
only temporarily visiting Delaware with her slave Rhoda failed to sway
the society. The society demanded she post a bond against her removal
of Rhoda from "further than Worcester County"; if she did so, the committee would detain the vessel of transportation. Whether the society
had the legal right to enforce Delaware law is debatable, but Collyer
apparently believed it did, for she posted a bond of $550.[64]

From the 1810s on, partly in response to the success of voluntary
manumission in the state, the abolition society shifted direction and focused on the plight of free blacks. With more than 75 percent of Delaware blacks freed by 1810, and many others promised their freedom
in the near future, the society increasingly chose to expend its energy in
helping the newly freed slaves adjust to freedom. The members felt that
it was a duty incumbent on white society:

> Let it be deeply impressed on our minds that we owe the descendants
> of Africa a debt of immense magnitude. We are bound by the laws of
> equity, by the solemn requisitions of justice to pay that debt. Can we dis-
> charge our obligations in any way so effectually as by communicating to
> the children of those (from the sweat of whose brows we have derived
> many of our external comforts) a portion of that knowledge which has
> been the source of our enjoyments and our power? . . . In places where
> our exertion for the liberation or personal preservation of the African
> is no longer necessary, we may discharge a portion of our debt by open-

ing the book of knowledge, and extending to their minds the blessings of education.[65]

But even after the shift in policy, the society continued to appeal for state-mandated abolition, but like earlier campaigns, these petitions failed.

The repeated defeat of the abolition bills did not unduly discourage the society; rather, it resolved to continue the fight until the end. The society clearly expressed this sense of perseverance in the report to the ACPA of 1823, promising to use "every favourable opportunity . . . to endeavour to attain the object so long sought for, until the laws of the State shall no longer tolerate Slavery."[66]

### Natural Rights versus Slavery

During the era of the American Revolution, protests against slavery emerged throughout the new nation. From New England to the southern states, citizens raised questions about the propriety of enslaving others while affirming freedom as the natural right of all mankind.[67] The rhetoric of the American Revolution played as important a role in fostering abolition as did religion and the economy; it was no accident that courts and legislatures often phrased abolition decisions and laws in the language of the American Revolution.

By the turn of the century, states north of Delaware had followed through with laws that abolished slavery either outright or gradually. Vermont led the North by abolishing slavery in its constitution, Massachusetts and New Hampshire ended slavery through judicial interpretation, while Pennsylvania in 1780 and Rhode Island and Connecticut in 1784 did so through gradual abolition laws. Not until the turn of the century did New York (1799) and New Jersey (1804), both of which had much higher slave populations, move to adopt gradual abolition laws.

Even the South with its large slave population and plantation economy did not completely escape the effects of republican doctrine. Prominent citizens of the South debated abolition, recommended an end to the slave trade, and urged the easing of manumission laws. Several southern states relaxed manumission regulations, and the number of free blacks increased notably. Unlike the North, however, the South failed to abolish slavery. The importance of slavery in the southern economy, the large capital investment in slaves, and the political influence of slave owners conspired against antislavery efforts there.

Delaware fits neither of these regional profiles: the state was not so strongly antislavery as to mandate abolition or so proslavery as to curb voluntary manumissions. Because a rigid stalemate prevailed between abolitionists and proslavery advocates of Delaware, neither side could firmly sway the state its way. Caught between these opposing forces, the state, by default, concurrently supported two contradictory philosophies. At the same time that the legislature energetically supported and encouraged voluntary private manumissions, it continued to affirm the in-state rights of slaveholders to their slave property.

Like many in the new nation, the citizens of Delaware debated the merits of abolition, using arguments as spirited as those employed in the rest of the nation. The tenor of the debates reveals that many in Delaware found it difficult concurrently to justify slavery and advocate liberty as the natural right of all mankind. But an equal number of Delaware citizens disagreed, claiming to see no inconsistency. Advocates from both sides examined slavery in its relation to the principles of Christian charity, natural rights, property rights, and the rights of the freed men and women. Predictably, those on opposing sides arrived at opposite conclusions.

On the eve of the 1789 election, "Querist" in the *Delaware Gazette* sparked an extensive debate on slavery and abolition which brought forward for the public's consideration the full spectrum of proslavery and antislavery argument. "Querist" raised a critical issue when he asked "whether men who in open violation of the laws of God and Nature, hold their fellow men in abject slavery, are fit persons to represent or govern a free people?"[68] He reminded his fellow citizens that according to the Declaration of Independence, which Delaware had signed, governments were instituted to secure the governed certain inalienable rights among which were life, liberty, and the pursuit of happiness. As such, said "Querist," slave owners were guilty of violating the rights of slaves. Electing a slave owner to political office was double offensive, "Querist" maintained. As an individual the slaveholder had infringed on the rights of his slaves, while as a representative he was in violation of the very reason why representative governments were created. Two anonymous replies to the "Querist" appeared in the 9 September 1789 *Delaware Gazette*; the first cited biblical sanction for slavery, while the second found justification for slavery in the absence of condemnation or prohibition of the institution by either president or Congress.

The ensuing debates, usually carried on in the legislature and state newspapers, divided equally between those for and those against slavery. On the question of whether slavery violated the laws of God, both sides found ample citations in the Bible to support their position. The original "Querist" likened slaveholding to stealing, an act contrary to God's word as written in the twenty-fourth chapter of Deuteronomy: "If a man be found stealing any of his brethren of Israel, and maketh *merchandize* of him, or *selleth* him, then that thief shall surely die, and thou shalt put away evil from among you." "Querist" preached Christian charity, appealing to the golden rule and its command that we "do unto others as ye would they should do unto you." But "Camillus," a proslavery writer, preferred the section of the Bible that states: "And he said, cursed be Canaan, a *servant* of *servants* shall he be to his *brethren*." "Camillus" explained it was God's plan "to make one vessel unto honour and another unto dishonour." But as the "Querist" pointed out, "Camillus" failed to prove "that negroes are vessels of dishonor."[69]

Contested readings of the doctrine of natural rights remained crucial to this debate. Antislavery writers like "Querist" defined the principle as applicable to all persons regardless of color or condition: "I stand forth," he declared, "an advocate for the unalienable rights of the human race." But "Camillus" and other proslavery writers thought differently; they insisted that liberty had to be earned, not given, that slaves were of an inferior race and thus undeserving of the rights of liberty, and indeed were "unconscious of liberty and incapable of enjoying it." "Humanus," a proslavery writer, not only subscribed to this view but recommended the removal of ex-slaves from "civilized" society. He believed that "negroes are in general in a savage state, they are altogether uncivilized"; therefore, before being freed, "they should be prepared for being organized into a separate government."[70]

Proslavery writers objected to emancipation not only because of their belief that blacks lacked proper preparation for it, but more so because they abhorred the notion of granting equality to blacks. The example of the American struggle for independence, "Camillus" said, should warn white Delawareans of the logical consequence of emancipation: freedom and equality. As free persons, ex-slaves must be taxed, and if taxed they must be represented; except, of course, "Camillus" could not bring himself—and doubted whether other white Delawareans were willing—to accept such radical notions of racial equality. "Camillus" maintained that God and nature had designated the white race as master over the black race; to reverse this order, he said, was not only tantamount to heresy but would certainly invite Armageddon.[71] His views were not peculiar to Delaware, for all over the nation proslavery writers expressed similar fears of racial equality.

According to the proslavery camp, slavery constituted a necessary tool by which masters controlled and directed the labor of the slave for the benefit of white and black society. To mandate emancipation would only release a host of "lazy free Negroes" into the Delaware economy. "Humanus" expressed this belief when he urged slave owners to resist abolition since "the person who manumits his negroes, does an essential injury to the neighborhood where he lives." Free blacks, he continued, "have a rooted aversion to work"; thus, it would be impossible for them to "procure a livelihood by their own industry the consequence of which is, that they must steal and rob in order to get a subsistence."[72] However groundless the fear of "Humanus," it was shared by many and was a contributing factor in the state's resistance to mandated abolition.

Belief in the sanctity of property formed a major obstacle in the fight against slavery. The same Revolution that promised liberty to mankind also affirmed the rights of citizens to their property. Since the law defined slaves as property, it raised the question of universal freedom versus the guaranteed property rights of citizens, even slaveholders. Antislavery writers tackled this issue by differentiating between legitimate and illegitimate property, with only the former deserving the protection of the law. Believing that slavery involved manstealing, antislavery writers accused slaveholders of acquiring illegitimate property in the form of slaves, so that they were not legally or morally entitled to its protection.[73] The charge of manstealing, said "Eugenius" of Delaware, applied with equal force to "the man who buys them, and he who brings them to market, or he who holds slaves born here, and he who buys them on board the Guinea ships." As was to be expected, "Camillus" argued otherwise: he charged opponents of slavery with turning the golden rule upside down and with fostering dissension. "Can you consistent with that [golden] rule," he asked the abolitionists, "calmly endeavor to destroy the peace and happiness of your country, sow the seeds of discord and confusion throughout the states, and rob thousands of their quiet and their property?"[74]

While some debated the issue, many Delaware slaveholders quietly responded to the incongruity between slavery and freedom by freeing their slaves. Slaveholders who bothered to explain their action often cited the principles of natural rights as the reason for freeing their slaves. In 1790, "being sensible that it is not only contrary to the principles of justice, and humanity, but likewise to the sacred law of God, to hold Negroes in perpetual bondage," Anna White of Kent County immediately freed her slave Candice and promised Candice's four-year-old son Zava freedom at age twenty-one. Sarah Brown stated that she freed her two slaves because she thought "it Wrong and Highly oppressive to hold Negroes in bondage." Benjamin Yoe of Kent County offered freedom to his slaves in 1789 "for divers good Causes and Considerations." And in 1799 James Scotton, "being convinced of the errors of slavery," freed his slave Benjamin with no restrictions; so did Richard Cooper of Kent County, who in 1816, "being actuated by benevolent and conscientious principles," freed Sarah with no qualifications attached.[75]

Well into the nineteenth century Delaware slaveholders continued to cite the ideology behind the American Revolution as justification for emancipating slaves. In 1803, a slave named George was freed by America Rogers of Sussex County out of a conviction that "Liberty is the Right of all human creatures and Especially Natural born citisons of these United States of America." In March 1827 Thomas Marim for "divers good causes" freed eleven-year-old Joe, while in 1849 Elizabeth Orrell of Duck Creek "from motives of benevolence and humanity" freed Ann Brown and her four children. In 1812 Thomas Parker, a farmer in Kent County, for "divers good causes" promised to free sixteen-year-old Hester after she served eleven years and six months.[76]

Although they were unable to legislate abolition, state actions during the early years of the Republic reveal legislators deeply affected by Enlightenment principles. When the legislature enacted the state's most comprehensive manumission law—the 1787 act—it gave full credit to abolitionists and the ideology of the Revolution. The legislators admitted in the preamble to receiving "information, that sundry Negroes and Mulattoes, as well freemen as slaves, have been exported, and sold into other states"; they decried this as "contrary to the principles of humanity and justice, and derogatory to the honour of the state." It was within the context of redeeming the state's honor that the legislature chose to restrict the import and export of slaves severely and to ease manumission regulations.

By rendering decisions that favored the new climate of freedom, the state judiciary also played a crucial role in the growth of manumission. The new tone of judicial interpretation encouraged slaves to seek relief from the courts. From the early national period, Delaware courts gradually reversed their earlier policy of classifying all blacks as slaves; now many judges refused to accept color as an irrefutable mark of bondage. As the number of free blacks surpassed that of slaves, the courts increasingly put the burden of proof on those who claimed to be owners, requiring anyone trying to assert a legal right to the labor of a black to prove his or her case.

In the case of *Allen v. Negro Sarah et al.* (1836), the superior court's decision expanded the boundaries of freedom to the children of a female slave, Amelia. In 1799 Amelia's owner illegally sent her to Maryland, thus qualifying her for freedom under Delaware law. Amelia, however, never sued for her freedom, and after an unsuccessful attempt to escape her bondage, she spent another thirty years in slavery. In 1836, more than three decades after the fact, the children of Amelia sued for freedom on the grounds that their birth after the 1799 incident meant that they were born free. Unanimously, the state supreme court affirmed the lower court's decision by ruling in favor of freedom for Amelia's children. As the court's decision explained,

> It is true, where a negro has been claimed and held as a slave in this state, the presumption of law is that he is a slave, and the onus pro-bandi rests upon him to show that he is entitled to his freedom. But this, like every other legal presumption may be rebutted. And when a negro claims to be entitled to his freedom in consequence of his having been exported from this state, contrary to the provisions of the statute, and proves the exportation, the burthen of proof is then shifted upon the master, and he must satisfy the court that the negro was lawfully exported.
>
> 2d. The court are of the opinion that "the fact of Amelia's remaining in the service of Allen for thirty years," does not bar the right of her descendants to freedom, if any such right ever existed. Nor can the doctrine of laches, neglect, and a sleeping upon one's rights be made to apply to questions involving the liberty of a human being.[77]

This presumption of freedom until proved a slave was well stated by the court in the case of *The State v. William Dillahunt* (1842). Race played only a minor role in this case, for the victim, defendant, and witness in question were all blacks. At stake, however, was the status of the state's witness, Charlotte Green. In an attempt to exclude Green's testimony, William Dillahunt's attorney challenged Green's free status, implying that she was a slave and thus disqualified from bearing witness, according to state law. The court presumed Green free, for it accepted her "reputation" of being free "as proof of freedom." In its opinion the court asserted that

> at the common law there was always a strong presumption in favor of freedom. In the first settlement of this country, the fact of the existence of the negro race in a state of bondage to the whites, and a large majority of that color being slaves, was considered sufficiently strong to outweigh the common law presumption, and to introduce a legal presumption that a colored person is prima facie a slave. Yet that state of things has changed. . . . There are in this State about 20,000 persons of color; of whom 17,000 are free, and 3,000 slaves. A large majority of all persons of color in the United States are free. In point of fact, therefore, there is no reason to presume slavery from color; in opposition to the strong common law presumption, that every man having the human form is a freeman. And such has been the decision of this court on several occasions. But additionally, it has always been the practice to take reputation as proof of freedom.

The precedents for this holding appear in the May 1792 case involving George Perkston. When Perkston sued for his freedom, the court summoned his "owner" David Maxwell to appear in court "to answer the complaint of negro George Perkston, . . . that he is unjustly detained in servitude by him said David." Should Maxwell fail to appear in court, the court warned, he would be fined £100 and Perkston declared free.[78]

The same assumption prevailed as late as the decade before the Civil War. When Daniel Webb sued for his freedom in 1851, his "owner" William S. Turner was required to produce at the hearing "the bill of sale or written contract or transfer by which . . . [Webb was] sold or transferred" to him. Turner either failed to produce the bill of sale or did not provide sufficient proof, because "the court on hearing the proofs and allegations on the part of the Petitioner, adjudge[d] and decree[d] that Daniel Webb or Webster the petitioner is and shall be free." Webb was awarded court costs.[79]

### Tobacco versus Grain

Changes in the Delaware economy proved equally vital to the struggle for the abolition of slavery. As the value of slave labor depreciated, slaveholders explored the most efficient means to employ their surplus slave labor. Owners experimented with the hiring, sale, and indenturing of their slaves. But ultimately, and quite often unintentionally, all these varied responses to the changed economy advanced the cause of freedom for the Delaware slave. Henceforth, the freeing of slaves in Delaware no longer remained the prerogative of religious groups or Enlightenment idealists; rather, it became a necessity for tobacco farmers.

By the end of the eighteenth century, Delaware agriculture had come full circle; from grain to tobacco, and back to grain. Often, a transition from one crop to another is initiated by a decrease in demand and/or falling prices. But when Delaware farmers switched to tobacco at mid century, they then reacted instead to a rapid decline in the quality of tobacco they were producing. Although profits and demand remained high, the voracious tobacco plant had exhausted Delaware's soil after a century of farming.[80] Poor soils yielded low amounts of tobacco and produced an inferior crop, and in the competitive tobacco market, Delaware farmers could not survive. They had no choice but to seek viable alternatives: crop rotation, a change of staple crop, and migration to new and fertile lands.

Delaware farmers did not stand alone in this predicament, for Chesapeake tobacco farmers were forced to make similar adjustments.[81] Still, Chesapeake planters possessed more options: they could, and often did, resolve the problem of depleted soil by seeking fertile land through internal and external migration. Delaware tobacco farmers lacked both options. The state had neither internal nor external frontier since it was bordered on the east by the Delaware Bay and the Atlantic Ocean, north and northwest by Pennsylvania, and west and south by Maryland. Delaware farmers still committed to tobacco culture could move out of state to the new western lands. However, from the 1780s state laws severely circumscribed slaveholders' ability to migrate with their slaves. Without the option of freely moving with one's slave laborers, migrating to fertile tobacco land made little economic sense.

Restoration of fertility to the tobacco-depleted soil required a fallow period of up to twenty years; this was not an option for tobacco farmers operating in diminutive Delaware. Wheat, the grain crop to which Delaware farmers switched, presented fewer problems: even on soil destroyed by tobacco, one idle year after two years of producing wheat could sufficiently restore the soil's potency.[82]

Tobacco farmers who chose to remain in Delaware, and many did, had to diversify: they could switch to cultivating grain on the tobacco-depleted soil and still make a decent living. Farmers unable to produce high-yield or marketable tobacco found grain provided a feasible alternative: both the price and market for grain remained favorable, while soil and labor requirements for the crop were relatively undemanding.

Delaware's transition to grain was gradual. Oftentimes, farmers combined or rotated tobacco and wheat. Still, by the American Revolution many tobacco farmers had completely switched to grain. When James Tilton described the state of Delaware agriculture in 1788, he identified wheat as the principal crop of the state. Christopher Daniel Ebeling corroborated this observation in his 1799 manuscript history of Delaware, confirming that "wheat is the grain most cultivated . . . in the whole peninsula . . . it is not only sought by the merchant sellers of the state but is also preferred in distant markets." Delaware farmers also raised Indian corn and barley, while tobacco was "cultivated by almost every planter though for his own use merely."[83]

Each change Delaware made in its staple crop affected the demand and use of slave labor. Tilton exaggerated when he said that grains "are so disposed of as to require no further care after the seeds are put into the ground," but grain production certainly required less labor than tobacco cultivation.[84] Because tobacco required continuous attention throughout the entire period of planting, harvesting, and processing, Delaware farmers chose to employ slaves as the primary labor on tobacco farms. However, once the farmers switched to less labor-intensive grain farming, slave labor became superfluous.

Data from newspapers provide further insight into how irrelevant slave labor became in Delaware's post–1780 economy. In the late eighteenth century farmers advertising slaves for sale began to indicate their willingness to accept low prices. An owner in 1790 promised to sell "on easy terms a strong, hearty, active young Negro who has been brought up on a farm." Another owner candidly acknowledged the problem of surplus labor, announcing: "For Sale, A Negro Girl, about twelve years of age. To be Sold for want of employment." One advertisement announced the sale of the "time of a stout, active black girl, who has about ten years to serve. The only reason for which it is desired to dispose of her time, is the want of employment."[85]

Grain cultivation could not support the high financial costs involved in slavery. The labor needs of grain could best be met through the employment of seasonal, indentured, and unbound labor. Slave labor posed insoluble problems for wheat farmers: a cycle which saw excess labor unneeded and unwanted for the greater part of the year, followed by a critical shortage of labor at harvesting, when wheat farmers needed labor the most. Delaying the harvest until sufficient labor could be arranged was out of the question because wheat has a relatively short harvesting period. Only by employing a large labor force could farmers guarantee a successful crop. According to Carville V. Earle, "the maturation of wheat allowed only about ten days in July for harvest"; "reaping at the maximum rate of an acre a day, a slave was hard-pressed to finish ten acres of wheat." Hiring additional labor, especially wage labor, "assured that the harvest would be completed on time."[86] Economically, it made better sense for wheat farmers to dispose of their surplus slave labor through emancipation and hire free labor or utilize indentured labor as needed. To judge by the rapid pace of manumission in the state, this is the course Delaware farmers followed.

It would be incorrect to assume that manumission was the preferred choice of Delaware farmers. Rather, it became the logical consequence of the slaveholders' quest for the most efficient means of utilizing surplus slave labor without breaking state law. Only by promising future freedom to their slaves could slaveholders legally and perhaps safely hire out the services of their half-free slaves in the labor markets of nearby states. The reverse also brought freedom: slaveholders who tried to defy state codes by illegally hiring slaves out of state created opportunities for slaves to sue and win their liberty.

Initially, slaveholders attempted either to hire or to sell off the excess labor. However, there was no market for in-state slave hire or sale, since nonslaveholders and slaveholders alike neither wanted nor needed full-time slave labor. Except during planting and harvesting, the very time the owners needed their labor, slaves could not be effectively employed.

Using slave labor in other sectors of the Delaware economy apparently was not profitable, since not even during the height of the institution did Delaware owners systematically utilize slave labor in the nonagricultural economy.

Delaware slaveholders could easily cross state lines into the Chesapeake in search of markets for their excess slave labor. But neighboring slave states, Maryland and Virginia, also suffered from tobacco-related labor problems and thus did not provide a good market for slave hiring or sale. Here, too, manumission became a rational alternative, and indeed the Chesapeake counties that switched to grain reported a higher proportion of free blacks than the remaining counties.[87]

Delaware slaveholders might have found a demand for slave labor farther into the Deep South had state law not all but closed this option to them after 1787. As the economic pressure of surplus slave labor escalated, Quakers, Methodists, and the state's abolition societies successfully joined forces against slaveholders trying to hire or sell slaves out of state. The resulting laws closed this avenue to slaveholders by banning the sale of slaves out of state without the permission of the courts. Failure to obtain court or legislative authorization freed the slave. Under the watchful eyes of Quakers, the abolition societies, the courts, and the slaves themselves, surreptitious out-of-state sales and hires proved a risky alternative.

The explosive expansion of the cotton kingdom and the resulting increased demand for slave labor did not occur until the beginning decades of the nineteenth century. That market might have provided a golden opportunity for Delaware owners to sell or hire their surplus slave labor. However, the cotton boom occurred after many slaveholders had already freed their slaves and many more had executed binding deeds of manumission promising freedom in the near or distant future. Delaware slaveholders could not revoke their word had they wished to do so, not when the watchful Quakers and abolition societies meticulously scrutinized state abolition records to ensure that slaveholders kept their commitment. By 1820, when the cotton economy took off in the Deep South, over 74 percent of black Delawareans were already free. It was too late to resurrect slavery in the state.

Still, some daring slaveholders defied the law, choosing to sell or hire their slaves out of state illegally. If they hoped to escape notice, they were disappointed: vigilant abolitionists, Quakers, and slaves sued in state courts that increasingly sympathized with the cause of freedom. In 1794 Negro Absalom sued and won his freedom because his owner had illegally hired him out in Maryland six years earlier. In the same year Negro

Isaac also sued and won his freedom because his owner had sold him "with intent to export."[88]

Hiring slaves out in the free northern states was not likely since demand for slave labor in the North always had been considerably less than in the plantation South. Further, by the turn of the century, all the states north of Delaware had either abolished slavery or were on the verge of doing so. Invariably, the gradual abolition laws enacted by the northern states either discouraged or outright banned out-of-state slaveholders from bringing slaves into the North or hiring them out there.

Even had the laws of Delaware and those of the free northern states permitted it, hiring out a bound person in a free state posed an unacceptable risk to most slaveholders. The possibility of such slaves unilaterally declaring their freedom was high, perhaps especially for slaves from Delaware. Both slaves and owners regarded the city of Philadelphia as a haven for Quakers, abolitionists, and the Underground Railroad; such a reputation must have given pause to Delaware owners thinking of illegally hiring their slaves out in that metropolitan center.

Delaware slaveholders unwilling to risk the loss of slave property inundated the legislature with petitions to export their slaves. Because the state courts and legislature did not automatically grant these requests but judged each case on merit, it fell to slaveholders to convince the authorities. Ultimately, owners willing to commute permanent bondage of their slaves to temporary servitude found favor with the courts and legislature. While the state did not mandate manumission, offering a contract of future freedom to the slave almost always won over a legislature known on occasion to reject slaveholder appeals or the state courts, which increasingly showed in its decisions that it favored manumission.

Apparently slaveholder Richard Cooper did not learn this lesson in time. In May 1800 he attempted to gain court permission to sell his slave Bob on the grounds that Bob was of "base morals" and had once absconded to Philadelphia. Fearing that Bob would escape again, Cooper asked the court to "grant a permit to . . . transfer and sell the said man out of this state."[89] The petition was denied, perhaps because Cooper failed to offer freedom, or else because he neglected to specify where he intended to sell Bob.

Unlike Cooper, slave owner Richard Lockwood first changed the status of his slave Eben to an indentured servant before seeking permission to export his labor legally into the Philadelphia market. Lockwood in 1811 assured the court that "the whole scheme and Idea" came from Eben "and is evidently calculated for his Benefit." Eben's temporary servitude in Philadelphia would ultimately end in freedom, Lockwood re-

minded the court; "instead of [Eben] being a slave for life, his term of
servitude will be limited to five-years and six-months." The court agreed
by granting Lockwood's request to indenture Eben in Philadelphia. Similarly, in 1811 John White, a resident of Philadelphia but the owner of
two Delaware slaves, was granted permission to send the two as servants
to Philadelphia. White bound Henry for five years, while Henry's nine-
year-old daughter, Winifred, had to serve an indenture lasting until she
was twenty-eight.[90]

Even slave hires not intended for the Philadelphia market often
ended with freedom as the result. Whether the hire was in Philadelphia
or not, Delaware courts favored petitions that promised future freedom
or where the move clearly would benefit the slave. To win a favorable
decision on his request to carry his slaves to Maryland, Peter Robinson
in June 1825 agreed that "before the sale or exportation of said slaves,
he will manumit them to be free."[91] The manumission deed, duly recorded by the court, granted freedom at age thirty for all the Robinson
slaves.

Whatever options were exercised by Delaware's slave-owning farmers,
the results remained the same: a decrease in the slave population and
the growth of the free black population. Blacks illegally hired out of state
sued and won their freedom; slaves freed at a future date and those
hired out legally ultimately gained their freedom at the expiration of
their indenture. In addition many slaves were freed outright with no
conditions attached. For whatever reason Delaware slave owners freed
their slaves, be it out of religious convictions, Enlightenment principles,
or changes in agriculture, they did so without any legislative compulsion.

*3*

# At the Margin of Freedom

AN ACCOUNT of Delaware's struggle to end slavery would be lacking without an assessment of how the voluntary system of emancipation, preferred by the state's slaveholders, operated. Slaveholders could not avoid coming to terms with the powerful social, political, religious, and economic pressures favoring emancipation. But the impact of these forces varied in time and place, thus dictating the distinctive pace of voluntary manumission in Delaware's three counties.

Long exposed to the direct influence of Quakers, Methodists, abolition societies, progressive politicians, and the economic ills of tobacco culture, the middle county, Kent, consistently led the state in manumissions. Many of the same factors fostered manumission in the northernmost county, New Castle, but initially not in the same dynamic combination or with the same intensity as in Kent. From 1790, however, New Castle steadily chased Kent in the march toward freedom, finally matching Kent by the 1840s. Seemingly least affected by the forces of emancipation, the southernmost county, Sussex, consistently reported more slaves and fewer free blacks than either Kent or New Castle County.

However compelling the forces fostering freedom, manumission in Delaware still was voluntary. It remained the prerogative of slave owners to choose the time and modes for freeing their slaves, if they decided to offer them freedom at all. Thus, slaveholder preferences exerted enormous influence on the terms and limits of freedom, with manumission decisions often reflecting such factors as the age, gender, and health of the slaves.

The majority of Delaware slaves did not receive immediate and unconditional freedom; most had to serve extended premanumission indentures. When slaveholders drafted manumission deeds that spoke of freeing slaves out of "divers good causes" or declared that they "absolutely manumit discharge and set free and at liberty" their slaves, reality often varied greatly from what the language of the deeds implied. Typically, complete manumissions occurred only after short indentures for adult slaves, but prolonged indentures for younger slaves remained the norm. This delay of freedom, a favorite strategy of Delaware slaveholders, was the secret to Delaware's success at inducing slaveholders to cooperate with the voluntary emancipation system.

As revealed in practice, voluntary manumission allowed slave owners the opportunity legally to relieve themselves of the financial burden of caring for old, indigent, and surplus slave labor. Owners who voluntarily freed their slaves but set the date of complete freedom in the distant future could recoup their financial investment in slaves without the burden of an unproductive slave system. By delaying the date of complete freedom, owners created a system of half freedom which assured them of the labor of the young half-free slaves—particularly during the most productive season—without the added burden of providing for surplus labor in a nontobacco economy.

Rarely did any economic loss ensue from voluntary manumission, for few slaves gained immediate and unconditional freedom. Even the few slaves freed in such manner created no financial hardship, since they were usually elderly, and their owners had long since gained maximum benefit from their labor. In the case of younger slaves, owners assured themselves through sale and/or indenture of profit in the form of money, labor, or both. The system offered owners other advantages: labor of youthful quasi slaves as needed, removal of barriers to out-of-state slave hires, perhaps even a curb on the temptation for the slaves to escape from their temporary bondage. Certainly, it soothed a Christian or an Enlightenment conscience, and with perfect timing the slave gained complete freedom just when age ended his or her period of useful labor.

Even slaveholders who questioned the morality or legality of slavery and thus advocated manumission felt quite comfortable with temporary indentured servitude. Many expressed uneasiness about permanent bondage, denouncing it as contrary to Christian charity and the rights of mankind. But temporary servitude, especially of minors and young adults, seemed permissible if excused as necessary apprenticeship or training for a useful trade. Many owners perceived temporary bondage

Table 5. Slave population in Delaware, 1790–1860

| Year | New Castle No. | New Castle % | Kent No. | Kent % | Sussex No. | Sussex % |
|------|------|------|------|------|------|------|
| 1790 | 2,562 | 28.8 | 2,300 | 25.8 | 4,025 | 45.2 |
| 1800 | 1,838 | 29.8 | 1,485 | 24.1 | 2,830 | 45.9 |
| 1810 | 1,047 | 25.0 | 728 | 17.4 | 2,402 | 57.5 |
| 1820 | 1,195 | 26.5 | 1,070 | 23.7 | 2,244 | 49.7 |
| 1830 | 786 | 23.8 | 588 | 17.8 | 1,918 | 58.2 |
| 1840 | 541 | 20.7 | 427 | 16.3 | 1,637 | 62.8 |
| 1850 | 394 | 17.2 | 347 | 15.1 | 1,549 | 67.6 |
| 1860 | 254 | 14.1 | 203 | 11.2 | 1,341 | 74.5 |

*Source:* Compiled from U.S. Bureau of the Census, Manuscript Returns for Delaware, 1790-1860.

as an acceptable compromise between citizen rights over property, human property in this instance, and the ideals of the Enlightenment and Christianity. Repeatedly, owners first affirmed their right by law to their slave property but, finding such a right to human property contradictory to Christianity and human rights, compromised by freeing adult slaves either immediately or after a short indenture while requiring that younger slaves serve temporary but quite often prolonged indentures.

### Manumission by County

Slavery existed in all three Delaware counties, with the slave population unevenly distributed among the three (table 5). Not surprisingly, the tendency of slave owners to free their slaves varied from county to county. By examining the manumission process in each county, further insight can be gained into the ways in which economic, religious, cultural, and ideological factors helped to bring about the decline of the institution of slavery.

Unlike the remaining slave states, the free black population of Delaware always was significant. Even in 1790, at the peak of slavery in the state, free blacks comprised 30 percent of the black population. Over the ensuing decades the proportion of slaves in the black population declined to 42.6 percent in 1800 and to 17.1 percent in 1830. By 1860 only 8.3 percent of the Delaware's 21,627 blacks were still held in bondage.

Sussex County consistently reported the largest number of slaves and the lowest number of free blacks in the state. Approximately 45 percent of Delaware's slaves lived in Sussex County in 1790 and 1800; by 1810 its share had increased to 57.5 percent, and this proportion continued to rise until 1860, when nearly 75 percent of the state's remaining 1,798 slaves resided in Sussex County. Kent County, which led the state in manumissions, reported the smallest number of slaves, with New Castle County not far behind.

A number of factors account for these regional differences. New Castle County shared a border and its culture with Pennsylvania. Like that state, New Castle was home to a significant Quaker, and later Scotch-Irish, population. Quakers in 1776 completely banned members from holding slaves, while the Scotch-Irish in New Castle County for the most part arrived as indentured servants and hence were rarely in a position to own slaves themselves. Moreover, wheat and mercantile interests dominated the economic life of the county, and since none of these required extensive use of slave labor, there was little incentive to own slaves.[1]

Reflecting the state norm, a majority of New Castle County slaveholders owned only a slave or two. Only a few owners held more than ten slaves, well below the definition for being a large slaveholder. In 1800 Cantwell Jones of Appoquinimink Hundred reported thirty-two slaves and two free blacks in his household; he was New Castle County's largest slaveholder in that census year. With a count of nineteen slaves, William Reynolds of St. Georges Hundred owned the most slaves in New Castle County in 1810.[2] New Castle County's largest slave owner in both 1850 and 1860 was Richard R. Lockwood; he reported thirteen slaves in 1850 and twelve in 1860.

New Castle County experienced an accelerated pace of manumission as evidenced by the census returns of 1790 and after. The county's proportion of free blacks in the black population in 1790, 19.9 percent, seems very moderate when compared to Kent County's total of 52.7 percent. But within the next two decades the gap between the two counties significantly narrowed. From 1790 to 1800 New Castle's slave population declined by 28.2 percent; the pace of decline almost doubled to 43.0 percent between 1800 and 1810. By 1860 only 3 percent of New Castle County black residents, the same as in Kent County, remained in bondage (tables 6 and 7).

The rate at which the slave population of the city of Wilmington declined was striking but not surprising. The city never manifested a strong demand for slave labor. In 1800 Wilmington reported 121 slaves, the

Table 6. Change in Delaware's black population, 1790–1860
(in percentages)

| | New Castle | | Kent | | Sussex | |
|---|---|---|---|---|---|---|
| | Slave | Free | Slave | Free | Slave | Free |
| 1790–1800 | −28.2 | +330.9 | −35.4 | +65.2 | −29.6 | +83.7 |
| 1800–1810 | −43.0 | +42.3 | −50.9 | +32.2 | −15.1 | +183.9 |
| 1810–1820 | +14.1 | +10.8 | +46.9 | −1.4 | −6.5 | −14.4 |
| 1820–1830 | −34.2 | +31.3 | −45.0 | +2.4 | −14.5 | +45.2 |
| 1830–1840 | −31.1 | +18.6 | −27.3 | +2.7 | −14.6 | −3.5 |
| 1840–1850 | −27.1 | +12.5 | −18.7 | +9.5 | −5.3 | −5.8 |
| 1850–1860 | −35.5 | +7.4 | −41.4 | +13.8 | −13.4 | +7.4 |

Source: Compiled from U.S. Bureau of the Census, Manuscript Returns for Delaware, 1790–1860.

Table 7. Slave and free black population in Delaware, 1790–1860
(in percentages)

| | New Castle | | Kent | | Sussex | |
|---|---|---|---|---|---|---|
| | Slave | Free | Slave | Free | Slave | Free |
| 1790 | 80 | 20 | 47 | 53 | 85 | 15 |
| 1800 | 40 | 60 | 26 | 74 | 69 | 31 |
| 1810 | 21 | 79 | 11 | 89 | 40 | 60 |
| 1820 | 22 | 78 | 16 | 84 | 42 | 58 |
| 1830 | 12 | 88 | 9 | 91 | 30 | 70 |
| 1840 | 7 | 93 | 7 | 93 | 27 | 73 |
| 1850 | 5 | 95 | 5 | 95 | 28 | 72 |
| 1860 | 3 | 97 | 3 | 97 | 23 | 77 |

Source: Compiled from U.S. Bureau of the Census, Manuscript Returns for Delaware, 1790–1860.

number fell to 14 by 1830, and in 1860 only 4 slaves belonging to two owners were reported. George Read Riddle, one of the two slaveholders, owned three slaves: a male aged sixty-eight and two females aged fifty-six and twelve. By state law the two adult slaves were well past manumission age, which perhaps accounts for their continued enslavement. Catherine Capelle, the other slaveholder, owned a seventeen-year-old female slave, who may well have been among the class of half-free blacks.

The decline in New Castle County's slave population was matched by a corresponding increase in the free black population. Starting from a low of 20 percent in 1790, the proportion of free blacks in the total New Castle black population increased threefold, growing to 60 percent by the census of 1800. Between 1800 and 1830 the proportion of free blacks increased to 88 percent, jumping to 97 percent by the Civil War (see table 7).

Wilmington experienced a spectacular growth in its free black population partly due to its own slaveholders freeing their slaves but mainly owing to free black migrants from rural Delaware and the South. By 1800, 78.5 percent of the city's black residents were free, climbing to 99.0 percent by 1830, and almost 100 percent in 1860, but for the four remaining slaves.

The rapid pace of manumission of slaves in New Castle was no accident. Many Quakers, two abolition societies, operators of the Underground Railroad, and abolitionists like Ferris and Garrett called the county home. As well, New Castle was the county closest to the freedom magnet, Philadelphia. Historian H. Clay Reed has attributed the county's progress in manumission "to such factors as the influx of Northerners with antislavery tendencies and the presence of a small but influential group of Quaker reformers."[3]

Alongside religious and Enlightenment influences, slaveholder responses in the face of the reality of early nineteenth-century New Castle County slavery helped to promote manumission in the county. It must have become apparent to slaveholders living in a county bordering free Pennsylvania that the best chance of reducing the incidence of escaping slaves lay in offering freedom coupled with an extended indenture, or risk losing their slave property through the active Underground Railroad. Additionally, the marginality of slave labor in the major economic pursuits of New Castle County made voluntary emancipation feasible.

Unlike New Castle, and in sharp contrast to Sussex, Kent County reported more free blacks than slaves in the First Federal Census of 1790: 53 percent (see table 7). And the segment of the black population that claimed free status continued to exceed that of the other two counties for the next half century. The proportion of Kent County slave owners and the average number of slaves they held were similar to those in the rest of Delaware; the difference lay in the rate of manumission in Kent County. From 1790 to 1800 the free black population in Kent County increased to 74 percent of its black residents; three decades later 91 percent were counted as free persons. On the eve of the Civil War, 97 percent of Kent County's black residents claimed free status.

The coming together of the forces of religion, the economy, and Enlightenment ideology in a fashion more dramatic than the experience in New Castle and Sussex counties explains this rapid pace of manumission in Kent County. Like New Castle, and to a lesser extent Sussex County, Christian conscience played a major role in the pace of manumission in Kent. Whereas the Quakers remained the primary religious group behind manumission in New Castle, and the Methodists played a similar role in Sussex, Kent County boasted a strong presence of both Quakers and Methodists. Their two-pronged religious assault on slavery had far-reaching results in the county, making it almost a certainty that Kent would lead the state in the pace of manumission.

Kent County was the home of the zealous abolitionist Warner Mifflin and the base of the influential Duck Creek monthly meeting. From 1774 on, the meetinghouse recorded well over six hundred manumissions, executed mainly by residents of Kent County, Quaker and non-Quaker alike. Not so easily determined are the exact numbers of non-Quakers freeing slaves or the count of slaves freed in response to Quaker persuasion. Perhaps the best testimonial is the hundreds of slaves who listed Warner Mifflin and other Kent County Quakers as friend or advocate in their freedom suits and also the large number of slaveholders who chose Kent County Quakers as witnesses to the manumission contracts.

By the 1790s Kent County Quakers could truthfully claim that they had eradicated the sin of slaveholding among members, yet Kent continued to lead the state in manumissions. Clearly, non-Quakers in Kent County were also manumitting their slaves, and Methodist antislavery must be credited for much of this. Even after the national Methodist church retreated from its earlier antislavery stand, Delaware Valley Methodist leaders, often in strong opposition to national leadership, continued to advocate abolition.[4] As a stronghold of Methodism in Delaware, Kent County benefited from this strong abolition stance.

The American Revolution inadvertently enhanced the cause of abolition in Kent County, for it brought Methodist leader and antislavery advocate Francis Asbury to Kent County. He spent the years from 1778 to

1780 near Dover, hiding from a possible charge of treason against the new nation. While in exile, Asbury wrote and preached his antislavery message to Delaware Valley Methodists, converting many who would later take up the causes of Methodism and abolition.[5]

Also aiding in the course of Kent County Methodist-inspired manu-mission was Richard Bassett, a local Methodist leader and a politician. Like Warner Mifflin, Bassett not only freed his numerous slaves but was also a founding member of the Dover-based abolition society. As a lawyer and state representative, Bassett championed the cause of abolition in the legislature by sponsoring the first major state law to foster manumission, the 1787 act.[6]

Antislavery politicians not necessarily religiously inclined also helped place the county of Kent in the forefront of the abolitionist movement. To Dover, the state capital, came lawyer-politicians, many of whom had been trained in Philadelphia and were, therefore, quite conversant with the abolitionist ideology of the day.[7] Richard Bassett was a prime example, as were two men who served as state representatives and later as presidents of the state, John Dickinson and Caesar Rodney.

Rodney's fight for abolition began in 1767, when he and his fellow representatives from Kent County unsuccessfully appealed for an end to the slave trade.[8] Later, as president of Delaware (1778–82) and as Speaker of the state senate (1783–84), Rodney successfully advocated the liberalization of voluntary manumission laws. Though John Dickinson was not a member of the Society of Friends, his Quaker background may help explain his antislavery beliefs. Out of a Christian conscience and duty, Dickinson in July 1775 freed all his slaves. Moreover, while president of Delaware, he recommended a state law providing

> that persons manumitting healthy Slaves not advanced in Years, should not be obliged to give Security for their Maintenance, and that Slaves should not be sent upon Sale or otherwise to Places distant from their usual Residence, by which Means affectionate and near Relations are cruelly separated from one another, and the Remainder of their Lives extremely imbittered. The Legislatures of several neighbouring States, moved by a deep Sense of the divine Favors to them in this Contest for their own Freedom, and by an enlightened Commiseration, have lately passed Laws for alleviating the Afflictions of this helpless and too often abused Part of their Fellow-Creatures.

Dickinson sincerely hoped that Delaware would follow the example set by neighbor Pennsylvania and legislate abolition.[9] His appeal was identical in content and wording to those submitted to the legislature by Quak-

ers and abolitionists, petitions that resulted in the enactment of the
1787 manumission law.

The shift in staple crop from tobacco to grain accelerated the pace
of voluntary manumission in Kent County. Predominantly rural and agricultural, Kent County by the Revolutionary era had replaced tobacco
with wheat as the region's principal staple crop. This considerably weak-
ened the demand for and use of slave labor, inclining Kent County slaveholders already facing a powerful barrage of antislavery forces—
Quakers, Methodists, abolition society, and politicians—to free their surplus slaves.

Sussex County was the southernmost county in the state and the bastion of slavery. It shared its northern border with Kent County and was
surrounded on its western and southern boundaries by Maryland. Almost half of Delaware's slaves lived in Sussex County in 1790; in subsequent censuses the actual number of slaves in the county declined, but
its proportion of slaves relative to Kent and New Castle counties increased. The much slower pace of manumission in Sussex and the rapid
freeing of slaves in Kent and New Castle counties combined to increase
the proportion of slaves in Sussex County. From 1790 to 1830 the county's portion of the total slave population climbed from 45.2 percent to
58.2 percent; by 1860, 74.5 percent of Delaware's slaves lived in Sussex
(see table 5). Although Sussex County reported the largest number of
slaves, the average number of slaves held by individual slave owners did
not substantially differ from that of New Castle and Kent counties.

Many reasons have been suggested for the persistence of slavery in
Sussex County. Its economic backwardness, its distance from Philadelphia, the relative lack of northern antislavery activism, and the absence
of Quaker antislavery influence proved detrimental to the cause of abolition in the county.[10] Further, the much higher number of slaves in Sussex
County proved an additional barrier, for it had almost twice as many
slaves as in either New Castle or Kent County.

The opportunity for Sussex County's slaveholders to dispose of their
surplus slaves, often illegally, also inhibited the freeing of its slaves.
When the shift to grain forced many Delaware slave owners to make
changes in their labor force, some Sussex County slaveholders eschewed
voluntary manumission in favor of the economically viable but unlawful
option of selling slaves bound for the Deep South through the neighboring slave states. Opportunistic Sussex County slaveholders could
accomplish such illegal sales with relative ease; their proximity to the
neighboring slave states provided an inviting conduit. Few enforcement
mechanisms were in place to check this illegal trade in Sussex County:

there were no strong Quaker or abolition groups to keep track of compliance with the state's slave laws, and the only appreciable antislavery group in the county, the Methodists, were strong on persuasion but weak on enforcement.

Delaware slaveholders, and in particular residents of Sussex County, were well aware of this illegal option. In 1837 a group of white residents not only condemned the restrictions on slave exports but blamed the regulations for engendering a sharp rise in the kidnapping and illegal export of slaves. In their petition to the legislature, these residents complained that Delaware's liberal manumission laws had "render[ed] slaves disobedient and consequently far less useful and valuable to their owners than they would otherwise be." Certainly slave truculence would reduce their value. The petitioners also noted that the law unintentionally had led to "the exportation of many slaves contrary to this law and to many and indeed to a great portion of the frequent cases of kidnapping."[11] The statutes prohibiting the export of slaves made Delaware—particularly Sussex County—with its convenient borders and devalued slave labor a fertile ground for kidnapping and illegal slave sales.

The kidnapping of blacks for sale to the Deep South reached epic proportions during the early nineteenth century. The abolition of the external slave trade in 1808, just at the time when the cotton boom took place, helped to create a voracious demand for slaves which legally could only be met through the domestic market. The upper South, its soil destroyed by repetitive tobacco cultivation and bypassed by the cotton kingdom, became the major supplier of slaves. As demand for slaves increased in the cotton-rich South, so too did the price paid for slaves, thus creating profits high enough to tempt many into illegally kidnapping both slaves and free blacks for sale farther South.

Delaware's location on the crossroads between freedom and slavery magnified this temptation. During the early decades of the nineteenth century, Delaware's most infamous slave and free black kidnapper, Patty Cannon, based her operations in Sussex County. The myths surrounding Patty Cannon makes it difficult to distinguish fact from fiction. However, all accounts agree that Cannon, her family, and her associates were responsible for numerous kidnappings from their headquarters, a house conveniently located on the state line. Because half of the house lay in Maryland, Cannon and her associates succeeded in thwarting Delaware authorities for many years.

Still shrouded in mystery is the exact number of kidnappings or the number of people killed by the Cannon gang during the commission of this illegal activity. Nevertheless, by the mid–1820s several family members had been convicted of kidnapping and punished with public whipping, pillory, and prison terms. Others, including Patty Cannon, moved from the state apparently to escape kidnapping charges. Not until 1829, when human skeletal remains were discovered on the former Cannon property, was Patty Cannon extradited from Maryland to face murder charges. The trial never took place: Patty Cannon died while in jail before the trial, sparking another controversy over the cause of her death.[12]

The series of antikidnapping laws passed by the Delaware legislature offers the most persuasive testimony of the extent of the problem. Laws in 1787 and 1789, passed in answer to Quaker and abolition society appeals, penalized convicted kidnappers and exporters of slaves with a fine of £100. An amendment in 1793 strengthened the law by prescribing corporal punishment rather than a fine: anyone convicted of kidnapping or aiding in a kidnapping would "be publicly whipped on his or her back with thirty-nine lashes well laid on, and shall stand in the pillory for the space of one hour, with both of his or her ears nailed thereto, and at the expiration of the hour, shall have the soft part of both of his or her ears cut off."[13]

Rarely did the state apply the full force of the 1793 law; in spite of numerous convictions, the courts tended to impose fines in lieu of the harsh penalties. In 1826 convicted kidnapper Rachel Scott temporarily lost her freedom as penalty for her part in a kidnapping. Initially her sentence followed the provisions of the 1793 law, but the governor chose to excuse her from receiving the mandated physical punishment. Still, Scott faced court costs of about $36; unable to pay the fine, she was sold into servitude for a period not exceeding seven years.[14]

Apparently, the kidnapping problem became so severe that even Delaware citizens not known to support the antislavery movement raised their voices in protest. One such complaint came from a New Castle County grand jury assembled in 1816 to study the problem of kidnapping. The jurors concluded that there "is ample testimony that the free colored man is insecure in his own house"; neither was "the master in possession of his slave," and all because "of the daring violation of Justice committed by those who are engaged in this nefarious business."[15] Thus, they recommended an exacting punishment for those found guilty of kidnapping.

The legislature seemed to agree, and by 1841 those found guilty of kidnapping had to "forfeit and pay to the State a fine of not less than one thousand dollars nor more than two thousand dollars." Plus, offenders would "be set on the pillory for the space of one hour; . . . publicly whipped with thirty-nine lashes on the bare back, well laid on, and to be imprisoned for a term not less than one year nor more than two years."[16]

Although severe, the 1793 act and subsequent antikidnapping laws did not end the practice of kidnapping. However, their effects were felt in certain circles. In very disparaging words, and quite unintentionally, slaveholder Thomas Rodney confirmed how effective the Quakers and abolitionists were in foiling kidnappings. He accused them of having

> long concealed their love of Tyranny and persecution under the mild, the meek, and the peaceable cloak of humanity. . . . They have lastly been seen advocating a savage, barbarous and cruel Law that would have disgraced even the reign of Nero—They have lastly been seen prosecuting to conviction under that Law and have been viewing the Whipping, Pillorying and Croping of the criminals with all that anxious and malignant satisfaction which a Tyrant feels at the execution of those they order to destruction, and all for only conveying negros out of our State into another which was remedial by civil process, while the negros incouraged by them are guilty of the most twisted and Iniquitous conduct and become pests to society.[17]

But even in Sussex County, where so many forces seemed to be working against abolition, the overwhelming majority of blacks gained their freedom. The census data reveal that Sussex County slaveholders freed their slaves at an impressive rate, albeit much slower than in both New Castle and Kent counties. From 1790 to 1800 the county's free black population increased by 83.7 percent, and by a phenomenal 183.9 percent over the next decade (see table 6). On the eve of the Civil War, Sussex County reported 77 percent of its black population as free (see table 7). Clearly, even Sussex County could not stem the tide running toward voluntary manumission of slaves in Delaware.

### Deferring Freedom

The records of manumission reveal that the occasion for freeing slaves was often as important as the deed itself. Apparently many owners linked manumission dates to events of significance to themselves, the slaves, or both. Owners freeing slaves out of a Christian conscience, for instance, chose Christmas and the New Year season to express their benevolence. The former, celebrating the birth of Christ and the Christian faith, and the latter, hopefully a better new year, seemed a fitting time to reflect on Christian conscience and to display a sense of charity and generosity. Both holidays symbolized new beginnings: a time for hope, a celebration of one's blessings, and a call to practice benevolence. They were also a time to remember the unfortunate and the unfree, and consequently slaveholders could demonstrate their piety by freeing their slaves at these times.

Slaveholders influenced by Enlightenment principles tended to choose the Fourth of July to depict their belief in liberty. The principles behind the holiday—freedom, liberty, and the rights of mankind—were not lost on slaveholders. The holiday and all it celebrated were the opposite of slavery, leading some slaveholders to live up to its spirit by granting liberty to their slaves. Other slaveholders rewarded good and faithful service with freedom, some timed manumission to follow their death, and many more owners offered no explanation as to the time or cause of the voluntary manumission.

Unquestionably, the Christmas season worked its special magic on slaveholder Spencer Lacey of Sussex County. On 5 December 1791 he executed deeds of manumission for all his slaves because he was "convinced of the greatest impropriety of holding . . . Fellow creatures in slavery." Complete freedom for all the slaves would be granted on Christmas Day, but in different years: emancipation for nineteen-year-old Mose would fall on Christmas Day in 1793; thirteen-year-old Sam would be free Christmas Day 1799; while eight-year-old Nice would receive her freedom on Christmas Day in 1803. John Fleetwood of Sussex County not only freed his slave Orange on Christmas Day 1794, but provided an additional Christmas bonus in the form of forty shillings; this, however, would not be paid until after Fleetwood's death.[18]

For several slaveholders named Moore, all residents of Sussex County, and possibly related—Isaac Moore in 1788 and both Solomon and William Moore in 1797—the New Year offered an opportunity to show mercy by freeing their slaves. Slavery, they all agreed, not only violated Christianity but also "the very principle of the late Glorious Revolution"; "therefore for these Good Causes and weighty considerations," they freed their slaves. None of the Moore manumissions were immediate, and the slaves in question faced extended indentures, but all the freedom dates fell on the first of January of the respective years.[19]

Slaveholder William Armor appropriately chose the first day of the new millennium—1 January 1800—to express his Christian benevolence. He addressed the manumission deed to all Christian people, informing them that he owned Cudjo Thompson "by an undefeasable right in Law and Equity," but that being so, it was his desire that Thompson be "sett free, and at full Liberty, in the full enjoyment of a perfect Emancipation." In the spirit of true Christian charity, Armor made the "perfect Emancipation" immediate and final.[20]

Freedom by last will with emancipation effective after the death of the owner was quite common. Slave owners who favored freeing their slaves but felt reluctant to lose their services during their lifetime often chose this method. In life, these slaveholders pleaded financial obligations or reliance on the services provided by their slaves as reason for delaying emancipation. But the death of the owner ended his or her need for the slave, making it possible to offer freedom. It was the "wish and desire" of Joseph Cannon that immediately following his death his three adult slaves and their children be "entitled to all the privileges of free negroes under the laws of the state of Delaware." Equally simple was the will of James Pettyjohn of Sussex County: it granted, following his death, unconditional freedom to all of his thirteen slaves.[21]

On occasion, freedom came not directly through wills but were incidental to a bequest. People who inherited slaves through the wills of relatives and friends but had no use for slave labor usually offered them their freedom. Forty-five-year-old Levin, for example, indirectly received his freedom through the will of John Phillip. The will required Levin to serve Phillip's wife Sarah and, following her death, to have the choice of selecting one of the Phillip children as his new owner. Levin wisely selected Spencer Phillip, who with "divers good causes thereunto moving," freed Levin in May 1799. Similarly, when Sally and Thaddeus Jackson became the owners of Will through the bequest of Julius Jackson, they for "divers good causes" offered him unconditional freedom.[22]

Good behavior and outstanding service provided another route to freedom. In 1796 Barkely Townsend of Sussex County freed a slave named Suck because "she hath been faithfull and have for twenty one years." Jacob, a slave, received his freedom in 1792 because he had "been the faithfullest slave amongst many and for which reason the subscriber hath given him his liberty." Jacob's owner, John Willbank, provided him a reference assuring prospective employers that they may depend on Jacob "being a faithful fellow of business except reaping." He was a good cutter, "an extraordinary hand to schear in and block of for a carpenter in giting timble steps port and rail fence," and he could "saw well in the pit with a whipsaw" and was a good farmhand.[23]

Slaveholders usually reserved immediate and unconditional freedom for adult slaves, particularly elderly slaves. Owners who freed their slaves in this manner most likely timed it just so they could escape the state deadline for responsibility for indigent ex-slaves. Although state laws eased manumission requirements, it still held slaveholders responsible if they freed unhealthy or indigent slaves. It is impossible to gauge with any degree of certainty the number of owners who tried to evade responsibility by offering immediate freedom or short-term indenture to elderly slaves. State law did not mandate manumission or require those who freed their slaves to justify their action, much less provide a truthful explanation.

Yet the existing records of manumission suggest that owners often chose this self-serving route. Certainly this explains the timing of the freeing of elderly slave Grace Baily by her owner James Latimer of New Castle County. Latimer meticulously documented his observance of the limits set by the manumission law of 1797:

> whereas in the Sixth Section of said Act, these words are contained, to wit; "And be it enacted that any Master or Mistress . . . may by any last will in writing, or otherwise Manumit and set at Liberty any Negro or Mulatto Slave above the age of Eighteen years & under the age of Thirty five years, who is healthy & no ways decripped or rendered incapable of getting his or her living, without giving the security required. . . ." And whereas I . . . now hath in my possession a black woman named . . . Grace Baily between the ages of Thirty four and Thirty Five years who I purchased a slave & has been maintained by me as such for a number of years past, but she now being desirous of obtaining her Freedom & I willing to grant her the same, well knowing that she has behaved her self honestly, soberly & industriously & that she is healthy & no ways decrippid or rendered incapable of getting her living.[24]

To evade the intent of the state law, some owners qualified the freeing of older slaves by compelling them to sign contracts relieving their former masters of any responsibility should the elderly ex-slaves become indigent. By the will of Edmund Lynch, his slave Philip would receive freedom a year after the death of Lynch. The will, however, required Philip to pay a bond of £100 in "security to indemnify the said County of Kent and the said executors from any damage that may arise to either the County or the executors by means of the said negro." In 1791 Philip bound himself to the county and the executors of the Lynch estate to the tune of £100.[25]

A minority of slave owners freed their adult slaves without demanding a term of servitude or cash payment. "Convinced of the errors of slavery," slaveholder James Scotton freed Benjamin and as testimony to his new convictions added no restrictive proviso to the manumission deed. Most unusual was Adam Black's manumission of his runaway slave Jacob. Apparently bearing no ill will toward the slave, Black freed the absconded Jacob, who was still at large at the time of the manumission, and further "defend the said Jacob Black in the peacable and quiet possession of his Liberty from the date hereof forever, against myself my Executors Administrators and every one of them under the Penalty of Two Hundred Dollars."[26]

Other slaves, though freed immediately, achieved this status with such unusual provisos attached to the manumission deed as to seriously compromise the meaning of freedom. James Miller in December 1803 freed his three male slaves out of the belief that freedom should be the right of all "civilised people and in particular the Natural born citisons of these United States of America." The manumission, though immediate, contained an unusual stipulation mandating that the "freed" men render certain specified and unpaid services for the lifetime of James Miller and, after Miller's death, the lifetime of his wife. As a condition of freedom, the three ex-slaves had to "agree to cut and hall into the Dwelling house of the said James Miller fire wood sufficient for his house use and cut five acres of hay marsh for the said James on his Marsh each of them for every year so long as the said James Miller doth live and his wife lives as his widow." And for the lifetime of James Miller and of his wife, the "freed" men agreed "to cut and spit Rales sufficient to keep the plantation in order the same length of Time and to give their personal assistance to help in finishing said James' Dwelling he now Dwells in."[27]

Daphne's manumission in 1797 was also very unusual; her freedom was contingent on her raising her son for a lifetime of slavery. To escape the financial burden of providing for an infant too young to work, Daphne's owner, John Marsh, freed her on condition "that she bring up her son Jacob to the age of nine years & provide him in the mean time sufficient food & clothing & then return him to me or my heirs and that shall be her discharge from all hire and service on the above conditions."[28] The deed made no mention of freedom for Jacob.

Rarely were slave children granted immediate and complete freedom; the few slave children freed outright were typically made the wards of parents who were either free, quasi-free, or freed at the same time as their children. These parents were expected to assume custodial responsibility for their children and to relieve the former master of any statutory liability. The manumission of twenty-seven-year-old Solomon, his twenty-one- year-old wife, Hannah, and their seven-year-old child, Zep, illustrates this point. For "divers good causes and considerations," their owner Rhoad Shankland of Sussex County executed a manumission deed that granted them immediate and complete freedom. The manumission deed for thirty-year-old Cottoh was more expressive: her owner Cornl. Paynter freed her and "all her descendants"; the freedom was to be clear of "restitution or limitation." In 1801 Anthony Heaveloe, also of Sussex County, freed a forty-seven-year-old slave named Madillah and at the same time "set free eight young Negroes which were born of the Body" of Madillah. All eight children, ranging in age from three to twenty-three, were given immediate and unrestricted freedom.[29]

Regardless of the rationale for the manumission, most Delaware slaveholders delayed the date of complete freedom for younger slaves. Slaveholder occupation or religion bore not at all on the terms of manu-

Table 8. Age structure of blacks in Delaware, 1830–60 (in percentages)

| | | Age | | | | |
|---|---|---|---|---|---|---|
| | | 0–9 | 10–23 | 24–35 | 36–54 | 55+ |
| 1830 | Slave | 33.3 | 44.2 | 14.7 | 4.9 | 2.7 |
| | Free | 32.5 | 29.2 | 17.3 | 14.3 | 6.5 |
| 1840 | Slave | 31.4 | 47.2 | 13.7 | 4.9 | 2.5 |
| | Free | 31.6 | 30.3 | 16.6 | 13.5 | 7.8 |

| | | Age | | | | | |
|---|---|---|---|---|---|---|---|
| | | 0–9 | 10–19 | 20–29 | 30–39 | 40–49 | 50+ |
| 1850 | Slave | 33.3 | 33.5 | 19.8 | 6.5 | 3.2 | 3.3 |
| | Free | 30.8 | 24.2 | 15.7 | 10.9 | 7.5 | 10.5 |
| 1860 | Slave | 29.9 | 33.9 | 19.1 | 8.0 | 4.0 | 4.5 |
| | Free | 28.9 | 25.4 | 17.0 | 10.5 | 7.7 | 10.1 |

*Source:* Compiled from U.S. Bureau of the Census, Manuscript Returns for Delaware, 1830–60.

mission, since both farmers and nonfarmers, Quakers and non-Quakers, delayed freedom for younger slaves. The most revealing result from the census (lack of data limits the analysis to the nineteenth century), the skewed age structure of the slave population, supports this conclusion. Slaves, more than free blacks, were concentrated in the most productive years, from the early teens through the early thirties (table 8). The explanation lies in the preference of slaveholders for young and healthy slaves and a tendency of owners to ignore the advantage of the state's manumission laws for those who freed young slaves. Instead, most owners delayed full freedom until the slaves approached age thirty.

A comparison of the age structure of Delaware's slave and free black populations confirms the slaveholder tendency to delay manumission. Both free black and slave populations reported a similar proportion of children aged nine or younger. But the census counted a disproportionately higher number of slaves than free blacks aged ten to twenty-three in 1830 and 1840 and ten to twenty-nine in 1850 and 1860, a clear indication that slave owners preferred holding their slaves during these productive years before releasing them. In 1830, for example, while 44.2 percent of Delaware slaves ranged from ten to twenty-three years old, only 29.2 percent of free blacks fell in the same group. Conversely, among blacks aged thirty and older, the proportion of free blacks exceeded that of slaves. In 1840 the state reported proportionately three times as many free blacks (7.8 percent) aged fifty-five years and over as there were slaves (2.5 percent) of the same age group. In both 1850 and 1860, the census recorded that the proportion of free blacks in the black population aged fifty-five and older was more than double that of slaves.

The 1802 manumission deed executed by John Hazzard of Sussex County—a document typical of many issued by slaveholders in the state—provides a graphic picture of the complexity and essence of the voluntary but delayed manumission system in Delaware. The deed included a variety of the indenture options open to Delaware slaveholders: older slaves were freed after a short or medium term of servitude, while young adults and slave children served until age twenty-one for females and twenty-five for males. The manumission deed for the ten Hazzard slaves declares:

> To all whom these Presents shall come Greeting. Whereas the subscriber is Possessed of sundrie Negroes that are Desireous of Freedom and being convinced that it is inconsistant with Christianity and Derogatery to that just and Equitable command of the Saviour of Mankind to do to others as we would in like circumstances they should do to us, to hold our Fellow mortals in slavery, Therefore I do grant unto the said several Negroes their Natural Right of Freedom as followeth . . . Negro Solomon aged about Twenty six years entirely at his own disposal after the Twenty fifth day of December next ensuing . . . Negro Cain aged about Twenty seven years entirely at his own disposal after the Twenty fifth day of December Eighteen hundred and three . . . Negro Rose aged Two years and Eight months entirely at her own disposal when she arives at the age of Twenty one years . . . Negro Caesar aged about fifteen years entirely at his own disposal when he arives at the age of Twenty five years . . . Negro Jacob aged ten years and three months entirely at his own disposal when he arives at the age of twenty five years, . . . Negro Isaac aged six years, Negro Abraham aged five years, Negro Phillip four years, Negro George aged two years and Eight months, Negro Cyrus Aged one year to be entirely at their own disposal as they and each of them arives at the age of Twenty five years.

Hazzard freed his slaves, he said, because the slaves wanted to be free. For himself, he found slavery contrary to Christianity and the principles embodied in the Declaration of Independence; thus, he believed that his slaves should receive their "Natural Right of Freedom."[30] But common to Delaware manumission deeds, these worthy sentiments did not preclude a prolonged delay in the natural right to freedom for the slaves, long enough to allow Hazzard to extract full value from his chattels.

Even Delaware Quakers known for their antislavery stand within and outside their society supported temporary servitude. However, unlike other slaveholders, Quakers insisted that indentures not differ by race. Delaware Friends accepted in principle that the bondage of blacks should not exceed that of white servants or the age of majority; thus, they offered adult slaves immediate and unconditional freedom but delayed freedom for minors until age twenty-one for male children and eighteen for females.

Israel Allston of Kent County, for example, not only offered freedom to his two slaves but believed it important that they serve no longer than white servants. When Allston purchased quasi-slaves John and Lydia, they had been indentured by their former owners to serve until age twenty-five and twenty-one, respectively; but being "convinced of the Injustice of such partiality in the Distinction between them and the Whites," he commuted their years of servitude, freeing them "when they arrive to lawfull age: that is when John arrives to twenty one and Lydia when she arrives to the age of Eighteen years."[31]

Similarly, when Warner Mifflin freed his slaves, females who were over the age of eighteen and males past age twenty-one received immediate freedom. But believing it his Christian duty to exercise "authority over the young ones, to raise and educate them till they arrive to lawfull age," Mifflin "reserve[d] the prerogative over the male till they arrive to twenty one years of age and the female till they arrive to eighteen years of age." Quaker-influenced John Dickinson offered unencumbered freedom to his adult slaves but delayed it for the young females until their eighteenth birthday and until his young male slaves were twenty-one.[32]

Yet even among Quakers there were some owners not willing to free their slaves at ages eighteen and twenty-one. The best the meetinghouse could hope for was to shame such members into compliance. When Samuel Hanson freed his slaves in January 1770, he claimed to be "convinced of the iniquity and injustice of detaining [his] fellow men in Bondage." But as the monthly meeting reported, Hanson's conviction did not include offering immediate freedom to his elderly slaves. Five years of committee visits finally forced Hanson to switch on his inward light and adjust the time of servitude, having come to believe with "full conviction that such Distinction made of reserving their Time longer

than limited by Law for whites to serve appears with too much Partiality."[33]

In October 1776 Thomas Hanson, another member of the Duck
Creek Meeting House, was identified as one of several Quakers guilty of
requiring blacks to serve longer than white servants. He agreed to free
his slaves but adamantly refused to emancipate any before age twenty-
five. It took further pressure from Duck Creek Quakers before he finally
reduced the servitude of his black "servants."[34]

Methodists and members of the abolition societies also seemed quite
comfortable with temporary indenture. Richard Bassett saw no contradiction in a system whereby temporary indenture preceded the grant of
complete freedom. Although Bassett freed all of his slaves, freedom for
the slave children he owned was never immediate. In 1793, for example,
he indentured his nine-year-old slave Maria to serve Mary Dally of Philadelphia for twenty-one years before becoming free.[35]

The case of Caleb Rodney of Sussex County illustrates the path chosen by many of Delaware's slaveholders. In December 1800 Rodney purchased the "right and property" to two slaves, thirty-four-year-old Sarah
and her twenty-month-old daughter. Apparently, Rodney felt uncomfortable about permanent bondage; thus, "from a Conviction that liberty
is the natural and equitable right of every person," he immediately and
absolutely freed Sarah. But even though Rodney seemed distressed by
the inconsistency between permanent servitude and the natural rights
of mankind, he had no qualms imposing a temporary indenture of over
twenty-three years' duration on her daughter. Therefore, he reserved his
right to the service of the infant Harriet "temporarily" until she arrived
at the age of twenty-five.[36]

Similarly, George Armstrong of Sussex County freed his slaves because "the holding [of] fellow men in perpetual slavery is contrary to
the Laws of God and the unalienable Right of mankind." The key consideration for slave owners like Armstrong was their perception of permanent or perpetual slavery versus temporary servitude. While he decried
permanent bondage, he had no misgivings about temporary servitude;
therefore, he ordered his adult slaves to serve additional terms of between four to six years and the younger slaves until age twenty-five for
males and age twenty-one for the females. Further, Armstrong made provisions for children born during the servitude: if "males to be free at the
age of 25 and females at the age of 21."[37]

Even provisions for freedom after the death of the owner held no
guarantees that the manumission would be immediate and complete,
especially not when friends and relatives could benefit from the servitude of the quasi-free slave. Mary Allfree's elaborate manumission deed

for her slave Zacharias is a case in point. Allfree stipulated an eighteen-year indenture for Zacharias; should she die before the end of his service, she designated her son Saul as beneficiary for the balance of the indenture. When she died four years later, Zacharias, only fourteen years old at the time, thus had to serve Saul until the expiration of the remaining fourteen years of his indenture. An additional provision in Mary's will specified that should Saul die before Zacharias's twenty-eighth birthday, Zacharias would receive his freedom with no additional reservations.[38]

Despite the owners' protestations of gratitude, slaves freed for good and faithful service also could not count on receiving immediate and unconditional freedom. Too often the recipient of freedom served an extended period of indenture before full freedom. Such was the case in 1789, when Margaret Gill of Sussex County "in consideration of the faithful services rendered . . . and for divers other causes" freed her slave, Negro Paris. Yet for all the praise of his exceptional service, Paris's freedom was not immediate; it would ensue the death of Gill. When Naomi Bruce in 1801 freed her slave Paris "in consideration of the services he had heretofore performed," she still made his freedom conditional upon "his future service during the term of five years."[39]

Indentures for older slaves often were of short duration, lasting from a few months to an average of two years. Usually, owners timed the servitude of older slaves to expire on the slave's next birthday or to coincide with the end of the year in which the manumission deed was executed; thus, the additional servitude imposed lasted between a few weeks and a few months. When Adam Short of Sussex County freed his slave woman Grace in February 1803, Grace was required to serve a very short indenture of only two months, setting her effective date of complete freedom in April 1803. It may be that the April date was her birthday, for Grace's son Nutter, freed on the same day, had his date of freedom tied to his birthday, his twenty-first. Slave owner Joseph Collins of Sussex County freed female slaves Grace and Martha under similar circumstances. Collins drew up the manumission deed on 23 December 1803 but delayed full freedom until 31 January 1804; he offered no explanation for the extremely short indenture.[40]

More typical in Delaware's system of delayed emancipation were older slaves who were required to serve short indentures of a year or two. Sarah Clarke's freeing of her two slaves aged forty and thirty-five is a case in point. She required that each serve a two-year indenture, and during this period, should they become unable to work—due to sickness or any other reason—they would be expected to make up the time with additional service beyond the initial two-year period. James Clayton also offered a short indenture of four years to his "Negro Man Caller," but with the stipulation that should Caller run away or stay absent during the indenture, "he shall be free only after he has made up over and above the said four years Three times as much time as is lost by his running away." Kent County resident Sarah Hoffecker freed her three slaves because of "gratitude and good will" and in that spirit urged the ex-slaves to enjoy "their perfect liberty and freedom." However, the "perfect freedom" would not occur until the expiration of a two-year indenture for Jacob Lebo, while John and Thomas Crosby, would serve eight and eleven years, of indenture respectively.[41]

Slaveholder John Maull's generous manumission terms for twenty-six-year old Cyrus were atypical. Maull, of Sussex County, freed Cyrus for "certain good reasons" with full freedom to occur at the expiration of four years of servitude. But contrary to common practice, Maull offered during the four years of indenture to "furnish said Cyrus with twenty Dollars worth of clothes and pay him twenty Dollars in cash for each and every year of the said four years that the said Cyrus work with or for me."[42] Offering payment in addition to freedom was not common in Delaware's system of delayed freedom.

Indentures for slave children and young adults were usually of longer duration, lasting until the age of majority for most, and well beyond for many. The manumission executed by Sarah Brown of Kent County stipulated freedom for seventeen-year-old Spencer when he turned twenty-one, but her female slave Rhodey, twelve at the date of the deed, would be freed at age eighteen. Joseph Collins of Sussex County granted two adult females full freedom after they served a monthlong indenture, and two male slaves were to serve eleven-year indentures. However, the "rest of the negroes, by the names of Philis, Rose, March and Harry, all girls to enjoy their freedom . . . at the age of twenty five years old—the boys by the names of Will, Joe and Jim to enjoy their freedom . . . at the age of eight and twenty years old."[43]

Usually, owners drew distinction between male and female slaves, imposing lengthier indentures on male slaves. Male slave indentures typically continued until they were somewhere in the range of twenty-one to thirty-five years old, with a statewide average of complete freedom conferred at 26.6 years of age. On average, female slaves served 3.3 fewer years of indenture than their male counterparts; the norm for females was servitude until age eighteen to twenty-five, with a state average of complete manumission granted at 23.3 years of age.

A slight variation existed on the county level, with Sussex County slaveholders imposing longer terms of service—an average of three additional years—on their half-free slaves than Kent County residents did. Sussex County slave owners freed male slaves at an average age of 27.5 years compared to age 24.1 for Kent County male slaves. The average Sussex County female slave served until age twenty-four while Kent County female slaves typically received their freedom at the age of twenty-one.[44]

Other slaveholders refrained from discriminating against male slaves; they instead imposed similar terms on both genders. Slaveholder Richard Green of Sussex County, for instance, required a similar duration of service to nine-year-old Caesar as he did for eleven-year-old Lydia. Both slaves were freed on the "express condition that they bind themselves to serve until they arrive to age of twenty eight years at which time it is the true intent & meaning of these presents that they enjoy the liberties & privileges that free Negro or mullatto may or Can do." Slaveholder Reynear Williams offered immediate freedom to two female slaves aged thirty-five and twenty-five but deferred freedom until age twenty-one for his younger slaves; specifying

> Prissilla a Negro Woman aged seventeen years to be [free] at the age of twenty one years—likewise a negroe Boy named Anthony aged tenn years to be free at the age of Twenty one years—also a negroe Boy called George aged seven years to be free at the age of twenty one years—likewise Elijah a negroe boy aged five years to be Free at the age of twenty one years—also a negroe Girl called Ailee aged two years to be free at the age of twenty one years—also a Negroe Girl named Comfort aged six months to be free at the age of twenty one years— also a negroe Girl named Jane aged four months to be free at the age of twenty years.[45]

On average, most slave children attained freedom before age thirty; few slaveholders delayed freedom past that age because owners had to guard against liability for freeing indigent and old slaves. But it was not unknown for some owners to delay freedom much longer. John Holland of Sussex County offered conditional freedom to his eighteen-year-old slave Sip with complete liberty to occur "after the Expiration of the term of thirty two years from the twenty second Day of November 1803."[46] In spite of the length of the indenture, Sip's time of servitude was clearly defined; should he live long enough, freedom would be his at age fifty.

For another slave named Benjamin, freedom day was not so definite but depended on the death of his owner, Hillary Coudwright of Kent County.[47] For "divers good causes and considerations," Coudwright freed the "Negro Man Benjamin he being about twenty eight years of age and he the said Negro to be free and at his liberty at My Death." Indenture ending with the death of the owner was indefinite, lasting from a few weeks to years of servitude. Such terms may well have encouraged slaves like Benjamin to yearn for the imminent demise of their owners.

Requiring female slaves to serve past their mid-twenties occurred rarely. However, a few slaveholders like Samuel Warren did so. Warren contracted to free his slave girl "Tamer when she arrive to the age of thirty years." At fifteen when the document was signed, Tamer had to serve an indenture of as many years' duration. From Sussex County, Jacob Wolfe, a physician, chose Independence Day 1803 to liberate his slaves. Wolfe's slave Rhoda, already twenty-nine, had to serve an indenture term of four years, or until age thirty-three. But in common with other Delaware slaveholders, Wolfe stipulated that Rhoda's four-year-old daughter Nancy serve until age twenty-one and her two-year-old son likewise to age twenty-four. Any children born by Rhoda during the four-year indenture would serve "Boys at the age of Twenty four and Girls twenty one."[48]

Not all Delaware manumissions were voluntary. Slaveholders who bought the time of quasi-free slaves were required by law to free them at the expiration of the indenture. When slaveholder Samuel Davis based manumitting his female slave Lark on "divers good causes and considerations," the key consideration was not benevolence but the contract of indenture, for he had purchased Lark at a sheriff's sale on condition that she serve for five years. Davis had no choice but to free Lark. Neither did Joseph Copes have an absolute choice in deciding the date of freedom for his slave Frank, whose purchase contract required that Copes free the fifteen-year-old slave at age twenty-eight. While Copes could offer Frank an earlier manumission date, he could not legally extend his service beyond the stipulated age.[49]

The chance to hire surplus slave labor in Philadelphia reinforced the attraction of voluntary but delayed manumission to Delaware slaveholders. Philadelphia's labor market, though not a cause of Delaware's manumission system, figured importantly in its development. It was the best market for Delaware owners seeking profitable indentures: demand for labor remained relatively high, and proximity provided an added advantage. But Pennsylvania's 1780 gradual abolition law outlawed slave imports, and decreed that any slaves brought into the state (except those belonging to diplomats and members of Congress) be freed within six months of arrival.[50]

However, Pennsylvania's ban against slave imports was not so final as to compel slaveholders to lose the labor of their half-free slaves. By taking advantage of a major loophole in the Pennsylvania abolition law, Delaware slave owners could legally hire their half-free slaves in the Philadelphia market. The Pennsylvania abolition law seemed more concerned with dismantling permanent rather than temporary servitude: it outlawed permanent bondage for incoming slaves but did not mandate immediate manumission, nor did it prohibit temporary servitude.

Technically, a Delaware slaveholder could free his or her slave, retain control of the labor of the former slave through an indenture, and still remain in compliance with the Pennsylvania law. Legally, the act allowed complete freedom to be delayed until age twenty-eight or, in the case of adult slaves, an indenture not exceeding seven years. The Delaware slaveholder who changed the status of his or her slave to an indentured servant could freely and legally hire the service of the half-free slave in the Philadelphia market.

The records of manumission and indenture kept by the Pennsylvania Abolition Society provide a valuable tool for assessing the hiring of Delaware slaves in Pennsylvania. But the records are by no means exhaustive. Only the manumissions and indentures that came to the attention of the society were listed; probably missing are many private indentures of Delaware slaves in Pennsylvania. Further, the available records provide very limited information; only a few of the indenture contracts supplied the names of all parties, the age of the slave, the terms of indenture, and the amount paid to the owner. But granted these limitations, the records still provide a useful glimpse into the world of delayed manumission.

The most striking observation is the similarity—but for different reasons—in the timing of manumission, whether in Pennsylvania or Delaware. Most slaveholders offered complete freedom by the time a slave reached age twenty-eight. However, in Pennsylvania, complete freedom by age twenty-eight was not a slaveholder choice but mandated by the state's gradual abolition law. From 1780 on, owners could impose a maximum indenture lasting up to age twenty-eight for the issue born to slave women, but the servitude could not be extended beyond.[51]

Delaware owners faced no such restrictions. But those intending to free their slaves had to accomplish this in time to escape their own state's sanctions against freeing old and indigent slaves, while those hoping to hire their surplus labor in Pennsylvania had to change the status of their slaves to a nonslave labor status. Inevitably, Delaware owners hiring their half-free servants in the Philadelphia market postponed freedom to the maximum allowed by Pennsylvania law, age twenty-eight for both male and female servants.

Illustrating this practice were the sales conducted by Samuel Dickerson of Sussex County. In 1794 he indentured the service of several of his half-free slaves in Philadelphia, hiring out the quasi-slaves aged eight to twenty-one for sums ranging from £15 to £45 with terms of service lasting until age twenty-eight.[52] Through the indenture, Dickerson suc-

ceeded in resolving several issues. As a nonslaveholder he cleared his
Enlightenment or religious conscience; he also gained permission to export his half-free blacks from Delaware, gained entrance into the Pennsylvania labor market, and at the same time made a considerable profit.

Some owners hired half-free blacks out in the Philadelphia market
only in reaction to their slaves' initiatives. On occasion, Delaware slaves
pressured their owners into selling their services in the Philadelphia
market and indirectly but ultimately thereby gained freedom for themselves. It is debatable whether slaveholder Joseph Buckmaster had any
intention of selling the service of his slave Manlove Butcher until compelled by circumstances. Butcher's escape and continued residence in
Philadelphia forced Buckmaster to seek from a Delaware court a "permit
authorizing him to dispose of the said Manlove to any person residing
within the City of Philadelphia aforesaid, to serve until he shall arrive at
the age of twenty eight years." By escaping to Philadelphia, twenty-four-
year old Sam also forced his owner, Joseph Ricketts of Sussex County,
into indirectly emancipating him. Legally, Ricketts could have forced
Sam to return to Delaware and to slavery, but he knew Sam, now calling
himself Parker Harris, could easily escape again. After considering his
options, Ricketts concluded the best course lay in selling the service of
the still "absconded Sam" into the Philadelphia market; thus, he indentured Sam to merchant Thomas Forte for four years at £65.[53]

Other Delaware slaves also gained freedom not because of slaveholder initiative but through their own efforts, at times with the help of
friends and relatives. Some purchased their freedom, others sued for
theirs, many appealed to religious and antislavery groups for help, and
many more unilaterally declared their independence by running away
to the free North, particularly to Philadelphia.

A precise count of the number of Delaware slaves who purchased
their freedom·is not possible; owners did not always openly admit to
receiving payment, although many vaguely alluded to "considerations"
received. Whether these considerations were monetary, in the form of
service, or both, or even just slaveholders' way to express the worthiness
of liberating slaves remains unclear. Thus, when slaveholder John Taylor
freed thirty-four-year-old Abraham "for divers good causes and considerations," what he left unexplained was the nature of the "considerations."[54] Like Taylor's, many Delaware manumission deeds were vague
on the kind of "considerations" exchanged.

Still, the manumission documents do contain many examples of slaveholders who explicitly admitted to the practice of freeing their slaves
in exchange for money, servitude, or both. Unquestionably, owners
saddled with old and surplus slave labor must have seen this as a viable

alternative to the more restrictive out-of-state hiring. Typically, slaves who purchased their freedom tended to be older, a logical consequence of the difficulty in saving for the purchase price. Perhaps it also reflected slaveholder inclination to allow older slaves to purchase their freedom, thus removing the possibility of being burdened with slaves beyond prime age.

Self-interest explains Wingate Jones's decision to allow fifty-year-old Jacob to purchase his freedom in 1802. Jacob's advanced age made him an unattractive prospective hire, and he was probably of little use to his owner anymore. Jones still claimed the manumission was issued out of "divers good causes," but no doubt the "good cause" was "more especially for the sum of Twenty pounds two shilling, . . . to me in hand paid by the said negro man Jacob." A reciprocal benefit ensued: Jones received cash payment for a laborer of doubtful value, while Jacob realized his desire for freedom.[55]

Most purchases were a simple and straightforward exchange of money or service for freedom, as in the case of Joseph Fernando who in 1728 purchased his freedom for an undisclosed sum. An unnamed Delaware slave more than paid for the amount invested in him; working as a hired hand, he earned for his owner $2,933.33, in consequence of which he gained his freedom. James Dickinson acquired his slave through the last will and testament of his father; he decided to free her for "divers good causes" but "more especially for the sum of fifteen pounds specie to me in hand paid by the said negro Patience."[56]

Through the early nineteenth century, the opportunity to purchase freedom remained available to Delaware slaves. When Burton West in August 1800 freed his "old mulatto woman" Jainy Waples, it was in "consideration of the faithful service" she had rendered, but equally as much in "Consideration of the sum of thirty five dollars." Pemberton and Priscilla Carlisle claimed to have freed their slave Jacob Hays for "divers reasons, considerations and causes"; later in the manumission deed, they admitted that it was "more especially for and in consideration of the sum of Twenty Five pounds" paid by Hays. The deed executed by Thomas Wilson was straightforward; he declared no other sentiment for freeing his slave Shadrich than receipt of a payment of £20.[57]

Free blacks with relatives still enslaved often worked toward the release of these family members. Spouses and parents, in particular, devoted themselves to reuniting the family in freedom. When one unnamed "Negro Woman" received her freedom, the $25 purchase price was paid by her free black husband, Neels Abraham. Slaveholder Henry Safford freed Newbold Rose and her two children in consideration of £30 paid by Joseph Rose, husband and father to the Safford slaves.[58]

Delaware slaves sometimes aggressively pursued their freedom by exploring all open avenues. For Adam, the route to freedom lay in capitalizing on his owner's mistake of illegally taking him to Maryland. In 1796 Adam sued for his freedom under the provisions of the 1787 act. Fearing that Adam would win his suit, the owner agreed to an out-of-court settlement. Adam's master agreed to free him at the end of three years if Adam worked the first year without pay and the second and third years at £20 per annum.[59] Adam chose to accept the certainty of freedom at the end of three years over the possibility of winning the freedom suit. Slave Peter Perzalion, on the other hand, first took the initiative of seeking legal aid from the Delaware abolition society but for unknown reasons decided he could not delay his liberty, even with the society's promise of legal aid. Rather, Perzalion decided that his best option lay in running away, an option he successfully exercised. Fortunee also appealed to the abolition society on the grounds of being illegally held a slave. Like Perzalion, Fortunee chose not to defer her liberty but escaped to freedom. Consequently, when the society received a letter from Dr. Thomas Martin claiming Fortunee as his and requesting her return to slavery, the society responded that they "are fully satisfied that there is no legal claim," and therefore they could not "accede to the proposition of Doct. Martin."[60]

A significant number of Delaware slaves obtained freedom by voting with their feet, as the numerous advertisements for runaways confirm. Escaping from Delaware was easier than from any of the other slave states; both the state's location and the existence of the Underground Railroad proved very helpful to runaways. Philadelphia, with its significant free black population and a viable job market, lay a short distance away. Plus, the Underground Railroad, with Thomas Garrett at the helm and many black operators behind the scenes, often helped freedom-seeking slaves escape to the North.

Even with all these advantages in their favor, slaves running away from Delaware nonetheless went to great lengths to ensure a successful escape. They changed their names and appearance, forged passes, and almost invariably headed to the free North where they could easily hide their identity among the large free black community. Such caution explains the actions of Stephen as he escaped from slavery in 1789. He had plentiful clothing, a forged pass, and a new name and headed for New York or New Jersey. His owner described him as wearing "a coarse grey cloth, coat of foreign manufacture, an old cloth Jacket with London brown fore-parts, and deep blue back-parts, half worn satinett Jacket and Breeches, half worn fine linen shirt, and half worn shoes with odd Buckles." Stephen's master suspected that the forged pass was "so well drawn that it will deceive, if not attentively examined," while the new identity it documented, as "Stephen Miller or Stephen Gibbs," was also intended to facilitate his escape.[61]

Ingenuity and versatility remained crucial to a successful escape, and Delaware slaves seemed well aware of this. Thirty-two-year-old Simon's mastery of disguise came in useful; he escaped from slavery dressed up as a woman. Simon also known as Dick most likely had little trouble adapting to the life of an escaped slave or finding work in the free North; his work experience during slavery included "working on a farm, but more especially house and kitchen work"; he also was "an excellent cook, can wash, spin, sew, knit."[62] The owner of runaway-slave Jack had no doubt that since Jack "has learning enough to write," he would increase his chance of escape by "furnish[ing] himself with a pass and chang[ing] his name and apparel."[63] No less ingenious was twenty-four-year-old Bill, who successfully eluded capture by presenting an old pass issued to his father, also a slave.[64]

Timing and opportunity were of equal importance to a well-planned escape, and escaping Delaware slaves revealed an acute awareness of both. Slaves Charles and Sam took advantage of the Christmas celebration to escape to Philadelphia. Borrowing passes from free black friends living in Wilmington, they used the fake identities until Sam was apprehended as he attempted to board a ship in Philadelphia. Charles successfully eluded capture. The New Year holiday provided the perfect opportunity for a second slave named Sam to escape from slavery. During the 1764 New Year holiday, Sam received permission to visit friends in Philadelphia; he knew the city very well, having been employed there as a slave. Sam chose to make the visit a permanent one, the beginning of his life as a self-made free black. Granted permission to visit a former owner, another slave, Joe, declared his freedom by permanently extending the visit; the last sighting placed him on the freedom highway, "King's road between Wilmington and Chester" on his way to the free North.[65]

Other slaves absconded when sent on business errands. Often such slaves had at their disposal both money and a pass, making it an ideal time to escape. Wilmington resident and slaveholder James Adams found this out when he sent his sixteen-year-old slave Ben Valentine on an errand to Kent County. Valentine had permission to travel in pursuit of his master's business; he had in hand a considerable sum of money with which he was expected to conduct the business; he could read and write; he was trained in the printing business and could easily find work in this industry in Philadelphia or other urban centers in the North.[66] The lure proved too tempting. Valentine chose not to resist; he took himself and his master's money off to the free North.

Runaways came from all three counties of the state, all job descriptions, both genders, and all age groups. From Sussex County came runaway Harry, about forty years old, employed as a carpenter and a miller, married to a free black woman, and father of several free black children. He ran away alone, but the owner had a strong suspicion that the family planned on reuniting in eastern New Jersey. Possibly because of this, Harry's free black wife was required to put up bail in the court at Sussex County. But she escaped as well, almost certainly to join her husband.[67]

Running away was not confined to male slaves; in 1747 Beck, a female slave, escaped from her New Castle County owner. She was well dressed, stole additional clothes, purloined her owner's bay horse, and ran away along with a white female indentured servant. And so did twenty-four-year-old Esther, who with her two-year-old daughter Flora on Saturday, 19 October 1789, escaped from slaveholder Thomas Crow of Wilmington.[68]

Philadelphia and the free North in general remained the magnet for Delaware's escaping slaves. Before the abolition of slavery in Pennsylvania, a few slaves did head instead to areas that were not controlled by the English, such as those held by the French or Native Americans. James Wenyam's 1746 escape to the French and Indian territory was indeed rare; he simply capitalized on an opportunity and his knowledge. He ran away from his master in Kent County, probably in company with another slave. Using knowledge acquired from an owner who often took him to the western frontier, Wenyam headed for the West where he planned to join and fight for the French and their Indians allies.[69]

Delaware slaveholders' practice of delaying complete freedom until a later date resulted in the creation of a large class of Delaware blacks who were neither free nor slave. These were the blacks whose manumissions were a matter of record but whose full freedom would occur sometime in the future. Usually, owners allowed these quasi-free blacks to live as free persons of color, responsible for their own upkeep. Legally, however, these half-free blacks remained in bondage with their labor, for a specified period being at the mercy of the former owner. This ill-defined half-free system prevailed from the 1770s until 1810 when the state finally clarified the status of Delaware's quasi-free slaves.

The change was instigated by Governor George Truitt who claimed that the status of the growing number of half-free blacks in the state simply demanded clarification. In his message to the legislature in 1810, the governor called on the state "to make the necessary provisions to meet the exigencies of the case." Truitt complained that

> it has become a frequent practice for masters to execute deeds of manumission to their slaves, by which they are to be permitted to go at liberty at a future period, and in the mean time their services are retained. So many are now in this situation, that it is a matter of great importance to ascertain what their condition is; for if it is slavery, the issue born of the female parents, are necessarily all slaves; on the contrary, if it is freedom, the issue at the moment of their birth are free and owe no services to the master. And is the master having no right to command their services for a single instant, bound to maintain them in their infancy —The mother cannot: and must the public be burthened with the expense?[70]

Responding to the governor's recommendation, the legislature passed a law which codified the informal voluntary but delayed system of emancipation.

The 1810 law balanced the interests of state, owner, and half-free black. Until the expiration of their servitude, these half-free blacks were to be considered slaves. From 1810 on, only those who had completed their indentures would be counted as free persons. Half-free blacks illegally absenting themselves from service could make satisfaction by additional service. Children born to these half-free blacks were also classified as slaves until they received full freedom at the age of twenty-five if male or twenty-one if female. Although classified as slaves, these half-free children faced shorter indentures than their counterparts in Pennsylvania, where owners had the right to impose indentures on both genders until age twenty-eight.

The 1810 law also provided protection for the half-free blacks. A provision similar to one in Pennsylvania's abolition law barred their children from permanent enslavement. Under penalty of a fine, owners were required, within twelve months of the birth of such children to record officially their names and birthdates so that the owners could be forced to abide by the mandated freedom date. Further, owners could no longer export these half-free slaves out of state except by grant of permission from the courts. Noncompliance carried a fine of $500.[71]

While the 1810 law did not mandate abolition, it promoted temporary over permanent servitude, thus firmly setting physical and permanent slavery in Delaware on course for ultimate extinction. Slaveholders who committed themselves to offering delayed freedom to their slaves could no longer renege on their promise or seek to impose permanent servitude on the children of these half-free blacks. By the 1820s, when the cotton boom rekindled the demand for slaves, a majority of Delaware slave owners had already executed and duly recorded manumission deeds, making it impossible to revoke the promise of freedom had they so wished. No longer would Delaware's half-free blacks face the hardship of permanent servitude. By this means, the day of complete freedom, even though delayed, would eventually arrive.

It is difficult to determine the precise proportion of Delaware free blacks who were in reality only half-free, and thus subject to the provisions of the new law. But since a majority of owners delayed freedom for the young and healthy, it must have been substantial. Hazarding a guess, perhaps as many as a third to one-half of Delaware's free blacks counted in the 1810 census were in that ambivalent half-free category. It is no surprise that in the very next census, 1820, Delaware's count of free blacks declined by 1.3 percent, while its slave population artificially increased by 7.3 percent. But 1820 was the only census in which Delaware experienced an increase in slave and a decline in the free black population; all subsequent censuses before the Civil War repeated the pattern of a growing free black population and a decline in the number of slaves.

The promise of freedom, whether at a near or distant future, did not guarantee a willing acceptance of temporary servitude by these quasi-free men and women. Like slaves, they ran away from their masters, often leaving their owners baffled as to the cause. In 1825 Jim's master professed complete bewilderment at his decision to run away, for Jim, though purchased as a slave for life, had just been promised freedom at the expiration of eight years of servitude. But to the owner's surprise, Jim "went off without any provocation or disturbance." Perhaps for Jim the "provocation or disturbance" was his bondage, however temporary. The same year, even with only nine months of service remaining, an unnamed Delaware slave chose to run away rather than complete his term of service.[72]

Although state law protected the future freedom of these half-freed persons, it did not always prevent owners from reneging on their promises, especially those made in last wills. A case in point was the contract between slave owner Mary Henry and her slave Molly Evans. The contract stipulated that after the death of Henry, Molly had to serve an indenture not exceeding eight years. When Mary Henry died in 1794, the administrators of her estate offered Molly's remaining indenture for sale.

Several purchasers appeared among whom was Samuel P. Moore of New Castle Hundred, who offered to comply with their proposals, and made

some generous protestations, without being solicited thereto; informing, that himself was a member of the abolition society; and had the
cause of the Blacks at heart, and pledged his honor several times for
the faithful performance of the agreement and that if she was a good
girl, he would release her sooner. Whereupon Molly chose to go with
him in preference to all others, merely for his humanity and generosity, and accordingly was sold for the term of 8 years, on Articles of
agreement, of which Moore had a counter part, and the original was
left in the hands of John Gregg . . . [who] is since dead.

Unfortunately for Molly, Moore was not a member of the abolition society, nor did he intend to free her at the end of eight years. The death of
John Gregg meant Moore was the only person with a copy of the terms
of sale. In 1802, a year after the Delaware Abolition Society got involved
in the case, it concluded on the advice of its attorney that there was no
hope of winning Molly's release from servitude. She remained a slave.[73]

For a variety of reasons, slaveholders in Delaware elected to manumit
most of their slaves, creating a free black majority among the Delaware
black populace. This widespread voluntary emancipation compelled
white Delawareans to consider the rights of citizenship for the growing
free black population. Few whites in Delaware were willing to grant
equal citizenship to free blacks. Responding to the wishes of its white
citizens, the state shifted its attention and the force of the disabling laws
onto the shoulders of those who had so recently been freed. As free
blacks of Delaware soon discovered, emancipation was laden with limitations. It fell to them to carve out real freedom, often in defiance of these
black codes.

# On the Bank of the River Jordan

PRIVATE AND voluntary manumission created a large class of free blacks whose very presence compelled public Delaware to grapple with the dimensions of citizenship rights. Ultimately, white Delawareans came to perceive the growing free black population as a threat to their racialized conceptions of civil society. Consequently, as the free black population exploded in the aftermath of the Revolution, the state legislature expressed the urgent need to affirm white privileges through the enactment of harsh black codes to regulate free black liberties.

Since the introduction of slavery to the New Sweden and South River colonies, custom and law had defined the proper station of black and white as that of slave and master. White citizens understood and accepted the view that unfree persons, particularly slaves, held no lawful claim to full citizenship rights. But by offering what increasingly amounted to universal freedom to slaves, Delaware owners unintentionally threatened to eliminate both the boundary between bondage and freedom and the very excuse that whites had used to justify an unequal society. Delaware white citizens faced the choice of whether to extend equal rights to the growing free black population or to develop a new rationale to justify the denial of equal citizenship rights to free blacks.

Even as Delaware white citizens voluntarily freed over 90 percent of the state's black population, they also fought to circumscribe that freedom. For Delaware's blacks, freedom coming at the end of voluntary and too often delayed emancipation brought with it the responsibilities but not the privileges and liberties of first-class citizenship. Whites did not expect freedom to change the supposed innate inferiority of people of African descent. Rather, Delaware whites expected free blacks to acquiesce in being treated as second-class citizens, quietly paying taxes without the benefit of franchise privileges and accepting their assigned role of providing cheap and seasonal labor for the benefit of whites. None characterized the status of Delaware's free blacks better than Chief Justice J. M. Clayton. The free black, he acknowledged, was only "nominally free, almost as helpless and dependent on the white race as the slave himself; he has few civil rights, being merely protected in his person and property by the law, and being allowed in some cases to give his evidence in a court of justice." And free blacks, Clayton continued, "can hold no office of honor, trust or profit; cannot act as a juror or legislator, cannot make or execute laws."[1]

Because white citizens of Delaware claimed that free blacks by nature were inferior, lazy, and too numerous, exerted a destructive influence on the remaining slaves, and placed a burden on the general society, they recommended strict control of free blacks. Through the force of the black codes, codes specifically regulating the lives of free blacks, white Delawareans hoped to establish effective control over the lives of the newly freed men and women.

The emerging black codes reflected both the economic ambitions and the racial fears of the white citizens of Delaware. Through the black codes the state sought to provide white employers, and in particular farmers, with inexpensive, reliable, and seasonal free black labor. Racism and racial anxieties often led to legal irrationality, for the black codes spared neither "lazy" nor hardworking free blacks. "Lazy" behavior predictably invited restrictive black codes. But free black autonomy and self-reliant actions also spawned harsh black codes, this time in response to "uppity" free blacks whose actions dared challenge the racial divide.

Delaware free blacks seriously pursued the responsibilities and privileges of freedom, but they could never persuade white Delawareans to abandon their fear of being burdened with a lazy and unproductive mass of free blacks. It was in this context that the Society of Friends, the abolition societies, the African School Society, and other sympathetic whites generously offered to help free blacks defend their tenuous freedom. Through petitions to the state legislature, legal aid when needed, education when possible, and other charitable work, these societies and individuals helped ease the burden that state laws imposed on the semifree and newly freed men and women as they journeyed toward complete emancipation.

### Defining the Limits of Black Freedom

It seems to have been inevitable that black and white citizens of Delaware would contest the meaning and limits of black freedom. Delaware free blacks understood and defined freedom as the antithesis of slavery, and so they expected to enjoy the same rights and privileges as all other free persons. Because slavery had deprived them of their liberty, the freed men and women hoped for full citizenship without reference to color or previous condition. But free blacks failed to achieve first-class citizenship, for color still determined status. Ultimately, they sadly admitted that they were "free men yet we are gilty of a [black] skin. A thing that was not in our power to controle yeat it was the will of him who made us to be his accountable creation."[2]

White Delawareans defined black freedom differently. Unlike blacks, they did not equate physical freedom with equal rights. Manumission and free status did not in their eyes necessarily imply social, economic, or political equality. Whatever inspired Delaware slaveholders to free their slaves, whether economic, humanitarian, or religious reasons, most shared the racial beliefs current at the time. They thus assumed blacks to be inherently inferior and not entitled to or ready for full economic, social, and political rights. White concerns about the effects of manumission on the traditionally racialized boundaries of citizenship underlay this negative reaction to the rapid growth of the Delaware free black population.

It was thus no accident that the 1787 act that removed almost all obstacles to private manumission also narrowly defined the bounds of black freedom. In fact, the law unequivocally excluded all free blacks from "any other rights of a freeman, other than hold property, and to obtain redress in law and equity for any injury to . . . person or property." Free blacks were denied the use of the franchise to effect change in their lives, for the law excluded all blacks from "the privilege of voting at elections, or of being elected or appointed to any office of trust or profit." Even simply observing democracy at work was denied to Delaware blacks. By 1825, whether free or slave, blacks were forbidden from being within half a mile of the polling stations on election day.[3]

Other equally galling black codes—nuisance laws fashioned to support racial social control—followed. One passed in 1826 mandating that free blacks carry passes seems particularly arbitrary and unnecessary, since neither the safety of white residents of Delaware nor the protection of slave property justified this enactment.[4] By 1826 free blacks outnumbered slaves by a ratio of three to one; roughly 74 percent of Delaware blacks were free. Obviously it was no longer necessary to use the pass system to differentiate between slave and free black in most of Delaware. However, such a system was very effective as a symbol of social control and a mark of caste; it defined free blacks as an "other," a class inherently unequal to whites.

Even the criminal codes discriminated by race, assessing disparate penalties against black convicts. The 1839 code regarding larceny, for example, prescribed between twelve and thirty-nine lashes and servitude of two to seven years for any free black convicted of larceny. However, it eliminated harsher penalties for whites convicted of the same crime: there was to be no servitude for whites, nor should their prison terms exceed three months. Two years later, another law defining the punishment for burglary mandated that white convicts be imprisoned for a term ranging from a month to a maximum of one year, "but if the person so offending be a free negro or free mulatto, in lieu of imprisonment, he shall be publicly sold to the highest and best bidder to satisfy the fine and costs."[5] Presumably, free blacks convicted of burglary could be sold (in-state only) into permanent servitude, for the law placed no limits on the terms of servitude.

At the heart of the conflict between whites and free blacks in Delaware lay a heated battle for economic power and social control: free blacks were in search of a racially just society, and white Delawareans were equally determined to defend their special privileges. Nowhere was this conflict more visible than in the realm of the labor of the ex-slaves. Labor had defined the relationship between slave and owner; once again, it served as the key determinant in the relationship between free blacks and Delaware whites. The struggle for control over the labor of the freed men and women is evident in the various petitions for vagrancy codes and the laws enacting them in the period.

Although a majority of Delaware slaveholders freed their slaves when slavery became a liability in the state's new grain economy, seasonal labor remained very much in demand at certain peak periods, particularly harvesttime. Even farmers who held on to slavery, or quasi-slavery, often needed additional labor during the height of the short harvest season. But such reliance on temporary free black labor would work for white farmers only if they had the means to control the mobility and labor of the ex-slaves, and only if they could make the labor of free blacks available when needed and at a price they could pay. The solution lay in vagrancy codes that restricted the ability of free blacks to travel outside the state and mandated that all free blacks remain "gainfully" employed. Free blacks not meeting the standards of the law could then be forcibly hired out to white citizens.

This reasoning is less apparent in the state's official explanation for enacting the vagrancy codes. Repeatedly, Delaware whites rationalized the vagrancy codes as necessary to protect the interests of both races, keeping "lazy" free blacks employed while saving white society from the burden of indigent and "lazy" free blacks. Following the logic of the argument, hardworking and self-reliant free blacks should have escaped the burden of the vagrancy codes, yet industriousness in fact brought no relief, only a renewed white backlash. Symbols of black independence, such as the acquisition of property and economic self-reliance, were not always welcomed by whites. Most ex-slaves dreamed of economic self-sufficiency—owning and living on their own land, free of bondage and white control—but only a few free blacks achieved such a degree of independence. Even this seemed too much for some Delaware whites who reacted unkindly to the independent spirit shown by these free blacks. When it became apparent that such self-reliance if unchecked would remove free blacks from the immediate control of whites, public Delaware sought to impede such enterprise.

The majority of free blacks could not immediately or easily attain economic self-sufficiency but had to depend on the state's white citizens for employment. In this situation, free blacks could achieve a degree of independence by insisting on the right to choose the best terms of employment. It was this free black insistence on defining the terms of employment that most angered white Delawareans. Whites construed such independent action by free blacks as impudent and threatening. Certainly, it jeopardized the ability of whites to exert effective control over the labor of free blacks.

Free blacks seeking better employment and a measure of independence could do so only if allowed to travel freely. The evidence indicates many did, moving from one Delaware county to another. While some headed to Wilmington, many more free blacks traveled to the most advantageous market for their labor, Philadelphia. Such behavior did not endear free blacks to the white citizens of Delaware. From the closing decades of the eighteenth century, the state's whites repeatedly complained of the inability to obtain a sufficient supply of free black labor, at a time when its slaveholders were offering freedom to thousands of slaves. The problem, therefore, was not a scarcity of free black labor but the difficulty of finding those willing to work under terms and conditions favorable to white employers. Despite the best efforts of their employers, free blacks not only found new employment but often refused to accept meager wages or to be bound by contracts they found unacceptable.

As early as 1786 Sussex County white residents complained about what they characterized as an aimless migration of free blacks both in state and out of state. The petitioners recommended that the legislature "enact, a prohibition of the negroes . . . from travelling especially from one county into another without written or printed pass or certificate."[6] The state did not immediately accede to the request, but what Sussex County residents failed to achieve in 1786 became possible during the early nineteenth century. By 1800 the demographic picture of Delaware's black population had fundamentally changed: over three-fourths of the black residents claimed free status, while many of those still enslaved were only quasi-slaves whose freedom was just a matter of time. Black Delawareans' insistence on favorable terms of employment, when added to the phenomenal growth in the free black population, 75.8 percent of the total black population in 1810 and 88.7 percent by 1850, intensified the resolve of white citizens to curb free black independence.

To assure black dependence on white employers, the state legislature not only restricted free black mobility but sought to impede free black ownership or rental of land. In 1807 Governor Nathaniel Mitchell initiated legislative debate over free black property ownership. Mitchell asked the legislature to curb free black liberties because "in some parts of the State, they are so frequently acquiring the possessions of lands, as tenants"; such industriousness, he claimed, was "undermining the white citizens, as to excite much solicitude." Mitchell insisted that "unless some suitable remedy" was devised, free blacks "would soon make a large proportion of the renters of land."[7] It may seem odd that Mitchell focused on renters but left unchallenged the ownership of land by free blacks. Possibly, because so few free blacks owned land, Mitchell thought it more appropriate to direct the force of the law against the relatively higher number of free blacks who rented land.

While Mitchell almost certainly exaggerated the extent of free black property leasing, he did accurately describe the racial fears that had began to gnaw at white Delawareans: a fear encompassing both "lazy" and hardworking free blacks. Inasmuch as white citizens fostered voluntary manumission, and indeed freed a majority of the slaves, they did not expect free blacks to vigorously pursue the symbols of freedom and were quite resentful of any who did.

The "suitable remedy" for this free black "impudence" was the 1807 black code, passed barely a month after the governor's speech. Called to regulate free black leasing and ownership of property, the legislature did not address these questions directly in the code it passed. Instead, it achieved the desired goal by further restricting the few options open to free blacks. Until 1807, Delaware free blacks could freely travel, presumably in search of better employment, and indefinitely remain out of state without penalty. Now, the new law limited free blacks to an out-of-state stay of two years, after which they would lose their resident status. The threat of losing citizenship, with little hope of gaining it elsewhere, was intended to discourage free blacks from seeking temporary out-of-state work. The legislature concluded the session by legislating against interracial marriages and sexual liaisons, declaring both illegal.[8]

Apparently the vagrancy codes did not produce the hoped-for results. Thus in 1811 a supplementary act decreased the time that free blacks could legally stay absent from the state from two years to six months.[9] Even this new law failed to satisfy white citizens, for in 1841 some Kent County white residents petitioned for a more restrictive code. The petition's graphic account of white concerns applied equally to all three counties. The petitioners complained that the

> citizens of this State, and especially our farmers, have encountered most serious embarrassments, occasioned by the difficulty of obtaining efficient and responsible hirelings and laborers, in the occupations of the field and household affairs: that the community is filled with complaints on this subject, and there is scarcely a farmer or housekeeper among us, who has not experienced grievances of this description: that the evils thus complained of are mainly attributed to the great number of lazy, irresponsible, lawless, and miserable free negroes and mulattoes, upon whom our citizens have mainly to depend for assistance in the cultivation of their fields, and their domestic concerns; and who having no permanent interest to fix them to our soil, and being by their indigence rendered irresponsible to the obligations of a contract, constitute a migratory tribe, without fixed abode; alternatively roving from city to country, as whim or necessity may drive them in their erratic and wayward course: that thus it too often happens that our farmers are deserted by the laborers they have employed in the cultivation of their crops, at the busiest season of the year: that as idleness is the parent of vice, these degraded beings, too indolent to work for a living, if left to their own volition, are driven by necessity into a predatory course of life, and by pilfering and depradations on our society, are compelled to mete out a scanty subsistence, with which, by honest industry they might be abundantly supplied: and that the consequences are, though there is an abundance of laborers amongst us, the farmers cannot get their work done even when ready to pay for it.

Because free blacks insisted on defining, sometimes even dictating the terms of their employment, the petitioners asked the state to compel free blacks "to enter into engagements for the month or year at the customary wages."[10] The customary wage was understood to be what white employers were willing to pay.

The preamble to the 1849 vagrancy code left no doubt as to the rationale and intent of white citizens: control of free black labor. After complaining about numerous inconveniences suffered by whites, it excused the law as necessary because "large numbers" of Delaware free blacks had acquired "the habit of leaving the State during the most important working seasons, when their labor is most necessary to the white population, and of returning within the term of six months allowed . . . destitute, diseased, with bad habits and bad morals to spend the winter among us in idleness and disorder, to the great inconvenience of the citizens of the State." The main concern of the legislature was not the supposed "bad habits" or "idleness" of the returning free blacks. Rather, it sought to ensure the availability of free black labor for Delaware farmers, and at a price that white Delawareans found acceptable. Twelve days later the legislature clarified its intent in an act entitled "An Act in relation to idle and vagabond free negroes."[11]

Under the previous vagrancy laws, Delaware free blacks could engage in temporary employment in Philadelphia and surrounding cities and states and still meet the stipulated residency requirement. Two years of seasonal work, later six months, provided ample time for free blacks to accumulate sufficient capital to support families left back home. Out-of-state seasonal employment gave some free blacks the opportunity to earn the necessary seed money for renting or purchasing farmland, the first step on the road to economic independence. For others, it meant earning sufficient funds to live on for the remainder of the year, as white Delawareans termed it, in "idleness and disorder."

By reducing the length of time that free blacks could legally remain out of state from six months to sixty days, the legislature hoped to prevent free black migration while assuring white citizens of the labor of the "idle" free blacks. The 1849 vagabond law empowered the authorities to hire out "idle" free blacks on the "best terms." Free blacks, male or female, failing to prove a "visible means of support" could be arrested, brought before a justice of the peace, and if deemed "idle," hired out as servants until the first of January of the ensuing year. At the expiration of the indenture, these free blacks had thirty days to find "some honest employment for a livelihood"; failure to do so incurred another forced service lasting until the first day of the following year. There is no doubt that some free blacks must have found themselves in this predicament year after year, since finding employment during the winter month of January was extremely difficult. Finally on 18 March 1863 the legislature reduced the time free blacks could remain out of state to a mere five days.[12]

At first glance, the vagrancy codes may not seem severely restrictive, for dissatisfied free blacks were always at liberty to leave the state permanently. However, this was not a realistic option, since free blacks were seldom welcome elsewhere. Most states, whether free or slave, legislated against free black immigrants, doubly so against free blacks insisting on carving out a livelihood that was separate and independent of white society.

What proportion of Delaware free blacks suffered under the provisions of these vagrancy laws is impossible to tell. But the benefits promised in the vagrancy codes and the frequent amendments afford a basis for speculating on how often white Delawareans appealed to the provisions of the laws. The 1849 code, for example, granted payment of three dollars to the informer for every free black so reported and hired out. The sheriff or authority in charge of arranging the hire received one dollar for drawing up the contract, as well as 10 percent of the wage for the free black in question. At the end of the forced indenture, the free black servant received the remainder of the agreed-upon wage, minus the deductions for the authorities and a list of owner-entitled deductions vaguely classified as "necessary costs and charges."

The rewards promised to informers, employers, and the authorities were surely intended to win the support of white citizens for full enforcement of the vagrancy laws. How often white Delawareans testified against free black "vagrants" is impossible to tell, but the few cases appealed to the state's high courts provide some insight. Illustrating this is the 1853 conviction of free black Elisha Proctor. On the testimony of Major W. Allen that Proctor "hath come into this State, after a voluntary absence of more than sixty days," Proctor was fined $51.55, "one-half to be paid to the said State of Delaware, and the other half to be paid to the said Major W. Allen, the informer." Two years later, a higher court overturned the judgment against Proctor. Similarly, based on information provided by white resident George Harris, the court adjudged free black William Burr guilty of abridging the vagrancy code and assessed against him a fine of $50. Later, a higher court reversed the conviction, but only because Burr's "offence" occurred before the effective date of the provisions of the 1851 act.[13]

Until 1811 free black children, except orphans or destitute children, were excluded from the provisions of the vagrancy laws. But when the free black population surpassed the slave population and white Delawareans panicked over the possibility of free blacks withholding their labor from the market, free black children, like their parents, faced the provisions of the vagrancy codes. These children could provide much-needed seasonal labor. After 1811 state law required free black parents to prove their ability to support themselves and their children. Failure to satisfy the justices of the peace meant the children could be bound to service under any terms, up to age twenty-one for males, and eighteen for females. Like the vagrancy laws governing free black adults, a monetary incentive of three dollars for each free black child bound to service—payable by the employer to the justice of the peace—made it tempting for the authorities to find black parents financially incompetent.[14] By the terms of the act, all free black parents had to prove themselves economically worthy and capable before authorities whose economic interests clearly dictated that they decide otherwise.

The law pertaining to the labor of free black children was amended in 1827. On the surface, the revised law seemed less restrictive, for it exempted children ten years of age or older whose parents could offer surety equal to a bond of $200, as well as pay the authorities the same fees due them had the child been bound out. In reality, the amendment offered little relief to the majority of free black parents. As late as 1860 only a few free black parents owned properties worth over $200. Only by utilizing their ingenuity did free black parents discover a way out of this predicament. They bypassed the intent of the vagrancy code by arranging for friends to bid for the services of these children. However, in 1861 the state ended this practice by declaring it unlawful to bind out free black children to other free blacks.[15]

Often, external events adversely affected the limited freedom of Delaware free blacks. During the 1830s the Nat Turner revolt in Virginia and the inauguration of William Lloyd Garrison's radical antislavery campaign heightened the fears and anxieties of white Delawareans. Locally, as Thomas Garrett's efforts gathered momentum, his Underground Railroad activities further inflamed white fears. White citizens responded with additional restraints on the rights and liberties of Delaware blacks.

That the Nat Turner revolt was organized by slaves in another state, a slave revolt in which black residents of Delaware, free or slave, were not culpable, did not comfort white Delawareans. Much of the burden of the resulting white fears and anxieties fell not on the dwindling number of Delaware slaves but on its free blacks. It seemed such a perfect opportunity for whites to discipline and disarm the growing free black population, 82.8 percent of the total black popualtion by 1830. White citizens justified the 1832 law as a necessary precaution, a safeguard of society's interests. But free blacks offered a different explanation: it was a law spawned out of racism and designed to maintain a caste system based on color.

The circumstances surrounding the 1832 act disarming free blacks were as revealing as the law itself. The August 1831 Nat Turner revolt sent shock waves throughout the nation, especially in the neighboring states. Delaware's proximity to Virginia exacerbated the anxieties of white citizens, first, out of concern that Nat Turner—not captured until October 30—or other escaping revolt leaders might seek asylum in the state, and second, perhaps more troublesome, out of fear that Delaware blacks might launch a similar revolt.

In this tense racial atmosphere a rumor surfaced claiming that several armed blacks were about to descend on the Sussex County town of Seaford on election day in October 1831. White Delawareans readily believed the rumor, creating widespread panic. The "armed blacks," it was later established, were white men disguised in blackface.[16] The disclosure of the warped prank did not alleviate the fears of Delaware's white citizens. Rather, it served as a reminder of the dangers that could ensue should Delaware blacks revolt, thus intensifying the resolve of the state legislature to avert such an occurrence.

White citizen petitions to restrict free black liberties came from all over the state. Three days after the election, in spite of the disclosure of the real identity of the "armed blacks," Sussex County white residents petitioned that in light of the "many dark plots and treasonable conspiracies among them," free blacks should be banned from using firearms. It was the "indispensable duty of the legislature to disarm" free blacks, they said, for only then could the state "prevent such a catastrophe as has transpired in a sister state."[17]

Petitioners from New Castle County not only supported the call for disarming free blacks but recommended an end to "all *nocturnal* assemblies, of our coloured population, under any pretence whatever." Further, they urged that "the ingress of free blacks into this State, upon the plea of preaching, be also made unlawful." The petitioners wished it understood that they were not opposed in principle to religious instruction of blacks. They preferred, however, that such instruction be conducted by white ministers, for only then would blacks be "carefully instructed in *religious* duties," rather than "as they are *now,* by their ignorant and fanatic black preachers." From Kent County came petitions that also recommended enactment of laws prohibiting free blacks from possessing firearms or holding meetings at night.[18]

The alarm and anxiety of white residents over a possible black revolt formed the central theme of Governor David Hazzard's annual message to the legislature of 1832. Hazzard first acknowledged the concerns of white citizens but noted with much satisfaction that none of Delaware's blacks were involved, for "they [knew] too well how certainly it would bring down speedy destruction on themselves." The governor then recommended passage of a law that would prevent such a revolt in Delaware.[19]

Passed in February 1832, the resulting law prohibited free blacks

from possessing firearms without first obtaining a license from the authorities. Each free black application for a firearm permit had to be
endorsed by at least five white citizens. Free blacks could not meet in
groups of more than twelve after ten o'clock at night unless three or
more respectable white citizens were present. Nonresident free blacks,
unless endorsed by five white citizens of the state and a justice of the
peace, were prohibited from preaching in Delaware. Finally, the authorities were given a financial interest to enforce the law with monetary compensation awarded for each warrant issued under the act.[20]

Free blacks did not willingly accept the black codes and the limitations on their freedom. While unlike other free persons they could not
vote for change, they could protest and repeatedly did to the "Legislature in which we have no voice, except that of our Heavenly Father."[21]
Free blacks appealed to the state both before and after passage of the
black codes. They did so at first to avert enactment of the codes, and
when that failed, as it often did, to fight for repeal of the law, but usually
without much success.

Following passage of the black code of 1832, free blacks petitioned
for repeal of the code. Beginning with a summary of the many adversit-
ies they faced, free blacks begged to be spared from the burden of further restrictions, for

> in addition to the many difficulties under which they labour, arising
> from their Caste and Colour being debased by slavery—this act appears
> to have visited upon them evils of the greatest magnitude—it has a de-
> moralizing effect upon the free People of Colour, for by placing them
> under suspicion—making them to feel that the eyes of the white people
> are continually over them, whether for good or ill—it is not for them
> to say—it takes from them one of the strongest inducements to virtuous
> actions: it, moreover, interferes with their religious privileges, violates
> their rights of conscience—and exposes them to all the horrors of per-
> petual slavery for the act of worshipping their Creator, according to the
> dictates of their consciences.

The code was unjust and "entirely without foundation," the petitioners
said; it was an act enacted out of a false alarm engineered by "a few
designing persons, who found a profit in thus exciting the prejudices of
the white population against the people of Colour." They appealed to
the conscience of the state, asking that the principles of the constitution
be equally and justly extended to them.[22]

The petition for repeal of the 1832 black code failed, but free blacks
continued in succeeding years to speak against the hardships of the
black codes. When the state in 1849 imposed a pass law on all blacks,

free blacks launched a campaign against the code. The petitioners described numerous incidents of abuse, harassment, and arrests suffered for failing to observe the pass laws. They questioned the merit of the law and challenged the state's proffered excuse, particularly in light of the state's willingness to accept as satisfactory a pass signed by any white man "though his character be mutch blacker than our skins."[23] Their protest fell on deaf ears.

One of the most revealing petitions on the plight of free blacks appeared before the 1853 legislature. It described the black codes as "heavy and hard to be borne in this enlightened age and land," found it burdensome that "the hand of oppression is stayed from all except our unfortunate race," and prayed that Christian charity would guide the legislature toward a repeal of the codes. Black residents wished it understood that like whites, they also aspired to be upright citizens and

> endeavor to perform the duties of good, orderly citizens, and it bears hard on us not to be allowed the privilege of seeking to do better elsewhere without losing our residence and being subjected to arrest, fine, imprisonment and sale. . . . We, like our white brethren, are seeking the consolations and peace of the christian religion, and not to be permitted to assemble together, as we have been accustomed, to ask counsel of God for the salvation of our souls hereafter, and for making us more upright in this life, works against both our spiritual and temporal interest; and to have our little ones taken from us upon slight pretexts by those desiring their services without adequate reward, is very hard, and causing all those to emigrate who can conveniently leave the homes of their ·families and childhood.[24]

The 1853 petition suffered a fate similar to other free black appeals; it brought no relief from the white backlash which free black initiative and success, however minimal, had provoked.

### Philanthropy beyond Manumission

Even as free blacks petitioned for equal citizenship, they concurrently labored to maintain their precarious freedom by denying the state the excuse and opportunity to apply against them the full force of the black codes. For Delaware's free blacks the initial joy over their manumission soon led to serious concerns about survival as free persons in a slave state where being charged with not being "gainfully employed," failing to carry a pass, or committing minor offenses could lead to "re-enslavement." It was a predicament to be avoided at all costs. To overcome these barriers to freedom, the ex-slaves were helped by sympathetic whites, both individuals and groups.

After leading a successful campaign in support of private manumission of slaves, Delaware Quakers and abolition societies next expanded the fight to the protection and bolstering of the tenuous freedom offered to Delaware's free blacks. On behalf of free blacks, these societies pressured the state for repeal of the black codes, fought against the kidnapping of free blacks, mediated in disputes between black and white citizens, and with the state unwilling to support education of black citizens, stepped in with schools to instruct blacks, free and slave.

The abolition societies, Quakers, and other sympathetic whites joined free blacks in pleading for repeal of the repressive black codes. As white citizens and voters, their appeals to the state at times achieved some amelioration of the black codes, even if the goal of complete repeal could not be reached. Illustrating this is the partially successful campaign to repeal the 1811 black code. Claiming that the excessive and unfair provisions of the act had provided a perfect cover for the more unscrupulous white employers illegally to export convicted quasi-free blacks out of state and into permanent bondage, the abolition society asked the legislature to repeal that code. "There is strong ground to believe that the punishment of *sale* and *servitude* mentioned in this Act," the abolition society concluded, "has opened a door for the exercise of a traffic in the Persons of those subject to its penalty."[25] The state did not repeal the code but plugged the loophole in 1816 when it prohibited the sale of convicted free blacks out of state and penalized offenders with a fine of $500.[26]

On a related issue, the societies fought against the growing trade in kidnapping of blacks—slave and free—for sale in the Deep South. Although kidnappers seized both slaves and free blacks, they more often tried their wiles on free blacks, a class not particularly liked or as protected by the law as slaves.[27] Owners of kidnapped slaves easily and readily appealed to the law as a remedy against those guilty of kidnapping their property because the force of the law favored slave owners, while their color, white, almost invariably secured them access and sympathy in court.

But kidnappers of ex-slaves had a better chance of escaping capture and or punishment. Once transported out of state, free black victims had little or no recourse to legal relief, for many states denied blacks the right to bear witness against whites. On occasion, sympathetic whites intervened on behalf of free black plaintiffs, but compassion did not always guarantee success or victory. Once sold into the Deep South—even if allowed access to court—proving one's free status in the cotton-rich states with their dependence on slave labor and strong belief in slavery as a "positive good" for slave and society usually proved an impossible task.

Where courts allowed the testimony of free blacks, it still remained the word of black against white in a society that decidedly favored the latter, even when they were kidnappers. Delaware's free black victims faced the burden of proving their free status and, if successful, then fighting for the right to testify against their white kidnappers. Since 1787, state law prohibited free blacks from testifying against whites, making it impossible for black victims to testify against white kidnappers. Only gradually did the courts, on a case-by-case basis, allow blacks injured by whites to testify against the accused.[28]

From its founding in 1800, the Wilmington-based abolition society launched a crusade against kidnapping. Through petitions to the state and appeals to the public, the society hoped to stop the "nefarious crime of kidnapping." But should appeals to conscience fail, the society prepared to seek justice under the law through indictments and lawsuits against those found guilty of kidnapping. A special meeting in June 1802 sought to "raise funds for the relief of one or more people of colour, lately taken clandestinely out of this state." Over the ensuing months and years, the society persisted in its fight against kidnapping, periodically raising funds to aid free black victims.[29]

Free black victims whose cases came to the attention of sympathetic whites before being transported out of state were sometimes saved from the clutches of kidnappers. In August 1805 a free black, George Wheatly, joined the ranks of the lucky few to escape such misfortune. Through the timely intervention of his neighbors and the abolition society, Wheatly not only escaped from a threat of slavery but saw the perpetrators brought to justice. Peter Staats, the employer of ex-slave Levin Carney, foiled a kidnapping attempt on Carney. Ever fearful that the same kidnappers would try a second time, and perhaps this time succeed, Carney sought and received protection from the abolition society. To deter the attempted kidnappers, the society initiated a lawsuit for damages, but it later abandoned the strategy when its investigation revealed that none of the kidnappers owned property or the means to pay should damages be assessed against them.[30]

An even smaller number of free black victims were rescued after being transported out of state. The November 1803 report of the acting committee of the abolition society celebrated its success in saving an unnamed free black woman from kidnappers. Not only did the committee return her to Delaware, but it also "arrested the purchaser who is now in New Castle Jail." Also through the effort of the society, free black David Pennock's days of "slavery" came to an end. Pennock's plight came to the attention of the society in November 1816; by January 1817

his release and that of "sundry other people of colour" were firmly secured, and they were waiting for "a safe convey home."[31]

Unfortunately, the case of Henrietta typified the experience of many
free black kidnap victims. News of her predicament reached the society
only after her illegal sale and removal to Georgia as a slave for life. Societies based in Georgia and Delaware petitioned the Georgia courts for
her freedom, but after three months of investigating and closely following the case, the members of the Delaware Abolition Society sadly concluded "that after making inquiry into the probability of success in
obtaining their object, the prospect appeared so discouraging as to induce them to decline any further procedure in the business."[32] Henrietta, and many like her, most likely remained slaves for life.

With limited access to state courts and a color that remained a barrier
to equal justice, free blacks readily welcomed the society's self-appointed
role as mediator in disputes between free blacks and whites. Typical con-
flicts revolved around the labor of free blacks, specifically over the wages
and terms of service. Since state law either completely forbade or severely restricted free blacks from testifying against whites, the mediating
role played by the abolition society was extremely crucial for those free
blacks seeking justice through the courts.

Certainly, it is doubtful that the unnamed black sailor who suffered
abuse by his captain would have received the rest of his wages, about
$18, had the abolition society not intervened on his behalf. Lowden Wil-
liams also owed his eventual freedom to the services of the society. Although Lowden paid the full purchase price for his freedom, $50, his
former owner, Joseph Ross of Wilmington, refused to honor the contract
until the society successfully interceded on Lowden's behalf.[33]

Education was one of the many rights denied to Delaware's free
blacks. While state law did not specifically bar free blacks from seeking
education, the state made no provision for the education of blacks, nor
were blacks welcomed in the white schools. In fact, Delaware failed to
provide its black citizens with equal access to public education until it
was mandated by the 1954 *Brown v. Board of Education* decision. Consequently, whatever education free blacks obtained came through the services provided by the Society of Friends, the Delaware Abolition Society,
the African School Society, and later the church-affiliated schools run by
free blacks.

Advancing and promoting educational opportunities for black Delawareans remained fundamental to the abolition society's larger goal of
aiding ex-slaves in their transition to freedom. But the society encountered several obstacles, of which the most serious were its meager fi-

nances and the sustained opposition of white Delawareans. As a result, the scope of the society-sponsored free black educational efforts were quite limited. Frequently, only one school, based in Wilmington, remained in operation; rarely did blacks in rural Delaware have access to education. And in addition, the school faced continuous financial problems which on occasion compelled that it be closed; at other times, the society could afford to operate it only half time or on weekends. Frequently, inadequate finances conspired with inclement weather to keep the school or schools closed throughout the winter months. Yet for all the difficulties encountered, these abolition society-run schools were for decades the only avenue open to blacks searching for education.

The first school for Delaware blacks opened under the leadership of John Thelwell, a Methodist and member of the abolition society. Its origins were very modest, with Thelwell devoting a part of Sunday afternoons for the education of a handful of blacks. In its report to the ACPA of 1801, the society spoke of a school "kept here [Wilmington] on the first day of the week by one of its members, who instructs them [blacks] gratis, in reading, writing and arithmetic." Although "seldom more than twenty scholars attend," they remained "generally attentive." Contrary to the prevailing racial myths, the society maintained that black students "appear to receive instruction as readily as white persons labouring under similar disadvantages."[34]

During January 1802 the society launched a recruitment drive for potential black students, and a special committee was appointed to visit and impress upon blacks the benefits and opportunities of education. Within three months the committee reported a successful conclusion to its mission: it had visited and persuaded several black families, "and in consequence the school has increased considerably."[35]

By January 1804, however, the society found itself with its finances depleted but black interest in the school remaining high. Its members considered various plans for accommodating the growing black interest amidst the financial crisis. Finally, they settled on a plan which allowed the school to operate while minimizing cost: a committee of ten members, all volunteers, would rotate instruction duty, with two teaching each Sunday. Future plans, subject to improved finances, provided for the hiring of a full-time teacher at a salary not exceeding $15 a month.[36]

In the interim the plan to staff the school with volunteer rotating teachers not only kept the school open but exceeded expectations. The school reopened in May 1804, and except for one day, it met each Sunday from 2:00 to 5:00 P. M. until 21 October, when it closed down for the winter. On average, thirty students attended each session of the Sunday summer school; their conduct, "a few children excepted, was orderly and attentive, evincing in general a capacity and disposition to profit by the opportunity."[37]

When the society met to plan the 1805 school year, finances were in better shape; thus, it seriously pursued the recommendation of the ACPA of 1804 calling for greater strides toward improving black education. With the experience of the past year's successful rotating instructor system, the society voted to expand the scope of the black school by paying a committee of three to teach the regular summer Sunday school, as well as a session of Sunday school during the fall season. However, severe and cold weather continued to keep the school closed during the winter months.[38]

The society's annual reports on the status of the black school continued to be optimistic, particularly on the question of black interest and response to the school. Indeed, as the summer school opened in 1807, Thelwell reported an increased demand for education, recommended the opening of an evening school, and asked for an annual allowance. The society's financial status remained healthy enough to support both suggestions, and it opened an evening school and granted Thelwell an allowance of $10. A visiting committee to the school in 1808 reported that "the talents of the Master appear to be adequate to his undertaking & they are of the opinion that the establishment may prove imminently serviceable." It also recommended the appointment of a standing committee with the authority "to have the supertendance of the school with power to grant such pecuniary aid as they may deem usefull."[39]

But 1809 opened on a bleak financial note, leaving the school's survival very much in doubt. The abolition society acknowledged that its pursuit of black education had "not proved intirely in vain" but did "lament that their beneficial effects, have not been more generally experienced."[40] With an extremely low school fund and no hope of monetary aid from either the state or the white citizens of Delaware, the school could not be expanded to meet black interest and demand for education. And although free blacks appreciated the school, they could offer little financial support.

The society's frustration was very evident in its annual report of 1809. It blamed free blacks for the school's problems, claiming there was "little disposition on their part to aid us in our friendly endeavours to promote their happiness." Three months later, depleted funds forced closure of the school, and as tersely reported to the society, "the school has been discontinued."[41] The education committee was released, and the school closed, with no indication as to how the society would next proceed.

The events of 1809, however, did not end the educational opportunities for black Delawareans. Even as the abolition society officially abandoned its operation of the black school, a new society "for the express purpose of educating black and coloured children" was founded in the same year. Membership in the African School Society, based in Wilmington, was dominated by many of the same persons affiliated with the Society of Friends and the abolition society: Thomas Garrett, Benjamin Ferris, Isaac Starr, and Jacob Alrichs, to name a few.[42]

The records of the early years of the African School Society have been lost, but from 1815 onward the abolition society often covered the school's progress in its annual reports. The 1815 report praised the African School and the thirty regular students; their achievements, though modest, were "silently, but certainly undermining the prejudice which has existed unfavourable to their capacities," a feat made more significant by the race of the teacher, a black man. The abolition society, impressed with the accomplishments of the African School, voted to sponsor a library for the school.[43]

Financial problems plagued the African School, as they had its predecessor. Determined not to reduce services or discontinue the school this time, members of the African School Society instead planned to save it through an act of incorporation, which "would enable them legally to hold and enjoy real estate" and, more important, to raise funds through "bequests and donations, as persons friendly to the institution might be disposed to invest in them."[44] However, a state still hostile to the concept of black education denied the African School's request for incorporation.

State opposition notwithstanding, the students and teacher of the African School continued to improve, said the abolition society in 1817. Approximately forty students of both sexes enrolled that year with a course offering of reading, writing, and arithmetic. The school's black teacher received high praise for his instruction of over five hundred black students in five years. Additionally, the school now owned a library, courtesy of the abolition society, and could also boast of "a house and a lot which furnished a very comfortable accommodation for the school and also for the teacher and his family." The quality of the building led the abolition society to rank the school "in many respects much exceeding the schools in which our Ancestors were taught or those for white children in remote situations at the present."[45]

Still, thousands of blacks, both in Wilmington and rural Delaware, continued without access to formal education. The remedy, the African School Society maintained, lay in expanding the school's portfolio; thus, in 1824 it resubmitted the petition for an act of incorporation. Luckily, this time the state approved the request, granting the society the right to hold property to the value of $5,000.[46]

The demand, growth, and popularity of the school explains the African School Society's request in 1843 for a revision of the school's original charter. Society members believed they could easily raise additional funds but felt constrained by the limit imposed by the charter of 1824. Thus, they petitioned for the right to hold property worth $15,000. As the association explained to the state, of the sum allowed by the act of 1824, it "expended nearly one half of that amount on the purchase of lots and in the erection of two school houses thereon, capable of receiving about forty children each: one for the boys and one for the girls." And while the school had appropriate facilities, "the income from the remainder of their property is sufficient for the support of one school only," unnecessarily forcing them "to discontinue their school for girls."[47]

A nonresponsive legislature sparked another round of petitions in 1847. This time two similarly worded petitions were submitted to the legislature: one came from the African School Society, and the other from thirty-two free black petitioners. Whether from additional donations or because the legislature granted their request, in March 1847 the Female African School reopened.[48] The Female African School operated as a subsidiary of the African School Society, with students instructed in reading, writing and sewing. From its beginnings, the female school faced inadequate financial support, lack of students, and difficulty in finding teachers. Yet the school survived to serve as one of the few avenues for female free blacks to acquire education.

The schools remained in full operation through the 1850s to the Civil War. Writing in 1856, Thomas Garrett maintained that he had "for 20 odd years, spent much time in establishing and attending the colored schools here, as the colored children were not admitted to schools with white children." By 1856 much had improved in the educational opportunities for Wilmington free blacks; they had access to "2 large schools almost entirely supported by the Society of Friends, both Hicksites & Orthodox & four private schools for colored children, all taught by colored teachers."[49] There was still no education for free blacks living outside the city of Wilmington.

On their own, Delaware free blacks established schools to complement those founded by the abolition and African School societies. Very little is known about these early schools sponsored by free blacks, except for a few scattered reports in the papers of the Delaware abolition society. The first mention of the school owned and operated by free blacks appeared in the 1826 annual report of the abolition society. It spoke of a school "established in this place [Wilmington] through the laudable exertions of the colored people themselves." The school's teacher, the report continued, was "one of their own colour." The following year's report commended both the free black and the African Society schools for "continu[ing] to afford the opportunity of instruction to a large number of the descendants of Africa."[50]

Given Delaware's disinterest in the education of its black citizens, it is no surprise that out of the 14,403 schoolchildren reported in the 1850 census, only 1.3 percent (187) were free blacks. Ten years later the proportion of black schoolchildren remained unchanged, still standing at 1.3 percent, or only 250 black children out of a total 18,672 schoolchildren. The location of the few black schools—mainly in Wilmington and a few other smaller towns—further restricted educational opportunities for black Delawareans, rural black children in particular. Predictably, a majority of the state's free black children attending school in both 1850 and 1860 lived in Wilmington: 43 percent in 1850, increasing to 65 percent by 1860.[51]

Free black adults fared no better. Only a minority could read or write. In 1850 free blacks constituted 55 percent of Delaware adults unable to read or write, yet blacks comprised only 20 percent of the state's total population. Ten years later there were signs of improvement as the illiteracy rate among free blacks dropped to just under 50 percent.[52] Lack of education did not necessarily prevent enterprising free blacks from managing their business affairs or lives, but it did limit their choices, and black illiteracy was constantly cited to excuse their exclusion from the rights of citizenship, especially the right to vote.

Education was one of the most lasting gifts bestowed on free blacks by white philanthropists. Not until 1875 did the state of Delaware assume partial responsibility for the funding of black schools.[53] Until then, the schools established by the abolition society, the African School Society, and free blacks remained the only schools open to Delaware blacks in search of education.

# 5

# Carrying Their Own Weight

OPPONENTS OF de jure emancipation often cited the supposed inferiority and lazy nature of free blacks as justification for opposing equal rights for them. These supporters of retaining slavery maintained that even when freed, peoples of African descent were by nature "worthless, lazy, irresponsible, lawless and miserable," making it imperative either to enslave them or to control them by retaining the threat of reenslavement. Rejecting such disparaging assessments of their character, Delaware free blacks instead called attention to "the uniform correctness of the[ir] lives," insisting that they were neither lawless nor miserable but had always "conducted themselves as peaceable and quiet inhabitants of the State." Whereas whites impugned the character of virtually all blacks, free blacks countered with a positive image, pointing out that they had "acquired real and personal property, by their industry and exertions."[1]

Obviously, white and black Delawareans did not see eye to eye regarding the readiness for citizenship of nonslave blacks. The actions and achievements of free black Delawareans from the late eighteenth century to the Civil War vindicate them against charges of laziness and lack of preparation for citizenship. Forced to carve out a living on the margins of a racially hostile society, free blacks knew that their freedom was at best tenuous; they recognized that only through hard work and upright behavior could they hope to maintain this limited freedom. They appealed to the conscience and laws of the state, questioned their second-class citizenship, and fought against the limitations imposed on them.[2]

Not until the twentieth century did Delaware blacks receive the basic rights of citizenship. Until then, Delaware free blacks struggled to create a viable, if often precarious, life-style of their own. Like other free blacks in the nation, Delaware ex-slaves celebrated their freedom in various ways. Perhaps none was more satisfying than to engage in activities so long forbidden, exercising an element of control over residence, employment, and social, religious, and family life. And while free blacks did all this to express their liberty, it was also to bolster their freedom in a Delaware society willing to free them but equally determined to withhold the privileges of full freedom and first-class citizenship.

## Passage to Self-Sufficiency

Regardless of the invaluable support offered to Delaware free blacks by white philanthropists, the ultimate responsibility for the day-to-day lives of the freed men and women remained their own. Delaware slaveholders, like others in the nation, typically freed their slaves with little regard to how, or whether, the ex-slaves successfully accomplished the transition into the free world. Usually, slaveholders considered it sufficient goodwill to free their slaves. As a result, rarely did slaveholders offer the tools of freedom alongside the "gift" of manumission. A majority of the newly freed men and women walked away from slavery with only their freedom papers and the determination to maintain that freedom. It was with these and not much else that free blacks in Delaware had to start a new life of freedom.

In making the transition from slavery to freedom, the newly freed men and women had to choose residence and employment. Their choices included whether to maintain residence in state, permanently to move out of state, or to adopt a middle position of calling Delaware home but seeking employment in the neighboring states. The decision for those choosing to remain in state lay between living in the major city of Wilmington or in rural Delaware, while those preferring residence elsewhere had to decide on a final destination. Whatever the choice, these decisions were influenced by personal preference, by the availability and nature of employment, and very often by family ties.

One of the cherished rights that came with emancipation was the liberty for newly freed blacks to establish and maintain durable and legal family relationships. Slave codes rejected the legitimacy of slave families and affirmed the legal right of owners to separate their slave property through sale. But with manumission came the opportunity and legal right for free blacks to create and sustain families not dependent on the whim of a master or directly controlled by whites.

However, translating a legal right to a family into reality required that the newly freed men and women possess the financial means to support an independent household. Few free blacks found the means to sustain a self-sufficient household immediately following their emancipation; only after years of planning and savings could such a course become feasible. But if immediate financial independence remained unattainable for most, resourceful free blacks could turn to alternate plans such as temporary residence in white households or sharing housing with other free blacks.

Although poor data prevent an appraisal from the documents of the First Federal Census of 1790, the censuses from 1800 to 1860 provide evidence for generalizations regarding the residential preference of Delaware free blacks. The most striking finding from the available census data is the degree of determination that free blacks manifested to fashion an independence—beginning with their choice of residence—free of white control. Remarkably, as early as the census of 1800 the proportion of Delaware free blacks living in all-black households reached as high as 72.0 percent, increasing further to 84.2 percent by the eve of the Civil War (table 9). Census data less clearly delineate the extent of kinship ties among residents of these all-black households. In some instances a close family relationship can be inferred, for example, through a shared surname. Also, the presence in the same household of an adult male and/or female plus younger children strongly suggests the makings of a nuclear family (table 10). For other ex-slaves the ties of a shared experience and history seem to have provided a basis upon which to build a common household. By pooling their meager resources and sharing a common residence, these ex-slaves could realize as nearly as possible the experience of freedom and independence.

Other freed persons from choice and circumstances embarked upon their life of freedom as part of white households. While the majority of the state's free blacks, typically over 75 percent, managed within a few years of freedom to establish their own households, others less affluent, too young, or too old continued to make their homes in white households. Although continued residence and work in the homes of former masters or other white employers may not have been emotionally satisfying, it provided one of the most accessible means of economic support and offered the poorest free blacks the chance to save toward self-sufficiency.

An analysis of the ages of free black residents in white households,

Table 9.  Residence pattern of free blacks in Delaware, 1800–1860

| Year | Living in all-black households | | Living in white households | |
| --- | --- | --- | --- | --- |
| | No.* | % | No.* | % |
| 1800 | 5,843 | 72.0 | 2,268 | 27.9 |
| 1810 | 7,097 | 71.4 | 2,834 | 28.5 |
| 1820 | 9,283 | 76.1 | 2,906 | 23.8 |
| 1830 | 12,184 | 76.8 | 3,669 | 23.1 |
| 1840 | 12,561 | 74.0 | 4,403 | 25.9 |
| 1850 | 14,125 | 78.1 | 3,948 | 21.8 |
| 1860 | 16,698 | 82.2 | 3,131 | 15.7 |

*Source:* Compiled from U.S. Bureau of the Census, Manuscript Returns for Delaware, 1800–1860.
*These figures include all of Delaware except where the census failed to distinguish between free black households and free blacks living in white households.

whether in Wilmington or rural Delaware, confirms that the vast majority were children and young adults aged twenty-five or younger (table 11). Their status differed from the quasi-free blacks whom Delaware law mandated be counted as slaves. Rather, these black children and young adults were fully free but serving apprenticeships or indentured as servants to white families, typically until the age of majority.

Most of these children and young adults contracted to serve as servants, laborers, and domestics. The very nature of their employment, rendering personal service, plus their underage status, dictated that they reside in the households of their white employers. Five-year-old John Miller, for example, was apprenticed to James Denny of Dover to learn the "art, trade or mystery of Farming" until Miller reached age twenty. Under similar circumstances nine-year-old William Henry Miller was apprenticed to Eugene Ridgely of Kent County until he reached the age of majority, twenty-one, to learn "the art, trade and business of a servant" while residing in Ridgely's household. Nine-year-old Kitty Manlove was also apprenticed to learn the "business of a servant," but her contract expired at the customary time of majority for females, age eighteen.[3]

Table 10. Free black households in selected Delaware hundreds, 1820, 1840, and 1860

| | 2 parents, child(ren) (%) | Married, no children (%) | Female headed (%) | Male headed (%) | *Other (%) | No. of Households |
|---|---|---|---|---|---|---|
| **New Castle** | | | | | | |
| 1820 | 75 | 12 | 9 | 0 | 4 | 57 |
| 1840 | 82 | 14 | 1 | 0 | 3 | 77 |
| 1860 | 71 | 16 | 6 | 1 | 6 | 86 |
| **Duck Creek** | | | | | | |
| 1820 | 81 | 7 | 6 | 3 | 2 | 167 |
| 1840 | 83 | 10 | 5 | 0 | 2 | 167 |
| 1860 | 75 | 7 | 10 | 3 | 5 | 208 |
| **Cedar Creek** | | | | | | |
| 1820 | 84 | 8 | 8 | 0 | 0 | 76 |
| 1840 | 76 | 14 | 4 | 5 | 5 | 80 |
| 1860 | 75 | 10 | 10 | 2 | 6 | 108 |
| **Wilmington** | | | | | | |
| 1820 | 68 | 16 | 10 | 0 | 6 | 154 |
| 1840 | 60 | 12 | 14 | 2 | 12 | 326 |
| 1860 | 58 | 10 | 18 | 2 | 11 | 389 |

*Source:* Compiled from U.S. Bureau of the Census, Manuscript Returns for Delaware, 1820, 1840, 1860.
*This category includes persons living alone and unrelated persons sharing a household.

For a much older George W. Rap, nineteen at the time of his indenture, the nature of his employment fixed his residence in a white household. Rap's contract, a two-year indenture ending at age twenty-one, required that he serve Abraham Pearce as a house servant, a duty clearly necessitating his residence in the Spearman household. And when twenty-year-old free black Azail Johnson voluntarily contracted with Jo-

Table 11. Free blacks in white households, New Castle, Duck Creek, and Cedar Creek hundreds and Wilmington, by Age and Gender, 1820–60

| | Males Aged | | | | Females Aged | | | | |
|---|---|---|---|---|---|---|---|---|---|
| | 0–15 (%) | 16–25 (%) | 26–44 (%) | 45+ (%) | 0–15 (%) | 16–25 (%) | 26–44 (%) | 45+ (%) | Total (No.) |
| **New Castle** | | | | | | | | | |
| 1820 | 15.1 | 24.0 | 14.2 | 4.4 | 11.7 | 17.1 | 9.8 | 3.4 | 204 |
| 1850 | 22.7 | 28.7 | 13.1 | 2.5 | 11.6 | 13.6 | 4.5 | 3.0 | 198 |
| 1869 | 19.6 | 26.3 | 10.0 | 3.7 | 14.6 | 12.5 | 7.1 | 5.8 | 239 |
| **Duck Creek** | | | | | | | | | |
| 1820 | 15.5 | 19.5 | 14.8 | 4.7 | 6.7 | 22.2 | 10.1 | 6.0 | 148 |
| 1850 | 29.0 | 25.7 | 5.6 | 1.9 | 17.4 | 12.5 | 3.9 | 3.6 | 303 |
| 1860 | 28.2 | 24.4 | 5.2 | 1.8 | 17.3 | 15.9 | 5.8 | 1.0 | 495 |
| **Cedar Creek** | | | | | | | | | |
| 1820 | 12.5 | 27.2 | 6.8 | 10.2 | 17.0 | 15.9 | 9.0 | 1.1 | 88 |
| 1850 | 35.5 | 30.7 | 2.8 | 0 | 13.4 | 11.5 | 2.8 | 2.8 | 104 |
| 1860 | 22.4 | 21.5 | 6.0 | 3.4 | 18.1 | 15.5 | 7.7 | 5.1 | 116 |
| **Wilmington** | | | | | | | | | |
| 1820 | 18.2 | 8.5 | 7.4 | 5.7 | 25.7 | 17.1 | 13.1 | 4.0 | 175 |
| 1850 | 9.0 | 10.5 | 6.8 | 1.4 | 17.0 | 32.9 | 14.8 | 7.2 | 276 |
| 1860 | 5.0 | 6.6 | 6.1 | 1.1 | 15.0 | 41.3 | 15.2 | 9.4 | 360 |

*Source:* Compiled from U.S. Bureau of the Census, Manuscript Returns for Delaware, 1820, 1840, 1860.
*Note:* The age categories for 1820 were 0–13 and 14–25.

seph G. Oliver to "learn the art, trade or mystery of Manufacturing Black oak Back," he also agreed to "dwell with and serve" Oliver until he arrived at the age of twenty-five.[4]

At the expiration of their service and/or after they attained the age of majority, many of these young black servants moved out of the white households into their own or shared housing with others of their kind.

This explains the extremely low numbers of free black adults aged twenty-six to forty-four still resident in white households. Conversely, a higher proportion (not in actual numbers, but as compared to the general black population) of older free blacks—past age forty-four—made their homes in white households. Perhaps, freed so late in life or too old to launch a life of economic self-sufficiency, these few elderly free blacks realized that continued residence in white households provided a safer economic situation, if not a satisfactory emotional environment.

The census data also confirm that Delaware free blacks used the opportunities afforded by their newly won freedom to fashion meaningful family relationships. In a sample of three rural hundreds in Delaware— New Castle Hundred in New Castle County, Duck Creek Hundred in Kent County, and Cedar Creek Hundred in Sussex County—in 1820, 1840, and 1860, free black families with both parents in the home clearly predominated. From 71 to 84 percent of black households in the three hundreds were headed by both parents (see table 10).

A minority of black families were headed by either a single female or male parent, with more of the former than the latter. The highest proportion of male-headed households was 5 percent in Cedar Creek Hundred in 1840, while female-headed households ranged from a low of 1 to 10 percent. Another 7 to 16 percent of black households were those of married couples without children. Approximately 2 to 6 percent of free blacks sharing no kinship ties but bound by race and experience joined to create households freed of white control.

Differences existed between free black families living in urban and rural Delaware. In both the city of Wilmington and the countryside, free black households headed by two parents or consisting of married couples without children predominated. But when compared to rural Delaware, Wilmington free blacks reported a lower proportion in both categories and a significant decline in the percentage of two-parent-headed household by the Civil War. Conversely, the number of female-headed households in the city remained higher than in rural Delaware. Indeed, by 1860, 18 percent of black households in Wilmington were headed by females as opposed to half that number in New Castle, Duck Creek, or Cedar Creek Hundred.

The explanation most likely lies in the varied demands of urban versus rural work, but issues of race and gender also complicated matters. Without question, white Wilmington households preferred black female house servants; thus skewing the free black sex ratio in the city in favor of black females. The census of 1820 confirms that free black females constituted a majority, 60 percent, of free black residents in white Wilmington households. The proportion of free black female residents in white homes rises slightly to 61 percent among younger blacks aged twenty-five and under. By 1860, among this same group, the proportion of black females had climbed to 81 percent of the whole and to 83 percent among younger free blacks (see table 11). Even in all-black Wilmington households, a similar pattern of a higher female to male ratio prevailed, but on a smaller scale: 57 percent of free blacks in the city in 1850 were females; ten years later the proportion of black females reached 59 percent.

Rural Delaware with its agricultural economy needed the labor of young and adult male free blacks. Here white farmers showed a marked preference for young males, whom they employed as seasonal farm laborers. Accordingly, in rural Delaware black males twenty-five years of age or younger greatly outnumbered females of the same age category. In 1820, in contrast to the pattern found in the city of Wilmington, 58 percent of free blacks aged twenty-five and younger still resident in white New Castle Hundred households were males; by 1860 the proportion had increased to 62 percent.

When compared to other major northern cities, Wilmington did not seem as attractive a city for free blacks. Perhaps its relative lack of desirable work and possibly the better opportunities available in nearby cities dimmed Wilmington's attraction for Delaware's free blacks. In 1800 only 5 percent of the state's free black citizens lived in Wilmington, compared to twice as high a proportion of Pennsylvania's free blacks who called Philadelphia home.[5] By 1860 the proportion had more than doubled to 11 percent, but even with the increase the percentage of free blacks residing in Wilmington still remained well below the average reported in neighboring northern seaport cities.

The finding is no surprise. Unlike Philadelphia or Boston, Wilmington never had a significant slave population. At the peak of slavery in Philadelphia, about one-fourth of its households owned slaves, but not in Wilmington, where urban slavery was never significant. Passage of Pennsylvania's 1780 gradual abolition law further added to the number of free black residents in Philadelphia; so did runaways from Delaware, attracted to a city with the reputation of being a haven of freedom. Wilmington reported only a negligible slave population by the early nineteenth century, yet to many free blacks a Wilmington free of slavery still could not match the magnetism, reputation, and opportunities offered by the city of Philadelphia. Moreover, competition from Scotch-Irish immigrants for the same type of low-paying, unskilled, and semi-skilled jobs reduced the employment opportunities for Wilmington's free blacks, particularly the men. Instead, many free blacks in search of better jobs and a dynamic free black community headed for the maritime ports of the North, primarily to nearby Philadelphia.

Delaware black codes mandated that all free blacks be "gainfully" employed.[6] Free blacks not working or failing to meet the state's definition of "gainful" employment found themselves subject to forced hires until the first day of the next year. Accordingly, finding gainful employment became crucial to the welfare of Delaware free blacks: not only did it afford economic security but also the means to defend their freedom. However, because poor education, gender bias, and race discrimination excluded free blacks from many occupations, they found it very difficult to find the type of work that offered both emotional and financial satisfaction and still complied with the state definition of gainful employment.

A disproportionate number of Delaware free blacks made their living as laborers, be it in rural Delaware or Wilmington. Free blacks dominated the ranks of the unskilled labor force. Although blacks comprised only 20 percent of the total Delaware population, they numbered over one-half of the laborers in the state. The proportion of black laborers rises sharply when the comparison is limited to the free black workforce. Location seemed to have had little effect; whether in rural or urban Delaware, a majority of free blacks made their living as laborers. The only significant difference lay in the nature of the work performed, laboring on farms in rural Delaware versus the service-oriented labor that typified Wilmington. The 1850 census counted 3,546 free black workers in rural Delaware, 2,697 or 76.0 percent of whom were employed as laborers, primarily as farm laborers. In the city of Wilmington, laborers also remained the majority in the free black workforce, 93 percent in 1850.

A decided shift in free black employment had taken place by 1860. In both rural Delaware and Wilmington, black occupations became more diverse, although laborers still dominated the free black labor force. Between 1850 and 1860 the number of rural free blacks listing their occupation as laborers experienced a 17 percent drop. In 1860 only 3,576 (59.4 percent)—though still a majority—of the 6,014 free blacks employed in rural Delaware still classified their occupation as laborers.[7] Improvement in the finances of rural blacks may account for this decrease, for many free blacks considered laboring jobs as only the first step toward self-sufficiency. It is significant that the decline in the number of free black laborers coincided with a proportional increase in the number of rural free blacks now listing their occupation as farmers and tenant farmers. This relationship probably suggests that free black initiative had begun to achieve the results desired by blacks and feared by whites, namely, the acquisition of the financial prerequisites of independence by free blacks.

A similar change, no less striking, occurred in Wilmington. The city reported a marked decline in the proportion of free black laborers, from a high of 93 percent in 1850 to the much lower figure of 71.5 percent (869 out of a total free black workforce of 1,215) in 1860.[8] Like rural Delaware, the change ensued from a more diversified free black employment, a strong indication of the improved economic status of Wilmington free blacks.

Although Delaware black codes did not exclude free black women from the laboring class, the census very rarely classified them as such, perhaps reflecting the tendency of census takers not to categorize women as laborers. Instead, census takers tended to identify by name the specific task performed by free black females, for example, by listing them as domestic workers and washerwoman. Men employed in equivalent tasks generally fell in the catchall category of laborers.

The censuses of 1850 and 1860 lists rural and urban Delaware free blacks employed in a variety of occupations ranging from semiskilled to skilled. Trades employing free blacks included blacksmiths, masons, barbers, watermen, carpenters, and bricklayers. Many of these service-related jobs had employed blacks during slavery and continued to offer similar opportunities to the former slaves. But increasingly, free blacks began entering into new and more financially rewarding professions not traditionally associated with slavery: teachers, paper bleachers, weavers, pumpmakers, millwrights, shopkeepers, saloon keepers, and farmers.

A few occupations, by law and custom, remained out of reach of the free blacks. Free blacks seeking work in Wilmington's light industries, for instance, found that their color posed a barrier; preference was almost always given to native-born whites or to the immigrant Scotch-Irish labor force. Other occupations closed to Delaware free blacks—for instance medical practice—required a level of education and training unavailable to many newly freed blacks. Thus, except for a few individuals, such restrictions had a negligible impact on the majority of free black workers.

Free blacks living in Wilmington best exemplified the resourcefulness of free blacks in entering new professions. The city directories offer evidence of the changing nature of free black occupations during the first half of the nineteenth century. The 1814 Wilmington city directory, for example, listed sixteen different occupations employing free blacks; by 1845, this had increased to twenty-nine different professions, and by 1857 to forty-nine (table 12). These new occupations include grain measurers, hatmakers, sawmill workers, engineers, fishermen, and a fore-

Table 12. Occupations of free blacks in Wilmington, 1815–57

|            | 1814 | | 1845 | | 1857* | |
|            | No. | % | No. | % | No. | % |
|------------|-----|-----|-----|-----|-----|-----|
| Laborers   | 55  | 68.7 | 198 | 70.9 | 133† | 46.5 |
| Farmers    | 0   | 0   | 3   | 1.0 | 4   | 1.3 |
| Artisans   | 6   | 7.5 | 12  | 4.3 | 19  | 6.6 |
| Mariners   | 3   | 3.7 | 13  | 4.6 | 16  | 5.5 |
| Skilled†   | 9   | 11.2 | 19  | 6.8 | 45  | 15.7 |
| Service§   | 7   | 8.7 | 34  | 12.1 | 69  | 24.1 |

*Source:* Compiled from Wilmington city directories for 1814, 1845, and 1857.
*The city directory for 1857 did not list all the adult residents of the city or provide the occupation of each free black adult.
†The 1857 directory incorrectly listed only 133 free black laborers, even though the 1850 census counted 440 free black laborers in the city.
‡This category includes teachers, seamstresses, grain measurers, foremen, and grocers.
§Included are servants, washerwomen, domestics, and waiters.

man. Once finances and opportunity allowed, free blacks moved from the unskilled laboring jobs to skilled and semiskilled occupations, which they preferred because they were more financially rewarding. Further removed from slave-associated work, these occupations also probably allowed a greater measure, or perhaps a perception, of independence from white control.

With the improvement in the occupational status of free blacks came a corresponding increase in their financial independence, and consequently in their confidence in themselves. Often they expressed this by acquiring property and creating institutions to cater to their communal social needs. Since most free blacks began a life of freedom with empty hands, admiration for their achievement might seem appropriate. But predictably, white Delawareans remained unimpressed and continued to allow their assumption of black inferiority to interfere with fair evaluation of free black success. Quite possibly, the relative wealth of whites as compared to black Delawareans may explain this unenthusiastic white response to free black achievements.

The censuses of 1850 and 1860 provide sufficient data to support an assessment of free black property holding, but none of the pre–1850 censuses evaluated either real or personal property. However, the county

Table 13. Tax assesments of Red Lion, Little Creek, and Broadkill
hundreds, 1804–52

|  | Blacks | | | | Whites | | | |
|  | Landowners | | Nonlandowners | | Landowners | | Nonlandowners | |
|  | No. | % | No. | % | No. | % | No. | % |
|---|---|---|---|---|---|---|---|---|
| **Red Lion** | | | | | | | | |
| 1804 | 1 | 4.5 | 21 | 95.4 | 65 | 39.3 | 100 | 60.6 |
| 1837 | 7 | 7.3 | 88 | 92.6 | 80 | 33.7 | 157 | 66.2 |
| **Little Creek** | | | | | | | | |
| 1804 | 7 | 6.8 | 95 | 93.1 | 161 | 48.3 | 172 | 51.6 |
| 1828 | 14 | 13.7 | 88 | 86.2 | 179 | 53.1 | 158 | 46.8 |
| 1836 | 16 | 13.4 | 103 | 86.5 | 168 | 54.0 | 143 | 45.9 |
| 1848 | 16 | 28.0 | 41 | 71.9 | 177 | 34.5 | 335 | 65.4 |
| **Broadkill** | | | | | | | | |
| 1809 | 3 | 9.0 | 30 | 90.9 | 342 | 55.7 | 272 | 44.2 |
| 1822 | 7 | 5.6 | 116 | 94.3 | 343 | 52.4 | 311 | 47.5 |
| 1844 | 25 | 17.2 | 120 | 82.7 | 370 | 48.2 | 397 | 51.7 |
| 1852 | 33 | 39.7 | 50 | 60.2 | 455 | 55.2 | 369 | 44.7 |

*Sources:* Compiled from tax assessment lists for Red Lion, Little Creek, and Broadkill hundreds, Delaware State Archives, Dover.

tax assessments offer a rudimentary picture of the worth of Delaware's free blacks in the period before 1850. Any conclusions must be tentative, since the tax assessment records are at best incomplete and are not available for all hundreds and counties for the same years. Consequently, only three hundreds, one from each of the three counties, with the most complete data have been selected for closer scrutiny.

In the three hundreds under study—Red Lion in New Castle County, Little Creek in Kent County, and Broadkill in Sussex County—the gains made by free blacks were moderate but striking (table 13). Much to their credit, these former slaves had begun to acquire land and other property as early as the beginning of the nineteenth century and possibly earlier. In all three hundreds, the number of free black property owners increased with time, as did the value of the property they owned. By the 1850s about one-third or more of rural free black families owned property in the sample hundreds. The 1850 and 1860 census returns provide additional evidence: out of 542 free black farmers listed in the 1850 census, 118 (21.7 percent) owned land. By the 1860 census the figure had increased to 31.3 percent (167 out of 533 farmers).

For many free blacks the road to financial stability and independence from white control would prove difficult. Often they embarked upon their life of freedom without money, property, or skill, effectively deferring their dream of financial independence. Most newly freed blacks started in whatever jobs they could find, usually males as laborers and females in domestic work, while striving to accumulate the capital needed for a more secure and independent future. The journey to personal autonomy of ex-slave Thomas Morris of Broadkill Hundred illustrates this point. Morris's date of emancipation is unknown, but he commenced his early life of freedom by working as a laborer on a farm. By 1844 he owned no land, but he had accumulated personal property in the form of two horses, an ox, a cow, two yearlings, a sheep, and four shoats. Four years later Morris was a proud landowner, having purchased nine acres of land valued at $13.50. Thus, from a very modest beginning, Morris managed to join the growing ranks of free black landowners.[9]

Land ownership did not necessarily bring instant wealth or resolve all financial woes, but it constituted the first major step in attaining the personal autonomy that free blacks so desired. Free black Jesse Dean of Little Creek Hundred in Kent County certainly understood this strategy. Dean began his life as a free person with fifteen acres of unimproved land and not much else in 1804. By 1828 he owned twenty acres of land plus two log tenements that needed repair. In 1836 he still owned the twenty acres of land, but seventeen acres were under cultivation. His old log tenement and stable remained in poor condition, but he also owned a horse, two colts, three cows, a calf, a sow, and two pigs.[10] Jesse Dean took thirty-two years to turn his unproductive property into a relatively successful farm and in the process enhanced his life and secured his economic independence.

Rather than owning land, the majority of rural free blacks rented it. The Reverend William Yates, an employee of the American Anti-Slavery Society, commented on this practice, claiming in 1837 that free blacks in Delaware were "not much inclined to invest money in lands in this state"; rather, they seemed to "prefer hiring, and as tenants there are those who are getting rich."[11] Yates's observation regarding the degree of free black tenancy was quite accurate; however, his explanation for the practice is faulty. Even among well-intended antislavery radicals, assessments of free black "intentions" need to be considered skeptically.

Yates's conclusion that Delaware free blacks were disinterested in land ownership is almost certainly unreliable. The steady increases in free black land ownership suggest that like lower-class whites, newly freed blacks saw land ownership as their ultimate goal. Like poor whites, free blacks unable to buy land tended to select tenancy over unskilled laboring jobs. This choice bore special meaning for former slaves because tenancy conveyed a significantly greater degree of autonomy from control and supervision of whites than did employment as an unskilled laborer. For persons recently freed from slavery, this precious margin of freedom signified a tangible improvement over their former status. Because of these factors, tenancy became the preferred means to accumulate the capital needed to realize various goals: land ownership, the establishment of an independent business, and out-of-state moves in search of even better opportunities.

Free black John Francisco of Little Creek Hundred, Kent County, used his tenancy for exactly such a purpose. Renting land in 1804, he was the owner of six horses, twelve colts, an ox, seven two-year-old cattle, eleven one-year-old cattle, six calves, thirteen sheep, ten shoats, one sow, and seven pigs, all valued at $475.83. John Francisco's brother Benjamin, also a tenant, owned livestock appraised at $606.25. By the time the two brothers moved to Ohio in the 1830s, they had amassed an impressive amount of wealth. Yates recalled being told the story of the Francisco brothers, both of whom "were farmers, occupying land as tenants." The Francisco brothers had earned the reputation of being "laborious, saving and industrious" and apparently "took about $10,000 in cash with them" when they moved to Ohio.[12] Only a few free black tenants managed to accumulate as much wealth as the Francisco brothers, but many did significantly improve their financial situation.

Both the 1850 and 1860 censuses evaluated the real wealth of all free persons; thus, a more accurate comparative picture of the wealth of free blacks can be drawn. The 1850 census appraised only real estate, while the 1860 census listed both real and personal estates. The wealth of free blacks in the state was not evenly distributed; differences of wealth existed between individuals, as well as between those living in the rural areas and in the city of Wilmington. But on balance, it appears that each decade Delaware's free blacks improved their net worth.

A majority of free black property owners in rural Delaware listed their occupation as laborer in 1850. The census valued the real estate of these 183 property-owning laborers at $40,075, for an average of $219. But this wealth was not uniformly apportioned, for the free black laborers ranged from the relatively wealthy to those just emerging from the subsistence level. While James Andrew, a laborer from Baltimore Hundred in Sussex County, reported property worth $1,000, numerous laborers from the same hundred and county owned properties valued at only $100 or even less.[13]

By 1860 the number of property-owning rural black laborers had increased to 297. There were several laborers in 1860 who had accumulated substantial property. Gustavas Carney of Little Creek Hundred, Kent County, held the honor of being the wealthiest of these laborers with real estate valued at $3,000, plus a personal estate of $250. Six other laborers owned estates worth over $1,000, but again a majority of the laborers reported estates of only $100 or less.

Numbering only 15 and 9 percent of the rural free black workforce in 1850 and 1860, farmers were among the wealthiest of Delaware's rural free blacks. Only 118 of the 542 (21.7 percent) rural free black farmers in 1850 owned real estate, but it was worth a total of $103,180. Ten years later, 167 out of 533 (31.3 percent) free black farmers owned real estate valued at $181,389. Although the number of free black farmers decreased by 1.7 percent between 1850 and 1860, the actual value of their real estate saw a phenomenal increase of 75.8 percent.

With estates appraised at $11,000 and $6,000, respectively, Thomas Fitzgerald and Isaac Caulk, both from New Castle County, were the wealthiest black farmers in 1850. Only five free black farmers owned estates of more than $2,000 in 1850; four of them resided in New Castle County, while the fifth farmer made his home in Kent County. Not surprisingly, Sussex County, the stronghold of slavery in the state, seemed less attractive to wealthy free black farmers.

Although the 1860 census reported fewer free black farmers, it showed a significant increase in the number of farmers with estates worth over $2,000. Eighteen black farmers owned real estate properties valued at over $2,000 in 1860; ten resided in Kent County and owned a combined wealth of $30,600, while four each in New Castle and Sussex counties reported a total worth of $19,100 and $10,890, respectively. Again, the wealthiest free black farmers resided in New Castle County, possibly because the county contained some of the state's best farmland and was farthest removed from the center of slavery in the state. The richest free black farmer in 1860, Thomas Bayard, from New Castle County, owned real estate with a value of $8,000.[14]

Not all free blacks acquired their modest wealth through farming. Census data show that skilled and semiskilled jobs provided another avenue for wealth accumulation. Levin Sockums, a merchant from Indian River Hundred in Sussex County, listed property worth $1,000 in 1850;

by 1860 he had turned to farming and had accumulated $5,450 worth of real and personal property. By 1860 several individuals from this group had amassed an impressive amount of property, as for example Alexander Lee, a preacher from New Castle County whose property was worth $3,300 and Elisha Prettyman, a carpenter from Sussex County who reported property valued at $2,500.[15]

The 1850 census enumerated 2,156 free black residents in the city of Wilmington, 95 (4.4 percent) of whom owned real property totaling $42,595. Approximately 50 percent ($21,140) of this wealth belonged to 61 laborers, only 2 of whom owned properties of $100 or less. Further, skilled artisans and owners of small businesses added to the wealth of free blacks in the city. By 1860 the real estate assets of free blacks in Wilmington had increased to $66,925; the wealth belonged to 97 (4.3 percent) out of the 2,210 free black residents in the city. The number of free black residents and free black owners of real estate in 1860 showed little change from the 1850 figures, with an increase of only 2.5 percent. But the value of free black real estate in 1860 marked an impressive increase of 57 percent over the 1850 figure.

In addition to real estate, free blacks in Wilmington owned $27,375 of personal property in 1860. Of a workforce of 1,215, many of them laborers, 35 percent (427) owned the combined real and personal property. Edward Chippy, the wealthiest laborer in 1860, reported a real and personal estate valued at $2,600. Many more laborers in 1860 owned real estate properties of over $500 than in 1850: 21 in 1860 compared to only 6 in 1850.

By 1860 free blacks in the service trades, waiters and washerwomen in particular, were making significant contributions to the wealth of free blacks in the city. The 21 waiters and 45 washerwomen who reported real and personal property in 1860 owned 8 percent ($7,635) and 7 percent ($6,335) of free black wealth in Wilmington, respectively. In 1850 Michael Sterling, a master blacksmith, owned $2,000 of property; by 1860 his net worth had reached $3,200. Similarly, Robert Graves, employed as a shopkeeper with property worth $650 in 1850, had by the next census multiplied the value of his property to $4,000, but this time as a tailor. John Layton, apparently the only free black storekeeper in 1860 Wilmington, had accumulated $4,400 worth of property by that census year.[16]

Both individually and as a group, free black women made important contributions to the economy. Few free black women did not have to earn a living by work done either inside or outside their homes. The income they earned not only assured the survival of the family but also secured their freedom against the hostile black codes. Typically, free black women held employment as domestics, washerwomen, cooks, servants, housekeepers, and seamstresses; and it was in such occupations that they made their contribution to the free black community and to themselves. Sarah E. Richardson, a free black who listed her occupation as servant, is a case in point; in 1860 she reported an estate worth $950. Only occasionally were female farmers mentioned in the census, but the few there were held substantial property. Farmer Catherine Mason, for instance, in 1860 owned property worth $3,950.

With property valued at $6,000 in 1850, Amelia Shadd easily led all free black female property owners. The majority of the female free black workers held very little property or none at all. Fifty-eight-year-old Deliah Henderickson, employed as a servant and owner of a personal estate valued at only $70, typified many free black women. But however modest, the income of free black women helped to keep their families afloat.[17]

### The Founding of Free Black Institutions

The increased acquisition of real and personal property by free blacks confirmed the improvement in their economic status. Free blacks, however, did more than accumulate property; they used their new wealth and its attendant confidence to establish and utilize institutions to improve themselves individually and as a group. They aspired to educate themselves and their children, and they built and controlled their own churches and institutions. By the beginning decades of the nineteenth century, free black Delawareans had founded educational, religious, and social institutions which helped to mitigate the racial prejudice and hostility that free blacks faced.

The least successful free black initiatives during the first half of the nineteenth century were their attempts to create social institutions. Hindering their efforts were problems with funding and the hostility of white Delawareans. In 1820 Wilmington free blacks founded the African Benevolent Association of Wilmington for the purpose of "the diffusion of knowledge, the suppression of vice and . . . the inculcation of every virtue that renders man great, good or happy." In spite of the admirable intentions of the society, when in 1823 the members applied for an act of incorporation, the state denied the petition without offering any rational explanation. A second appeal in 1825 was also rejected. But even without a charter, the society continued to function and according to its members even "progressed successfully in their operations at least equal to their just expectations."[18]

The state likewise rebuffed a similar attempt by free black residents of the town of New Castle. When New Castle free blacks founded the

Sons of Benevolence in 1830, they did so with the noble intention of establishing "a fund for burying the dead and taking care of the indigent and sick among our coloured brethren." Like Wilmington free blacks, they failed in their bid for an approved charter. This time the legislature noted vaguely that it found approving the petition "inexpedient."[19]

In religion the black struggle for independence proved very successful. Here they wrenched autonomy from the white churches, but not without a mighty struggle. It was within the Methodist church, the denomination that attracted most Delaware blacks, that the black struggle for religious autonomy was waged. For blacks, Methodism seemed the most compatible religious denomination: it was available in both urban and rural Delaware, many leaders of the church condemned slavery, its emotional style of worship appealed to them, and its liberal policy of allowing black lay preachers, slave or free, to preach to racially mixed congregations proved equally attractive.[20]

But however liberal Methodist practices were, they failed to satisfy the newly, confident, sometimes educated, and relatively wealthy (by the standards of the black community) free blacks. Methodist liberalism, for example, did not extend to desegregated churches; instead, black members were allocated separate seating and received no voice in the running of the church. Rather than accept such practices, free blacks in almost every state and major city left the white-controlled churches to build their own. But the movement to build separate black churches reflected more than a simple reaction to the discriminatory practices of white churches; it was partly fueled by the desire of free blacks to control their own institutions.[21]

Two Methodist-influenced former slaves from Delaware led the founding of the nation's first black churches, perhaps a tribute to the possibilities and limitations of Methodism in the Delaware Valley. When in the 1790s free blacks from Philadelphia initiated the movement toward independent black churches, they were led by Absalom Jones and Richard Allen, both former Delaware slaves.[22] At home, Delaware free blacks led by Peter Spencer, and under circumstances very similar to those in Philadelphia, launched their movement for a separate black church.

From the early nineteenth century, a series of racial incidents coupled with the ambitions of the free blacks propelled them to build separate churches. The first of the black churches to be built in Delaware was Ezion in 1805. Then in 1813, in response to continuing racial strife, a second break occurred, bringing into being not only a separate church structure but an independent and black-controlled conference.

While racial incidents provided the immediate cause, Wilmington free blacks had long before the final break taken the first steps toward separation from the parent church, Asbury Methodist Episcopal Church. Although the founding members of Asbury included many Wilmington free blacks and black membership at the church ranged from one-third to one-half of the total membership, Asbury, like many white-controlled churches, maintained a segregated policy. By custom, black members occupied the seats in the gallery, except at the end of the regular service when they had permission to use the main floor for class meetings.

As early as 1800, blacks revealed their displeasure with the policies at Asbury. They began holding separate services in the homes of black church members, serving notice of their intent to sever ties with Asbury. Alongside the discontent over Asbury's policy of segregation, the desire and determination of blacks to secure their independence in religious affairs guided their decision to separate from Asbury. Five months before blacks walked out of Asbury, they appealed through the Wilmington newspapers for public support to build their own church. Lacking the financial means to build the church they desired, these black members of Asbury called on "the public whose generous aid they respectfully solicit to enable them to accomplish this laudable purpose."[23]

The immediate incident leading to the separation occurred in June 1805. White members of Asbury accused the black members of defiling the church and consequently prohibited them from using the main floor for their class meetings. The incident marked the proverbial last straw for blacks who had hoped that the only institution that promised them equality in the eyes of God would fulfill this dream on earth. Disappointed over Asbury's racial attitude, and with their own ambitions driving them, about one-third of the black members left Asbury to create their own institution, Ezion Church.[24]

Capital for building Ezion came from both black and white Delawareans, including financial support from white members of Asbury church. In helping blacks build Ezion, white members of Asbury apparently believed they were aiding in what would be a simple extension of the segregated church policy, a separate building where blacks could worship in much the same way as they had in the gallery at Asbury. Certainly, Asbury had no intention of yielding its power over the black Methodists, and from the very beginning it insisted on exercising a supervisory role over Ezion. Asbury would allow Ezion some autonomy but still considered Ezion subordinate to Asbury. Thus, for instance, Ezion could appoint its own board of trustees, class leaders, and lay preachers but had to defer to Asbury on the question of pastors.[25]

Because these restrictions conflicted with the goals of the black founders of Ezion, dissension between Asbury and Ezion seemed inevitable. The symbolism behind the chosen name for the black church, Ezion, should have warned Asbury of black intent and resolve. It was no accident that free blacks named their church after the seaport city of Ezion-Gaber. According to the Reverend Joseph R. Waters

> the inference which may be drawn from this name is that as Solomon's fleet went forth from Ezion-Gaber in search of gold, so did our fathers go forth from this Ezion, in search, not of the gold that perisheth, but for the golden treasures of heaven which perisheth not; not to Ophir but to the land of the blessed. . . . The meaning of this name Ezion-Gaber, "the giant's backbone," is also very suggestive. In those days, when our race was oppressed and when in many parts it was a crime for our people to assemble even to worship God, it required not a weak backbone, but a giant's backbone to withstand the heavy pressure which was brought to bear against them.

The city of Ezion-Gaber was also the last stopping place of the Israelites in their wanderings before Kadesh (the wilderness of Zin), the place from which Israel after years of roaming in the wilderness finally entered the promised land.[26] Evidently, Ezion wished it known that it too was poised on the brink of entering the promised land of true freedom and had the backbone to accomplish this feat.

From 1805 to December 1812, relative peace prevailed between Asbury and Ezion. The uneasy truce ended in 1812 over Ezion's insistence upon rejecting "unsuitable" pastors. Although this disagreement provided the immediate spark to the second breakup, the root cause lay in the growing black determination to exercise control over Ezion, as well as in Asbury's refusal to grant the level of autonomy sought by Ezion. Ezion seemed willing to concede on the issue of pastor appointment but reserved the right to reject ministers who failed to meet its needs. However, a compromise with Asbury could not be reached, for James Bateman, the white pastor at Asbury, refused to accept the position taken by Ezion. The conflict came to a head in December 1812, when Bateman fired the entire board of trustees and class leaders at Ezion. Unable to reach an acceptable compromise, both sides appealed to the court at Wilmington.[27]

Out of financial consideration and a realization that Asbury would not grant meaningful autonomy to Ezion, Peter Spencer and his supporters abandoned the lawsuit in favor of complete separation from the white-controlled Methodist Episcopal conference. "We thought," said Spencer for the many disappointed members of Ezion, "that we could have the rule of our church, so as to make our own rules and laws for ourselves." Unwilling to accept the level of control white-led Asbury favored, several members of Ezion, led by Spencer, left for another black house of worship, one truly independent of the white Methodist Episcopal conference. These estranged members from Ezion erected by September 1813 the African Union Methodist Church, commonly known as "Old Union."[28]

Financial aid for the construction of Old Union came from blacks and from white citizens, particularly Quakers. No longer ignorant of the true intentions of the black worshipers, white-controlled Asbury offered little support. By the same token, Old Union took steps to avoid the misunderstandings that had plagued Asbury-Ezion relations. Old Union severed all ties to the white Methodist Episcopal conference and maintained that it was Methodist in faith but African Methodist, thus absolutely separate and independent of the Methodist Episcopal conference. Article 6 of the charter of Old Union very clearly restricted church membership and governance to "Africans and the descendants of the African Race."[29]

In the founding of Old Union, free blacks of Wilmington launched the establishment of an institution that transcended the existing landscape of separate Christian denominations. It signified an independence in the governing body, the beginnings of a separate conference of black churches: the African Union Methodist Protestant and the Union American Methodist Episcopal churches.[30] In this, Old Union preceded a similar move by Philadelphia's Bethel Church; not until three years later, in 1816, did Bethel truly become an independent black church.

The movement began by Peter Spencer and the Wilmington blacks slowly spread to other Delaware towns and the rural parts of the state. Gradually, in Delaware towns like Christiana, New Castle, Welsh Tract, and Summit, blacks separated from the segregated, white-controlled houses of worship to set up churches modeled after the African Union Methodist Church.[31]

Having fought so hard for their own independent churches, the black church became more than a religious establishment for black Delawareans. In addition, it served both political and social functions, providing leadership and guarding the welfare of black society. It was in this role as guardian of the black community that the leaders of Old Union mounted an intense and successful opposition to the American Colonization Society (ACS).

From 14 October 1823 when a chapter of the ACS was formed in Wilmington, members of the society with the blessing of the state launched a campaign to persuade free blacks of Delaware to migrate voluntarily to Africa. The goal of the Wilmington branch, like that of the national

ACS, was to promote colonization of free blacks in Africa or any other place designated by Congress. An address published in the 27 January 1824 *Delaware Gazette* explained the goals of the ACS and appealed for public support.[32]

A similar address submitted to the legislature of 1827 dealt with the issues of the growing free black population and the black codes. But unlike the Quakers or the abolition societies, the ACS did not seek a repeal of the unfair black codes, nor did it recommend a racially just society. Rather, the ACS maintained that the separation of the races was the result "of moral causes, the foundations of which . . . could not safely be remove[d]"; thus, it advocated the elimination of the "problem" through the colonization of free blacks. The ACS claimed that it favored emancipation but gravely feared the danger inherent in freeing slaves without awarding equal rights. It predicted two kinds of dangers: first, "will not crimes increase as rapidly as their numbers?" and second, "brought up, as these people are, in sight of our privileges, will they consent to be excluded from them?" The society's solution to this impending disaster was colonization of free blacks, which could be "effected with ease by the power of this nation."[33]

The ACS, unlike the abolition society, enjoyed widespread support among white citizens and the legislature of Delaware. In a memorial to the 1827 legislature, certain white Wilmington citizens expressed their approval; it was a subject, they said, "in which the present generation has a deeper interest, or which more urgently demands the attention of our statesmen."[34] Another white citizen, using the pseudonym "Alphonso," supported the society but found its goals too moderate; colonization of free blacks, he insisted, should be required of all free blacks.[35] There is no record of the Wilmington ACS ever settling any free blacks in Africa or elsewhere. It may well be that the unabashed support of the ACS by white Delawareans so alarmed free blacks that it strengthened their resolve to defeat the society.

The Wilmington-based ACS was the only society ostensibly promoting the "interests" of free blacks to receive the unqualified approval of the conservative state legislature. Indeed, the legislature predicted immeasurable benefits for free blacks: resettlement in their original homeland of Africa, in a land the legislature described as "luxuriant" and heavensent. In an 1827 resolution the state legislature praised the ACS for "endeavouring to execute one of the grandest schemes of philanthropy, that can be presented to the American people." The grand scheme in question was the ACS's "redemption of an ignorant, and a much injured race of men, from a degradation worse than servitude and chains" and its plans to colonize free blacks "in that country, on that luxuriant soil, and in that genial climate, pointed to by the finger of Heaven, as their natural inheritance." However, the legislature acknowledged that it was also swayed by the prospect of colonization relieving the "country from an unprofitable burden" while eliminating the threat of "the dreadful cries of vengeance that, but a few years since, were registered in characters of blood at St. Domingo." In the interest of promoting the prosperity and safety of white citizens, the legislature recommended "that measures should be taken for the removal, from this country, of the free negroes and free mulattoes.[36]

A legislature known for its fierce opposition to federal intervention and its quick appeal to the ideology of states' rights on matters relating to race, slavery, and abolition was not averse to recommending federal financial support for the ACS. Declaring the ACS's goals worthy of "public support," the legislature suggested "that they ought to be fostered and encouraged by the national government, and with the national funds."[37] Ironically, four decades later when Lincoln's compensated emancipation plan came before the Delaware legislature, the state argued to the contrary.

The 1831 Nat Turner revolt exacerbated the debate over colonization: white Delawareans intensified their call for removal of free blacks but were opposed by an equally determined free black Delaware bent on defeating such plans. Old Union spearheaded black opposition to the colonization schemes. The first meeting on record took place on 12 July 1831, when Peter Spencer and other Wilmington blacks met to consider the question of colonization. Contrary to the assertions of the ACS and the white citizens of Delaware, blacks found colonization not only "inimical to the best interests of the people of colour" but plainly an abridgment of their "civil and religious liberty, and wholly incompatible with the spirit of the Constitution and Declaration of Independence of these United States." Neither were they impressed with the white portrayal of Africa as a promised land. They were descendants of Africa, they acknowledged, but they refused to join in "a design having for its object the total extirpation of our race from this country, professions to the contrary notwithstanding."[38]

Out of the meeting came a committee of three with the duty of preparing an address to the general public and devising effective ways to educate free blacks on the true intent of the ACS. The resulting address reiterated free black claims to United States citizenship, called inaccurate the rosy picture painted of the Liberia settlement, and challenged the ACS to apply its Christian benevolence to free blacks at home rather than in "the burning sands of Liberia." Colonization would not solve the nation's racial problem, the committee continued, but education and moral improvement would certainly remove prejudice and promote equal justice.[39] Delaware blacks were solidly behind their leaders in this, for they spurned the arguments of the ACS.

The achievements of free black Delawareans, modest as they may seem, coupled with their fierce desire for independence from whites, make it more difficult to understand white hostility toward free blacks. With free blacks gradually uplifting themselves and in no way a financial burden on the state, this story of black achievement undermines the principal rationale for the state's refusal formally to end slavery in Delaware. Black Delawareans never wanted economic subsidies, and did not become an economic liability. Why then the state legislature's reluctance to break the decades-long slavery stalemate?

# 6

# "A Government of White Men for the Benefit of White Men"

IN A SMALLER but more prolonged version of the nation's battle over the institution of slavery, north and south Delaware fought their own bitter war over slavery and emancipation. Divided into two cultural war zones since the colonial era, the state maintained a rigid sectional balance of power that made compromise, particularly on the slavery question, virtually unattainable.

For much of its history, the political landscape of Delaware divided almost evenly into a northern, antislavery, Republican (earlier, Democratic-Republican) New Castle County and a southern, proslavery, Democratic (at first, Federalist) Sussex County, while Kent County found itself rent down the middle. Southern Delaware against northern Delaware, proslavery opposed by antislavery, Democrats versus Republicans; often, neither group could control the branches of the state government to the point of fully and consistently dictating policy. Because both the antislavery and proslavery sections of Delaware lacked the means to dominate the state, maintaining the political stalemate as a means to obstruct the opposing side while praying for an opportune political moment became the default solution for the two Delawares.

Consideration of the partisan implications of de jure abolition accompanied the state's decades-long debate over the death of slavery. In spite of a majority white population in Delaware, the black vote threatened to be the deciding vote in state races. Delaware whites divided almost equally between Democrats and Republicans and between southern and northern Delaware. Too often, statewide election results hinged on fewer than a hundred votes. Thrown into this election equation, black Delawareans who comprised approximately 20 percent of the total state population would tilt the delicate political balance in favor of one party. Black male voters, predictably voting Republican, had the potential clout to obliterate the political future of Delaware Democrats.

In anticipation of reaping the black vote, northern Delaware and its politicians pushed for the abolition of slavery and supported the franchise for black males. But northern Delaware found its way to abolition and the black vote blocked by the powerful intrastate rivalry. Because emancipation and a universal franchise threatened to undermine the political strength of southern and Democratic Delaware, it chose the opposite route. Staking its political future on a platform opposing abolition and black voting rights, southern and Democratic Delaware billed its party as that of "white men for the benefit of white men." Southern and Democratic Delaware opposed abolition out of fear, for the addition of even the most modest number of black voters might permanently tip the state's precarious balance of power in favor of its intrastate rivals.

It is this fear of partisan political demise, not the economic fallout from emancipation, that explains why from the American Revolution to the Civil War and beyond, Delaware Democrats resisted all attempts to legislate the abolition of slavery. In a postscript to the battle for ratification of the thirteenth amendment to the United States Constitution, Gove Saulsbury, a Democrat and the then governor of Delaware, confirmed this Democratic and southern Delaware fear. Saulsbury allowed that free blacks were "justly entitled to the sympathy and commiseration due to inferiors" but adamantly rejected proposals asserting that blacks have a "claim of right to the privilege of voting." Speaking for Democrats, Saulsbury declared that "the interests of both the negro and white man imperatively require that the distinction between the political status of the races should be as marked and distinct as the color ineffaceably impressed upon them by the Creator."[1] Saulsbury's assertion that the Democrats were seeking to protect the interests of free blacks by excluding them from the franchise is very questionable, but his comprehension of the impact of the black vote on southern and Democratic Delaware was very perceptive.

### The Campaign for Gradual Abolition of Slavery

In the era of the American Revolution, Delaware began seriously to consider the legality of the slave trade and slavery. Because slavery had ceased to be of importance in the Delaware economy, the state rather easily banned the external slave trade. The call for a ban on slave imports began in 1767. In that year Kent County representatives led by Caesar Rodney unsuccessfully petitioned the Delaware colonial assembly for an end to the slave trade. The movement to end the external slave trade was revived during the Revolution, initially with the intention of weakening the enemy, the British, through economic and political pressure. In 1775 the colonial assembly approved a bill prohibiting the external slave trade, only to have Governor John Penn veto the measure. The final word on the external slave trade came after independence; in 1776 the new legislature included a ban on the slave trade in the new state constitution.[2] Following the Revolution, the state continued its ban against the slave trade because a changed Delaware economy no longer had room for slave labor; fear of a slave revolt like that in Santo Domingo and, in 1808, a national ban on the Atlantic slave trade permanently ended that trade.

The mild opposition to the movement against slave imports contrasted sharply with the century-long and often fierce opposition mounted against the abolition of slavery. From the Revolution to the beginning of the twentieth century, a closely divided Delaware grappled with the implications of emancipation. The underlying issue lay in the connection between freedom and the right to the franchise. Freedom presupposed citizenship; citizenship, fairly applied by the standards of the time, implied a right to the franchise for all qualified males. Although not free of racial prejudice, northern Delaware and the Republicans supported the extension of the franchise to free blacks, fully expecting blacks to vote Republican out of gratitude to the party of emancipation. Not expecting to reap the black vote, Democrats held onto legal slavery, even if of only 1,798 blacks, for it provided the excuse to deny equal citizenship and the vote to the 19,829 free blacks. So long as legal slavery remained in place, it defined and embraced peoples of African descent as unfree persons, rationalizing the exclusion of manumitted blacks from the privileges of citizenship.

Delaware failed to keep minutes of legislative debates scrupulously; mention is made only of a final vote but not of the legislative process nor debates preceding that final vote. Consequently, it is difficult to say with any certainty why in some years abolition bills failed to reach the floor, while in others they progressed to the point of floor debate and a final vote. Still, much can be inferred from the final votes on the abolition bills.

Beginning in 1782 when Delaware's president John Dickinson called for the gradual abolition of slavery, the state repeatedly debated abolition. Abolition failed each time, until forced by the terms of the Thirteenth Amendment to the United States Constitution, which the state refused to ratify. The voting pattern on these bills for abolition of slavery reveals how the county and political affiliation of the legislators correlated with their positions on the bill. Invariably, representatives from New Castle County supported abolition. Sussex County politicians almost consistently opposed all forms of legislated abolition. Kent County representatives usually split their politics and almost equally divided their votes between these two opposing forces.

From 1782 until 1796 the state reviewed petitions for an abolition law almost every year. But on each occasion the legislature chose to shift the course of the debate away from the subject of mandated abolition and toward laws encouraging private and voluntary manumission. Although the legislators offered no explanation for their decision to evade debate on abolition, their actions suggest a desire to resolve through private acts of manumission what they could not, because of lack of sufficient votes, mandate. Perhaps the legislature hoped that its middle position of maintaining legal slavery while actively supporting private acts of manumission would sufficiently pacify the two competing sections of Delaware. But the legislature's position satisfied neither the proslavery nor antislavery side.

In 1797 the legislature began a serious debate on an abolition bill but after several readings chose not to call the question to a final vote. Claiming that the bill was "imperfect in its provisions" and if passed would adversely affect "the citizens of the state, and even [cause] distress to Negroes and Mulattoes," the legislature decided to postpone consideration and a final vote until the white citizens of Delaware had been given the opportunity to express "their wishes and opinion upon the matter."[3]

However, not until the beginning of the nineteenth century, in 1803, did the state resume debate on the abolition of slavery. The bill narrowly missed passage in 1803, failing by one vote. Abolition of slavery was debated again in 1805; this time, after a preliminary debate, the legislature decided to postpone consideration of the bill to the next legislative session.[4] Records of the next session are missing; if the legislature debated abolition, the measure failed, and most likely by the same evenly divided partisan vote.

The next mention of an abolition bill occurred during the session of 1812; however, beyond reading the bill and referring it to a committee of three, very little seems to have been accomplished.[5] A whole decade passed before the legislature resumed its discussion on abolition; data may be missing, or the silence may also reflect a state turning its attention to matters of war, the War of 1812. Then in 1822, several citizens and groups from the state submitted petitions for the abolition of slavery; in response, the legislature resumed debate on abolition. The proposed abolition bill of 1822 failed in the house by a vote of eleven to six. All Sussex County members voted against the bill, and Kent County split its vote, while all of the New Castle County representatives except two voted in favor of abolition.[6]

The following year a call for limited emancipation came from Governor Caleb Rodney. Calling slavery a "blemish upon the fair fabric . . . erected in this country to liberty," Rodney commended Delaware citizens for the successful voluntary manumission system and asked for the placement of additional restrictions on the domestic slave trade. An attempt by New Castle County members to introduce a gradual abolition bill was defeated eleven to nine by a coalition of Kent and Sussex representatives joined by one New Castle County member.[7] In 1825, and again in 1826, abolition bills were read, reread, and debated, but each time the bills were postponed to the next session. Following yet another attempt in 1827 to postpone debate on the abolition bill, the House finally called the bill to a vote; it lost on a voice vote.[8]

Debates on abolition seemed conspicuously absent during the decade of the 1830s. From 1831 to 1839 the legislature considered several issues affecting Delaware blacks, but not emancipation. In response to the fear and anxiety generated by the Nat Turner slave revolt, the state turned its attention to the elimination of the few rights enjoyed by free blacks. Rather than promoting freedom, a spate of laws denying free blacks the right to possess firearms, to travel freely, and to worship without hinderance became the focus of legislative debates.

The only break in this seemingly antiblack decade of the 1830s came from a group of over three hundred women from the city of Wilmington who in 1839 dared to appeal for an abolition law. Perhaps emboldened by the growing militancy among female antislavery members who were now demanding that the national society recognize the right of women to air their views publicly, these Wilmington women implored the Delaware legislature to eliminate from the state "a burden oppressive both to master and slave, and a dishonor to our common country." But these female petitioners did not help the cause of black Delawareans. A legislature famous for evading, delaying, and deadlocking on abolition bills wasted no time in answering these "misguided" women. On the very next day, and in no uncertain terms, the women were denounced for overstepping the bounds of womanhood with their "unwarranted interference in subjects that more properly should belong to their fathers, husbands, or brothers." It would be more beneficial for society, the legislature continued, were these women to confine themselves "to matters of a *domestic nature,* and be more solicitous to *mend* the *garments* of their husbands and children, than to patch the *breaches* of the Laws and Constitution."[9]

The national debate over the admission of Texas as a slave state provided the backdrop to Delaware's consideration of abolition bills during the 1840s. The state debated abolition in 1845, 1847, and again in 1849. In 1845 a gradual abolition bill offered by Stephen Stapler of New Castle was read, reread, and then indefinitely postponed on the motion of George P. Fisher of Kent, who during the Civil War changed his political affiliation to the Republican fold and became a leading advocate of Lincoln's compensated emancipation plan. The abolition debate resumed in 1847, but as in 1803, de jure abolition lost by a single partisan vote. Two years later, in 1849, members of a committee appointed to debate the abolition bill reported that "they deem it inexpedient to legislate upon the subject at this time," and the house unanimously approved their resolution.[10] Not until the decade of the Civil War did Delaware once again resurrect the abolition debate.

Of the state's repeated failure to legislate the abolition of slavery, two occasions stand above the rest, the defeats in 1803 and 1847. In both years the abolition bill lost by a single vote. These two debates are especially noteworthy because they reveal the rigid sectionalism within the state of Delaware over the issue of legislated emancipation.

In 1803, in a fashion typical of the Delaware slavery stalemate, the submission of an abolition petition by Quakers and the abolition society sparked the legislative debate. Unlike earlier debates, however, events in the Caribbean provided a strong external stimulus for heated discussion of the emancipation question. The petition began with the usual charge that slavery was contrary to the word of God and the spirit of the Revolution. But it next shifted to the Santo Domingo slave revolt, painting a graphic picture of the attendant bloodshed and destruction of life and property, and concluded with the plea that the state undertake "such steps as may lead to a gradual Abolition of slavery."[11]

Perhaps swayed by the passionate language of the antislavery petition, the legislature in 1803 agreed to take the matter to the bargaining table. The resulting gradual abolition bill, drafted out of the Quaker petition, was introduced by two representatives from New Castle County, William Poole and Philip Lewis. Predictably, the opposing motion to delay consideration of the bill until the next session of the legislature came from Outerbridge Horsey, a Sussex County representative. Even more predictably, the bill failed. The final roll call revealed a nearly straight partisan vote ending in a tie; the deciding vote of the Speaker of the House, Stephen Lewis, a Federalist from Kent County, broke the tie against abolition.

A tally of the voting reveals that all Democratic-Republican members supported abolition, while Federalists, except for three members, voted against the bill.[12] All six Democratic-Republican supporters of the bill were delegates from New Castle County; arrayed against them were the Federalist representatives from Kent and Sussex counties. One of the three maverick Federalists was from Sussex, and two were from Kent County.

Abolition in 1847 was also narrowly defeated, by a majority of one Democratic proslavery vote. The 1847 debate also arose in response to various antislavery petitions, but the national debate over the Wilmot Proviso provided an additional ground. Headed by Henry Swayne of New Castle County, the committee appointed to consider the question of emancipation submitted an elaborate report documenting why the state should speedily acquiesce in abolition. The report opened with an assurance to the white citizens of Delaware: committee members insisted that they were neither radical abolitionists nor outside agitators and that they strongly "condemn the incendiary attempts of all who, for any purpose whatever, seek to intermeddle with the question of slavery in other States in which they have no residence or interest." And the committee denounced the partisan nature of the abolition debate, calling it "one of the most melancholy evils of the day that it [slavery] should ever have been mixed up with the disturbing topics of party warfare." Its report and recommendations, the committee maintained, would remain strictly bipartisan, addressing "itself to no party feeling."

Second, the committee pleaded states' rights on the question of slavery, believing it to be a domestic issue that should be settled by the people of Delaware and their elected representatives. Third, it found slavery of little economic value to the state; awareness of its marginality seemed clearly evident in the growing number of manumissions. However, a voluntary system of emancipation, the committee insisted, would no longer suffice, for without the formal abolition of the institution, the

> stigma of slavery rests upon the State, and its moral influence operates
> perniciously, both at home and abroad; while its evils, as a system of
> long standing, weigh heavily and most injuriously upon our agriculture,
> and upon the prosperity of our people. Notwithstanding the cheapness
> and fertility of our soil, the mere reputation of being a slave holding
> State certainly prevents many useful and enterprising citizens of the ad-
> joining free States from emigrating to our State, and vesting their capi-
> tal in our land, and thus robbing us of the benefits of free labor and the
> stimulant of increased capital. The careless, slovenly and unproductive
> husbandry visible in some parts of our State, undoubtedly result mainly

from the habit of depending on slave labor. It is no longer a debatable question that slave labor impoverishes, while free labor enriches a people. We see it in our own State in the fact that agriculture and the arts flourish, and population increases, just in proportion as free labor prevails and slave labor recedes.

The committee moved beyond a simple recounting of the evils of slavery and sought to persuade the legislature that abolition could be easily accomplished. It was absurd, continued the report, for Delaware to endure "the stigma of slavery for a remnant so paltry in number as to leave us without excuse or apology for continuing an evil . . . every slave State in the Union would gladly get rid of if placed in the same circumstances." Because the committee believed that the public favored abolition, it urged the state to fix a date "after which every child born in the State, of whatever color or degree, shall be born free."[13]

The resulting gradual abolition bill went through the usual first two readings, and then on the third reading, representative John W. Scribner of Sussex County moved for an indefinite postponement of the bill.[14] Voting was strictly partisan: all the Sussex County representatives voted in favor of a permanent delay and were opposed by a unanimous New Castle delegation, with Kent County, as usual, torn between the northern and southern counties, two of its representatives in support of the Sussex position and five in opposition. With the majority voting against postponement, the house resumed debate on the abolition bill. On the final ballot, the house by a vote of twelve to eight approved the bill for gradual abolition of slavery. Voting followed county and party allegiance: the Whigs of northern Delaware voted in favor of abolition; the Democrats of southern Delaware were opposed. All of the New Castle County delegates supported the bill, Sussex County unanimously voted against it, and Kent County split its vote five to two between the forces of freedom and slavery.

In spite of this success in the House, abolition did not become law in 1847. It failed when it encountered powerful proslavery resistance in the Delaware senate.[15] After the second reading of the bill in the state senate, Samuel Paynter of Sussex County moved that the "bill be indefinitely postponed." The motion carried by a majority of one: with a five-to-four vote, the senate elected indefinitely to shelve the abolition bill. Opposed to the motion were all Kent County delegates, plus one from New Castle; support for postponement came from Sussex County and, curiously, from two New Castle County representatives, Samuel Burham and John D. Turner, who offered no explanation for their defection.

The national debates over slavery in the territories during the 1840s and 1850s provided a divided Delaware with an additional forum for airing its diverse views on slavery and emancipation. The state kept to form, responding to these national debates in true partisan fashion. On the question of slavery in the territories, northern Delaware and the Whigs argued in favor of the Wilmot Proviso, but southern Delaware and the Democrats opposed this plan which sought to restrict the expansion of slavery into the territories. Only days after the state defeated the abolition bill of 1847, Whigs and northern Delaware successfully fought for a resolution that stated the state's opposition to "the annexation of Texas with the view to the addition of slave power in our Union." The same legislature that defeated in-state legislated abolition now claimed to regard the acquisitions of additional slave territory as "hostile to the spirit of our free institutions, and contrary to sound morality." Thus, it advised the state's senators and representative in Congress "to vote against the annexation of any new territory which shall not thereafter be for ever free from slavery."[16]

### The Civil War and Universal Emancipation

The Civil War further sharpened Delaware's political and geographical divisions, thereby affecting the state's response to slavery and emancipation. Delaware, though a slave state, chose to remain in the Union. The decision not to secede encountered relatively little opposition from the two Delawares. The existing political animosities made it unlikely that Delaware could ever muster a secession majority. Northern and Republican Delaware supported the war as the best means to preserve the Union. Democrats and southern Delaware opposed the war; indeed, many favored the Confederacy but seemed unwilling to support disunion.

White Delawareans, Democratic and Republican, agreed it would be suicidal to secede. Given the state's size and location and the nature of its economy, its interest clearly would best be served within the Union. And at issue was the state's pride: Delaware boasted of being the first state to enter the Union and swore that if need be, it would be the last state to sever these ties. Hence, in answer to a call from Georgia to secede, the legislature replied that "as Delaware was the first to adopt, so will she be the last to abandon the Federal Constitution." On 3 January 1861 the Delaware legislature overwhelmingly voted against secession. And subsequently, the state supported various attempts intended to prevent secession, including the Crittenden Resolution and the Washington Peace Conference, both of which would have forever guaranteed slavery where it existed.[17]

Delaware's decision to support the Union unintentionally prolonged the life span of slavery in the state. Because it was a nonseceded state, the status of its slaves remained unaffected by Lincoln's Emancipation Proclamation of 1863. Not until ratification of the thirteenth amendment in December 1865 did the national government compel Delaware to grant universal emancipation to its remaining slaves.

While the decade of the Civil War presented Delaware with several opportunities to end legal slavery, the most promising came with President Lincoln's offer of compensated emancipation. Lincoln sought to appease loyal border slave states by offering compensation as a preparation to his larger policy of freeing the slaves in the Confederacy; he hoped thereby to bring the war to a close and to restore the shattered Union. Delaware as the smallest of the slave states was selected as the testing ground for Lincoln's emancipation plan. A slave state saddled with a devalued slave institution would seem ready to adopt compensated emancipation gratefully. But not Delaware; seemingly in defiance of logic, the state rejected the offer.

In November 1861 Lincoln drafted but did not submit to Congress a bill offering payment of $400 per slave (a total of $719,200) to Delaware to cover the cost of emancipation. The bill proposed the immediate freeing of all slaves thirty-five years of age or older, with other adult slaves receiving their freedom as they turned thirty-five. All remaining adult slaves would be freed on 1 January 1893 or some other negotiable date, perhaps 1872. From the effective date of the act, children born to slave women would be freeborn, but these children were required to serve the owners of their slave mothers until age eighteen for females and twenty-one for males. Colonization of the ex-slaves was not mentioned in this draft.[18]

During the same month Lincoln broached the compensated emancipation plan to Delaware representative George P. Fisher, now a Republican. Apparently, Lincoln made an offer of $300 per slave, but Fisher successfully bargained for $500, and plans were made for Lincoln to test the response of a Delaware slaveholder to the compensated emancipation plan. Subsequently, Fisher and a fellow Republican, soon-to-be Delaware representative to Congress Nathaniel B. Smithers, drew up an abolition bill which incorporated the provisions in Lincoln's draft, substituting the year 1872 for his 1893. In their plan the national government was expected to fund both the compensation of all owners and the colonization of the ex-slaves.[19]

Had it passed, compensated emancipation would have offered the remaining 587 slave owners of Delaware (86 in New Castle County, 66 in Kent County, and 435 in Sussex County) the chance to rid themselves of their 1,798 slaves and receive substantial cash compensation.

Compensated emancipation seemed to offer the perfect opportunity for Delaware's slave owners to make money while eliminating an unprofitable labor system. Delaware resident Charles I. du Pont thought so. He claimed that the compensated emancipation plan would "prove a God send to many a slave owner," especially "in Kent & Sussex counties, where they say, that now the hogs eat all the corn, the Negroes the hogs, and the Sheriff the master."[20] But the state spurned the offer.

Why did Delaware reject compensated emancipation? Certainly not because Lincoln's plan radically departed from any system of manumission known to the slaveholders of Delaware. Indeed, with the key exception of compensation, the bill closely matched the gradual abolition laws of the northern states and the practice of voluntary manumission so fashionable among the slaveholders of Delaware. While white Delawareans voluntarily freed slaves of all ages, they most often offered complete freedom to slaves aged thirty and above, while promising younger slaves their freedom at a future date, usually age twenty-one for males and eighteen for females. Lincoln's plan would have preserved this Delaware custom while reimbursing slaveholders for a portion of the fair market value of their slaves.

Repeating their response to past abolition bills, the public, newspapers, and legislature of Delaware voiced diverging opinions of Lincoln's compensated emancipation plan. The debate centered on the plan's effect on white Delawareans with little concern evinced for its impact on Delaware blacks, except perhaps to suggest, as the *Delaware Gazette* did, that the ex-slave would suffer because he was "not capable of making himself comfortable" without the direction of whites.[21]

Delaware's response to the compensated emancipation plan did not follow a neat slaveholder versus nonslaveholder division; rather, political and county loyalties remained the deciding factors. Many of the plan's most virulent detractors were nonslaveholders reacting out of a sense of loyalty to racial beliefs and allegiance to their party—Democratic—or to their home counties, Kent and Sussex. So did defenders of the plan—typically residents of New Castle or Republican in political affiliation—support emancipation out of loyalty to county and politics.

A leading supporter of compensated emancipation happened to be one of the state's largest slaveholders, Benjamin Burton. In 1850 Burton owned fourteen slaves ranging in age from six months to fifty years old; by 1860 his slave property had increased by two to sixteen. In politics Burton claimed a Republican affiliation, but he lived in the Democratic stronghold of Sussex County. When Lincoln expressed interest in enlisting the aid of a Delaware slaveholder, Burton was selected to meet with the president. Apparently, Burton attended the meeting with a few qualms about the plan's feasibility, but Lincoln's assurance of congressional approval removed any remaining doubts.[22]

Burton was said to have assured Lincoln of the plan's success in Delaware. If he did so, then Burton's declaration constituted a gross exaggeration. His campaign in his home county of Sussex failed dismally; only one small slaveholder, Hiram S. Short, the owner of one slave in 1850 and three in 1860 and a resident of the same hundred and county as Burton, publicly aired his support of the plan. Short's support was lukewarm; strongly convinced of the imminent universal abolition of slavery, he simply expressed his preference for financial settlement over uncompensated emancipation.[23]

If Burton, one of the state's largest slaveholders, supported compensated emancipation, many of his fellow slaveholders from the same county fought the plan and actively lobbied for its defeat. Although a Republican and a Union supporter, Caleb S. Layton of Sussex County voiced his opposition to compensated emancipation. Layton in 1850 owned a single slave, a male aged five; by 1860 he was the owner of two slaves, a forty-five-year-old female and the slave from 1850, now aged fifteen. Financial loss seemed the least of Layton's concerns, other factors determined his opposition. He challenged the constitutional basis of the plan for its attempts to deprive citizens of their property and to compensate slaveholders with public funds. But equally worrisome for Layton were the social and political ramifications of abolition. He offered an alternate plan, proposing that freedom be granted to the issue born of slave mothers: male children after serving indentures of twenty-one to twenty-five years and females after terms ranging from eighteen to twenty-one years. According to Layton, his plan guaranteed citizens the right of property, was cost-free, precluded interference with the labor needs of Delaware whites, discouraged the unloading of old and indigent slaves on taxpayers, and preserved existing social relations.[24]

His, however, was an unoriginal gradual abolition plan, similar in language and scale to the manumission bills defeated by past Delaware legislatures. Layton, a prominent lawyer and citizen, most certainly was aware of the repeated defeat of similar bills in the past; it is difficult to explain why he thought his bill would succeed where others had failed. Further, except for excluding compensation, his bill did not significantly differ from Lincoln's. Indeed, for Delaware whites, compensated emancipation held an advantage over Layton's bill, for it promised the colonization of free blacks.

Nonslaveholders of Delaware, the group least affected by the emancipation plan, also divided over the issue. A supporter using the pseudonym "Libertas" cautioned the state against its "blind devotion to slavery." It was an institution serving no useful purpose, he said, only saddling Delaware with "all of its evils and none of its benefits," a system kept in place solely for the benefit of "party purposes." He advised the remaining slaveholders to embrace the plan, for

> its terms are fair and just. It takes no man's property without paying full value. It buys what the owner cannot otherwise sell—what there is no demand for—what three-fourths of the slaveholders in this state are anxious to sell. They cannot sell them out of the State, for the law forbids it under heavy penalties. They cannot sell them in the state, for persons who do not own slaves, do not wish to buy. Every year diminishes the value. . . . The average price of the slave if sold in this State today —would not be $100 each.

If "Libertas" was correct, not only would Delaware slave owners eliminate the surplus labor by adopting compensated emancipation, but they would also make a handsome profit in the bargain. "Libertas" estimated the average price of a Delaware slave as $100, while Lincoln's plan offered between $300 and $500 per slave; on average, owners would have received three times the actual value of their slaves.[25]

But if "Libertas" anticipated profits for slave owners, supporters of slavery predicted financial disaster. The ability of the national government to fund compensation, the source of the funding, and the total cost disturbed opponents of the plan. Many worried about the combined cost of compensation and colonization and expressed great fear of an increased tax burden. Seemingly skeptical that the federal government actually would pay for the entire cost of compensation, Democrats warned that the financial responsibility would fall on the states. The use of federal funds to compensate slave owners also remained a sore point, with opponents arguing against using funds belonging to all citizens to compensate a few.[26]

Governor William Burton, a Democrat, calculated that compensated emancipation would cost a total of $112 million (at $300 per slave) to free slaves plus an additional $117 million to fund colonization; such a proposal, he said, would "deprive the country of about twelve hundred million dollars of laboring property, and to substitute . . . a debt of seventeen hundred millions bearing interest." Burton warned white Delawareans that the plan was a scheme to tax "the industrious, hard-working white man to pay for the emancipation of the slaves" and thereafter to support free blacks "either in the alms-house, county jail or otherwise." White citizens who thought differently, the governor charged, had their "judgement biased by fanaticism," not reality.[27] The *Delaware Gazette* shared the governor's skepticism of the national government's intentions, particularly regarding the compensation portion of the plan. The paper informed the federal government that Delaware slaveholders continued voluntarily and at no cost to free their slaves; therefore, Delaware citizens had no intention of being taxed "to effect immediately what time will certainly effect for them, in a few more years without cost."[28]

The Republican position as defined by Fisher promised benefits including financial gain, an end to the Civil War, and removal of all free blacks through colonization. Contrary to Democratic assertions regarding the high cost of emancipation, Fisher believed that abolition of slavery would save the national government the expense of the Civil War. It cost less to support compensated emancipation in Delaware, argued Fisher, than the expenditure for half a day of warfare. Were the national government to provide Delaware what it cost to fund the war for half a day, it "will not only pay for all the slaves at full prices, but will leave a margin to provide a fund for the removal . . . not only of the freed slaves, but the entire negro population, and colonize them in any country provided for them by the General Government."[29]

Opponents of compensated emancipation responded with additional objections. They denounced as unconstitutional the government's attempts to legislate on the slavery question; nor did they believe it appropriate to use federal funds for reimbursing slave owners. The compensation plan, they insisted, was an assault on the rights of a state, its people, and their slave property. Senator Willard Saulsbury, a Democrat and brother of Governor Gove Saulsbury, repeatedly charged that neither Congress nor Lincoln had the constitutional right to abolish slavery or use federal resources to fund the plan.[30]

Delaware's other United States senator, Democrat James A. Bayard, fully concurred. Like Saulsbury, he denied any congressional authority over emancipation and compensation. Reversing the Democratic position of the 1830s that called for federal funds to aid the ACS in colonizing free blacks, Bayard now argued that Delaware neither needed nor desired "from the Federal Government a dollar in relation to the question" of slavery. Rather, he and Delaware Democrats wished the national government would stop interfering in an issue that the state could resolve on its own.[31]

Such spirited defense of states' rights found backing even among those who favored compensation, except that they often qualified their support of the principle. Some like Fisher conceded that Congress had no constitutional right to interfere with slavery and that to each state must belong the "sole and exclusive jurisdiction over slavery within the state." But unlike Democrats, Fisher did not perceive Lincoln's proposal as an attack on the rights of a state. Rather, he portrayed it as "just to all, an infringement of no man's rights, and in no wise a violation of the letter or spirit" of the Constitution. The purpose of the plan, Fisher continued, was not to contend with states' rights but to make it possible for those states interested in compensated emancipation to afford the choice of putting the divisive issue of slavery on a "course of ultimate extinction."[32]

Had Republicans succeeded in assuring their opponents of both the plan's legality and the national government's ability to fund compensation without raising taxes, Democrats would still have opposed it on the ground that it lay beyond the duty of the state to legislate abolition. Delaware voters had not elected legislators "with a view to the passage of any act for the emancipation of Slaves," Democrats maintained; rather, it was understood, in agreements "either expressed or implied, that legislation upon the distracting subject was hostile to the public peace and therefore to be avoided." An anonymous writer, INF, a resident of Sussex County, pro-Union, and proslavery, shared these sentiments. Out of his fear that abolition would kindle the "infernal negro question" and increase the free black population, he warned the legislature that it "would be very much out of their duties to meddle with it [slavery], as that was not the issue upon which they were elected."[33]

Against the Democratic call for the state to abstain on the question of slavery, the *Delaware State Journal and Statesman* praised the bill and expressed hope for its passage. Far from calling for restraint, the paper wished the legislature to "screw its courage to the sticking point" and pass the measure.[34] So did Fisher, who portrayed the plan as "an olive branch of peace and harmony," a good-faith gesture to all the slave states. Not only would its adoption provide a "final settlement of all angry discussion and agitation upon this terrible question of slavery," but it would end the war between the states, paving the way for peaceful restoration of the Union.[35]

Conversely, Democrats insisted that compensated emancipation would build an impenetrable barrier to the readmission of the seceded states. Speaking for the proslavery side, Saulsbury described a Republican-hatched conspiracy engaged in changing the Civil War from a fight to save the Union to one designed "to elevate the miserable nigger, not only to political rights, but to put him in your Army, and to put him in your Navy." For as long as the policy remained in force, warned Saulsbury, "the Union will never be restored, because you can have no Union without the preservation of the Constitution."[36]

Out of the opposition camp came warning that Lincoln's plan would precipitate a short-term labor shortage. Opponents had little fear of emancipation and colonization affecting labor in the long term; they anticipated the eventual replacement of black with white labor. But such a radical transformation in the system of labor, they cried, required time, more time than Lincoln's plan would allow. Only through a more gradual plan of emancipation and colonization could Delaware farmers avert "very destructive loss to the crops and the productive labor generally."[37]

In rebuttal, Governor William Cannon, a Republican and a supporter of the plan, insisted it was possible to administer emancipation and colonization without adversely affecting the labor needs of white Delaware citizens. An emancipation plan combining gradual abolition and colonization but timed to the same pace as the replacement of black with white labor would successfully avert any disruption in the labor supply.[38]

Like Cannon, Fisher disputed the Democratic claim that a labor shortage would ensue from compensated emancipation. Instead, he offered a detailed analysis of the contrast between proslavery Sussex County, and he believed Kent, too, versus the antislavery county of New Castle. New Castle County, Fisher said, was a society based on free labor and a consequent thriving economy. In New Castle "there is but one slave for two hundred freemen," and as a result its "manufactures, arts, and agriculture" were "scarcely second to the most flourishing county in the Union." The county comprised "only about one fifth of the area of the State," Fisher continued, but "it is nearly equal to both the others in population, greatly superior to either in agricultural products, and far exceeds both in aggregate of industrial wealth."[39] By contrast, Fisher depicted the economy and society of Sussex and Kent counties as severely impaired by slavery; only by ridding their society of the institution could the two lower counties duplicate the successful economy of New Castle County.

The fiscal impact of emancipation, whether on slaveholders or the state, seemed the least important factor in deciding a person's stand on the issue. Both sides readily agreed on the insignificance of slavery in the Delaware economy. Although an opponent of the plan, Senator Bayard acknowledged that slavery was not "a valuable source of property" in the state; given a choice, white Delawareans would certainly select white labor over the labor of blacks, because white workers posed no social "threats," and they provided a "superior" labor capable of quadrupling the wealth of the state. Similarly, Gove Saulsbury acknowledged that slavery in the state had "never been one of practical importance, and never was worthy of much consideration, otherwise than as one involving clear constitutional right and duty."[40] Nevertheless, regardless of what white Delawareans might prefer, both Bayard and Gove Saulsbury concluded that the state could not afford the social and political consequences of emancipation.

When Democrats expressed fear that emancipation would transform Delaware's social structure, they did so not out of concern that 1,798 slaves would seriously alter the proportion of free blacks, certainly not with 19,829 blacks already free, nor out of belief that emancipation would upset the economic well-being of the state. However, the social and political impact of universal emancipation on Delaware remained of critical importance to both friend and foe of slavery. Whether Democrat or Republican, antislavery or proslavery, the people of Delaware acknowledged that slavery had been sustained in Delaware for reasons other than material interest. From the Republican camp Cannon, declared that slavery was being used to "perpetuate . . . a social institution or a political machine." Cannon's political rival Burton also agreed: he predicted that a universal emancipation "policy would produce a radical change, and indeed break up [Delaware's] social system."[41]

Much can be explained in light of this anxiety over, and contest for, social and political control in Delaware; actions that otherwise would seem irrational assume new meaning. In the 13 June 1862 *Delaware Gazette*, INF best summed up the fears and anxieties of proslavery and southern Delaware. "This abolition business," INF charged, "has gone about far enough, there are free negroes already enough within this State, according to population"; it would be a grievous error to increase the free black population through abolition. Although white Delawareans "look upon slavery as a curse," said INF, they "look upon freedom possessed by a negro, except in a very few cases, as a greater curse." Faced with the "two evils" of slavery and free blacks, INF recommended that "it is wisdom to choose the least," that is, slavery.[42]

Elaborating on the question of choosing between black freedom and black slavery, the *Delaware Gazette* asked whether Delaware through compensated emancipation could eliminate the financial burden of slavery and still avoid granting the privileges of citizenship to black Delawareans. The paper did not think it possible; thus, it cautioned white Delawareans about the difficulties of denying equal rights to free black citizens. Like the American Revolution's battle cry of "no taxation without representation," free blacks, the paper predicted, would launch a similar uprising if emancipation was offered without equal rights. If freed, blacks in common with other free persons would be taxed, and if taxed, blacks would demand the franchise as a moral and legal right, and with the vote, blacks would inevitably insist on equal power and representation. Would a white Delaware society that believed "the negro better off in his present state," the paper asked, really wish for "such an approach to equality?" Still, if universal emancipation and racial equality were unavoidable, the paper would rather compromise in favor of gradualism.[43]

In a similar vein Senator Bayard ascribed Delaware's failure to legislate abolition to what he called "the dangers of race." He did not blame the failure of abolition on the power of the slaveholding class; rather, he attributed it to what he called the "antagonism of race." Bayard claimed that the white citizens of Delaware understood that "where two races of men inhabit the same country . . . the inferior race must perish before the superior race, unless it remains a subject race." Therefore, although slavery as an economic system no longer remained viable, Delaware's social and political interests compelled the continual domination and enslavement of the "inferior" black race.

This "antagonism of race" Bayard truthfully admitted, lay behind Delaware's rejection of legislated abolition, including President Lincoln's compensated emancipation plan.

> It is the principle of equality which the white man rejects where the negro exists in large numbers. It is that which creates the antagonism of race. The antagonism of race does not take place where but few individuals exist who do not affect the structure of society. . . . It does not arise until the relative numbers of the two races are such as to affect the social relations and the whole body politic. We have felt it in our State, and we know what the antagonism of race is. Sir, the skilled labor of Delaware, the mechanics of Delaware, would scorn the idea of equality in their occupations with the negro. They would not permit the negro as an equal, whether he had equal rights by the law or not, to be forced into the same occupations in which they are engaged. No employer dare make the attempt. . . . The antagonism arises not from the fact of the difference of race, but from the assertion of equality on the part of the inferior race. The white man cares nothing that he labors in the same occupation that the slave does; but place the slave in the position of equality by making him a freeman, and you at once create the antagonism of race, if the two races exist in large relative numbers.[44]

In much stronger language, and expressing a similar fear of the social and political consequences of emancipation, Sussex County Democrats declared their opposition to the compensated emancipation plan. They announced their

> unalterable and uncompromising opposition to the proposition of the President of the United States for the abolition of slavery in the Border

States, with pretended compensation to their owners or upon any other terms or conditions whatever, except the free, unsolicited and unsuggested voice of the people. 2d. That we will inflexibly oppose all attempts at abolition of slavery in the State of Delaware, and do hereby declare that if we are intrusted with the confidence of the people, that the relation of master and slave shall continue in the future as it has in the past, and that this State shall continue to be governed in accordance with the precept and example of the good, the great and the wise who preceded us.[45]

Even supporters of the Lincoln's compensated emancipation plan often seemed lukewarm and on occasion proved extremely hostile to the social implications of universal emancipation. Frequently, defenders of the plan coupled their support with proposals to increase white control over Delaware blacks, while others made their support contingent on the colonization of all free blacks.

Fisher, though the leading supporter of compensation, always carefully qualified his support. Compensated emancipation, as he repeatedly reminded white Delawareans, included a provision for colonizing both the newly freed slaves and all other free blacks. He took great pains to dissociate himself from any charge of being a radical abolitionist or an advocate of racial equality. His avowed intention was the removal of the cause of dissension between North and South, between antislavery and proslavery, but never did he subscribe to the concept of a racially just society. In words reminiscent of some of the plan's harshest critics, Fisher contended that "the Almighty intended this Union as the home of the white race, created for them, not for the negro." Thus, it was incumbent on "every patriot to consider . . . under a full sense of his responsibility to his God and his country, how the separation of the two distinct races, which can never, and ought never, to dwell together upon terms of political and social equality, can be effected with the least jarring to the harmony and happiness of our country."[46]

Governor Cannon, the other leading supporter of the plan, also carefully qualified his endorsement; often he reiterated his disapproval of the growing free black population. Portraying free blacks as "not desirable," Cannon declared that they must remain "inferior being[s], under tutelage" of whites. Any person or group expecting to transform this social relation by advocating equal citizenship rights, claimed this supporter of emancipation would not only discredit but also insult the white citizens of Delaware.[47]

The struggle for control of Delaware politics remained inseparable from the struggle to defeat Lincoln's compensated emancipation plan and from the general concern over social change. Both Delaware parties saw winning the contest over compensated emancipation as vital because it offered long-term dominance in state politics. Republicans fought for the plan and their own political future, while with a parallel zeal and self-interest, Democrats labored for its defeat.

Whereas any social change ensuing from emancipation would touch, perhaps even equally, all Delawareans, the political consequence of the plan would affect the two major parties differently. Because of the existing delicate political balance, the slightest shift threatened one party or the other. Passage of the plan could promote the political careers of the Republicans but adversely affect the fortunes of the Democrats. Republicans and northern Delaware chose to court the black vote. They supported abolition and the right to the franchise for the freedmen, expecting that the freedmen's sense of gratitude would lead them to vote Republican. In a bid to entice white voters, Delaware Democrats and southern Delaware chose to raise the race wall. They identified their party as the white man's party, stood in rigid opposition to legislated emancipation, and resisted all plans proposing equal citizenship rights.

Democrats dubbed their opponents black Republicans, equated support for emancipation with a call for racial equality and miscegenation, and convinced voters that emancipation would lead to the destruction of white society. The effectiveness of racial politics was revealed not only through the rejection of the plan but in succeeding years when Democrats successfully employed the same tactic to defeat the Republicans. Supporters of the plan found it difficult to defeat such a heady combination of political opposition. Republicans and supporters of emancipation fought a losing battle against the Democratic-painted picture of a race-induced Armageddon. It was a potent political charge that state Republicans proved unable to defuse, and this failure made it impossible for Republicans to win outside New Castle County.

This stalemated and racially charged reality of Delaware politics obstructed passage of Lincoln's plan. The social and political composition of the Delaware legislature of 1861, and thereafter, virtually precluded the acceptance of an emancipation plan. An examination of antebellum Delaware politics, beginning with the contest over the election of 1860, provides the key to an understanding of the intense struggle over slavery and emancipation in Delaware during the Civil War era. So much bitterness was spawned out of the statewide election of 1860 that it spilled over into subsequent elections, thereby ensuring the defeat of all attempts at compromise on slavery and emancipation.

While Delaware whites disagreed on the presidential candidates of 1860, it was the state and local elections that created the most rancor.

The 1860 campaign produced the usual charges and countercharges of election fraud, intimidation, and corruption, but by the final count neither the Democrats nor the Republicans and their allies the People's party had acquired a clear majority in the state legislature. Thus, the success of abolition hinged on the ability of the Republicans and the People's party to persuade Democrats to their way of thinking, virtually an impossible task in Civil War Delaware.

One of the state's most hotly contested races in 1860 was fought over Delaware's single congressional seat. The victory, marred by controversy, went to George P. Fisher. A breakdown of the voting rolls reveals that Fisher won in New Castle County with the support of the Republican and People's party vote, lost in his home county of Kent, but posted a victory in Sussex County with a very narrow margin of seventeen votes. Fisher's success in the traditionally Democratic stronghold of Sussex County was made possible by a bitter dispute between two Democratic factions, one of which expressed its anger by casting its vote against the official party slate, thus handing the victory to Fisher. Democrats offered a different explanation for Fisher's victory; they charged election irregularities.[48] It was this Fisher, with a cloud of political impropriety over his head (so claimed Democrats), who was selected by Lincoln to sell the controversial compensated emancipation plan to a bitterly divided Delaware.

The race for representation in the state legislature boded further ill for Lincoln's compensated emancipation plan. The election produced a stalemate in the legislature. Democrats gained a one-vote advantage in the senate, but this was offset in the house where the People's party held a similar one-vote edge. As expected, New Castle County voted for People's party members. In a reversal of roles, Kent County elected a solid Democratic ticket, but the feuding Democrats of Sussex County split their votes. The breakdown in the senate revealed five Democrats versus four People's party members: three People's party members hailed from New Castle, three Democrats represented Kent, while Sussex County seated two Democrats and one People's party member. The Democratic advantage in the senate was offset in the house where the People's party, by eleven to ten members, enjoyed a majority of one. Repeating the pattern in the senate, the house members from New Castle County claimed affiliation with the People's party; Kent County members were Democratic; while Sussex County cast its vote in favor of three Democrats and by default elected four People's party members.[49] This deadlocked legislature now faced the task of debating Lincoln's compensated emancipation plan.

Before submitting the compensated emancipation bill to a formal vote, supporters tried to smooth its passage through informal canvassing and lobbying of representatives.[50] The results revealed a partisan legislature divided on both party and county lines. The Senate with its Democratic majority was expected to defeat the plan with a five-to-four vote, but the opposite occurred. Supporters of compensated emancipation successfully persuaded Wilson L. Cannon, a Kent County Democrat, to support the bill. Because the political division in the house favored the People's party by one vote, the bill was expected to clear the house and be enacted into law. Again, the unexpected won the day. For unstated reasons Robert A. Cochran, a People's party member from New Castle County, refused to support his party's stand on emancipation. Cochran's defection overturned the thin majority that had seemed so certain in the house. Rather than risk certain defeat, supporters resolved to delay formal voting on the emancipation bill until after 1861. With an eye to the 1862 election, they hoped that Delaware's political climate would change enough to allow passage of compensated emancipation. But future elections strengthened the Democrats, assuring its defeat.[51]

Lincoln's actions during early 1862 seemed to validate the Republican optimism. Apparently undeterred by Delaware's inability to entertain abolition, Lincoln on 6 March 1862 proposed compensated emancipation to the remaining border slave states and four days later met with congressmen from those states. Lincoln warned that a long-drawn-out war would certainly destroy slavery, while his plan would compensate for the loss of a property whose destruction was both inevitable and necessary for bringing an end to the war. Lincoln explained that "if the war continues long, as it must if the object be not sooner attained, the institution in your States will be extinguished by mere friction and abrasion—by the mere incidents of the war." It would be "much better for you and for your people," Lincoln advised the representatives of the border slave states, "to take the step which at once shortens the war and secures substantial compensation for that which is sure to be wholly lost in any other event!"[52] Had any of the border slave states, in particular Maryland, approved compensated emancipation, it seems likely that Delaware would have followed suit. Put simply, Delaware could not afford the burden either of being surrounded on all sides by free states or of remaining the only slave state in the Union. Because the remaining border states rejected Lincoln's compensated emancipation plan, legal slavery in Delaware survived until December 1865.

For supporters of emancipation the results of the November 1862 election proved extremely disappointing. Rather than the victory that Republicans had expected, Democrats intensified their hold on state politics, and the prospects of success for the compensated emancipation bill dwindled. With the exception of New Castle County's seats and the governor's race, Republicans experienced total defeat. The final count of the state election in 1862 revealed Democrats now in control of both houses of the state legislature, as well as Delaware's two seats in the United States Senate and one in the House of Representatives.

A successful use of racial politics by the Democrats plus Republican miscalculation had assured this Democratic victory in 1862. The Democratic platform juxtaposed two contrasting images. It accused Republicans of promoting racial equality, of supporting the elevation of blacks above whites, and perhaps most damaging, of favoring racial miscegenation. Against this image of Republicans fomenting the destruction of white society there stood the state's Democrats as protectors of the rights of the white citizens of Delaware.[53]

So effectively did racial politics work in 1862 that state Republicans felt compelled to downplay their support for the emancipation plan. But if Republicans hesitated to raise the issue of emancipation, their opponents did not shy away from reminding voters of the failed plan; it remained vital to their campaign strategy. The Democratic platform forcefully denounced state Republicans as the "Black-Republican-Abolition-Disunion party," engaged in a conspiracy to abolish slavery, to elevate blacks, while degrading whites. By comparison, the Republican campaign platform proved feeble and defensive: it condemned the South, denied that the Civil War was being fought to free slaves, declared its support of black troops in the Union army, denounced Democrats for playing racial politics, but remained conspicuously silent on compensated emancipation.[54]

Added to the usual election spectacle were two events, both instigated by the Republicans, that angered the Democrats and affected state politics long after the election. First, the national Republican government granted leave for Delaware Union troops to vote in the election; and second, Union soldiers were authorized to supervise the polling stations. Democrats rightfully questioned the special leave and delay of duty extended to Delaware troops just so they could cast their vote. Democrats did not, on principle, oppose troops participating in the electoral process; however, it seemed obvious that the special treatment of Delaware's troops, at the request of local Republicans, served the Republican cause. As a mainly volunteer force, those who freely joined Delaware's militia tended to believe in the cause of the Union and the Lincoln administration, and almost invariably they voted Republican.

Democrats found the use of Union troops to monitor the election— also at the request of Republicans—particularly galling. Not surprisingly, most of the polling stations manned by the Union troops lay in the Democratic strongholds of Kent and Sussex counties, while the bastion of the Republican party, New Castle, remained relatively untouched. Democrats bitterly complained that the action was unwarranted and that it did not protect democracy, as Republicans claimed, but instead intimidated prospective Democratic voters. The Democratic accusations held an element of truth: a subsequent investigation revealed Union troop improprieties ranging from obstruction of Democratic voters to the stuffing of ballots with fraudulent Republican votes.[55]

There were no unexpected surprises or major upsets in the 1862 race for local representatives. New Castle County voted the Republican ticket, and Kent and Sussex counties voted Democratic. The division in both houses of the state legislature now favored Democrats. The senate remained unchanged from 1860, still holding a five-to-four majority in favor of Democrats. The house, however, changed direction. Sussex County Democrats did not repeat the political infighting of 1860; hence, they voted a solid Democratic ticket. The house now had fourteen Democrats to seven Republicans; Kent and Sussex counties were aligned against New Castle County.

In the hotly contested congressional race of 1862, the margin of victory was extremely close. Only a statewide margin of thirty-seven votes separated the winning Democrat, William Temple, from the loser, Republican George P. Fisher. County and party loyalties decided this race. Temple, a Kent County native, easily carried Democratic Kent and Sussex counties but lost in Republican New Castle County. In reverse order, Republican Fisher won in New Castle but lost in Kent and Sussex counties.[56] That his support for compensated emancipation had cost him the election of 1862, Fisher had no doubt. Democrats directed the full force of their race-baiting campaign at Fisher, taunting him as a man "whose compassion for the negro slaves of Delaware . . . led him to exhibit an entire *want* of compassion for the poor white laboring population and advocated the ridiculous compensated emancipation scheme."[57] His support of such divisive issues as abolition, militia voting, and Union troop supervision of elections were effectively used against him; so were charges that he favored racial equality.

Clearly, Fisher miscalculated white Delawarean response to the compensated emancipation plan. He had expected a financially strapped slave state quickly and gladly to accept a proposal offering financial reimbursement. But Fisher underestimated the social and political importance of slavery. No matter how weak a financial institution, slavery buttressed perceptions of white and Democratic superiority. Formal removal of that edifice would shake the foundation upon which power and control in Delaware society had rested for so long. Democrats and the people of lower Delaware could not afford to make such a sacrifice.

The 1862 gubernatorial race also proved extremely close, but in this contest the victory went to the Republican candidate. William Cannon of Sussex County, a former Democrat now turned Republican, won with a statewide margin of only 111 votes. Cannon lost the election in Kent and Sussex counties but managed to overcome the Democratic challenge by carrying sufficient votes in the more populous Republican county of New Castle. However, that was not how state Democrats interpreted Cannon's victory; they claimed instead that Cannon won because of election fraud. That Cannon lost by only six votes in his home county of Sussex, a Democratic bastion, did not escape the notice or condemnation of Democrats. Democrats insinuated that the presence of armed Union troops spelled intimidation, fraud, and suppression of the Democratic vote in Kent and Sussex counties; conversely, they claimed that the absence of Union troop monitors in Republican New Castle fostered a wholesale fraud and election victory for Cannon. But for the use of Union troops, Democrats concluded, their candidate, Samuel Jefferson, would have won the race for governor.[58]

Certainly, the presence of Union troops partly accounts for the extremely close election in Sussex County, but the contest was further complicated by the background of the Democratic candidate, Samuel Jefferson of New Castle County. Sussex County voters seemed caught in a bind: should they assert county pride by voting for Cannon, a native son but a Republican, or should primary allegiance be given to the Democratic party through support for a fellow Democrat, but a "foreigner" from New Castle County? In answer, Sussex County closely split its vote, 2,421 to 2,415, between Democratic candidate Jefferson versus county native but Republican Cannon.

Kent County voters had little trouble deciding between the two gubernatorial candidates; here, neither Cannon nor Jefferson commanded county loyalty. The result was a strictly partisan vote in support of Democratic Jefferson with Cannon losing by the wide margin of 443 votes. Neither did New Castle County voters hesitate in putting Republican party interests over county loyalty; they threw their support to Republican Cannon of Sussex over Democrat Jefferson of New Castle.

By the end of the 1862 election, the only prominent political office still held by Delaware Republicans was that of governor. This at best proved a mixed blessing, for Cannon faced a hostile Democratic-controlled legislature displaying an animosity conceived out of existing political differences now exacerbated by the contentious election of

1862. The disputed election of William Cannon removed any hope for compromise on the question of emancipation. While Democrats initially used their opposition to emancipation as an effective weapon in the battle for control of state political power, now they had a second reason to oppose the measure: defiance of the "traitor" Cannon.

Cannon's relations with the Democratic-led legislature deteriorated still further with time. Charges of election fraud were leveled against him by the outgoing governor, and Democratic legislators set up a partisan committee to investigate these charges. Although Cannon was never indicted, it was not an auspicious beginning to his career as governor; neither did it help his campaign for emancipation. Ultimately, his attempts to revive Lincoln's plan met nothing but hostility from the Democrats. A governor elected through questionable means, Democrats said, had no moral authority to govern, and certainly not on such an important issue as slavery and its abolition.[59]

The irregularities of the 1862 election thus overall hurt the Republicans and advanced the Democratic cause. In turn, this Democratic control of state politics doomed any emancipation proposal, compensated or otherwise. Having seen how well the combination of a misrepresented emancipation plan and racial politics worked in the 1862 election, the Democrats would have been foolish to allow the measure to pass and thereby deprive themselves of such a winning card.

As events unfolded in the following year, 1863, Democratic belligerence toward Cannon and emancipation intensified. In May 1863 the death of Representative William Temple, a Democrat, added a new twist to the battle for control of state politics, opening up the state's single congressional seat. New elections were held in November 1863 with the choice between Republican Nathaniel Smithers and Democrat Charles Brown. Smithers and the Republicans won what on the surface looked like a lopsided victory: 7,299 votes for Smithers versus only 13 votes for Charles Brown. As was typical of Delaware politics, the story was not so simple, and the long-term loser was not the party defeated in this 1863 special election, the Democrats, but the Republicans and emancipation.

Paralleling the events of 1862, and once again over Democratic objections, the national Republican administration granted leave to Delaware soldiers who wished to vote in the special 1863 election. And as in 1862, Union troops manned the polling stations, again mainly in Democratic counties. Robert Schenck, the Union general in charge of the troops supervising the election, aggravated the situation by being overzealous in carrying out his orders. He compelled all voters suspected of disloyalty, meaning Democrats, to swear an oath of allegiance to the Union before being allowed to vote.

In protest against this blatant attempt to skew the election in favor of the Republicans, state Democrats decided to boycott the election. They miscalculated completely. Apparently, they had theorized that an election boycott would prompt a congressional investigation and ultimately a voiding of the results, but much to their dismay, the Republican-controlled Congress chose to honor the election of a fellow Republican. The outcome of this special election, however, boded ill not only for state Republicans, as Democrats sought to undo the damage of their ill-advised boycott, but in all issues relating to the Republican administration and, in particular, emancipation.[60]

Governor Cannon fared no better in 1864 in his attempt in August to authorize black enlistment in the Union army. This move provoked Democratic anger and became a hot campaign issue that year. Cannon proposed the enlistment of blacks as a way of meeting Delaware's quota of troops. Predictably, Democrats opposed the suggestion. Claiming the request was "unworthy of their consideration and unfit to remain on the files of either House," Democrats in a truly partisan vote chose to return the governor's message to him. Democrats opened their attack by accusing Cannon of secretly abducting "from their lawful owners negro slaves" for the harmful "purpose of arming them for the destruction of their masters." The governor's proposition, they warned, would "incite" blacks to "insurrection and murder" and breed a war between "civilized peoples" and "those as unfit for such service as the most savage tribes." To arm blacks, Democrats continued,

> would be in contravention of the settled policy of the State from its first organization to the present time. The African race has ever been considered by us as an inferior and subject race. While our laws have extended to them all the privileges to which the most prudent and humane could possibly consider them entitled in consideration of their condition and qualification for the enjoyment of political rights and privileges, and has afforded them the fullest protection in all their legal and just rights, vindicating those rights when infracted, and redressing all their wrongs where such have been inflicted, the enjoyment of certain privileges has wisely been denied. Public policy demanded, and legislative wisdom has uniformly declared that they should not be allowed the use of fire-arms and ammunition. The sentiment of the people of the State has uniformly approved this policy, and this General Assembly see no propriety in a departure from it at the present time.[61]

Contrary to Democratic assertions, Cannon did not propose arming slaves to fight against Delaware slaveholders, nor did he intend to deprive owners of their lawful property. In fact, slave enlistments from the state began almost a year before the governor's formal call for black troops. On 26 October 1863 the War Department applied the provisions of General Order 329 to Delaware, thus subjecting what it estimated on the basis of the census of 1860 to be 289 slave men between the ages of eighteen and forty-five to enlistment. The actual number of eligible slave men was no doubt much lower, for the government's estimate failed to take into account the decline in the slave population between 1860 to October 1863 caused by both voluntary manumission and slave escapes during the war. Cannon's proposal aimed at filling the quota gap by recruiting from among free blacks, 19,829 strong in 1860, of whom 3,597 were eligible for military duty. Ultimately, 954 Delaware black men, both free and slave, served in the Union army.[62]

Democratic Delaware expressed a similar anger over the enlistment of free blacks into the Union army. The prospect of these supposedly inferior recruits enlisting in the national army rankled Democrats. But they also feared that the enlistment of free blacks would threaten their chances in the upcoming 1864 election. Democrat Thomas F. Bayard warned white Delaware men to "consider that the negro substitutes they may furnish" may very well turn out to "be their guards at the polls—and their jailers in Bastilles!"[63] Should black troops monitor the election of 1864 in Democratic strongholds, it could upset state politics against the Democrats.

In truth, Democratic objection to black enlistment was only partially race-related, for sympathy for the Confederacy remained equally significant to its opposition. In sentiment many Democrats supported the Confederacy, so that they were not inclined to approve policies that would strengthen Republicans or the Union war effort. State Democrats repeatedly impeded the Union cause. The rejection in 1863 of Cannon's request for $25,000 to support the families of Delaware troops reflected partisan Democratic politics; politics, not the cost of the support, defined Democratic opposition. In February 1864, only a few months later, the same Democratic-led legislature allocated $500,000 as a general relief fund for white male citizens wanting to evade the Union draft. By federal law such persons had to pay a commutation fee of $300; Democrats planned to contribute $200 of the fine for each white citizen holdout.[64]

The 1864 presidential election further polarized a divided Delaware. As in 1862 and 1863, Union troops supervised the election, and again Delaware soldiers came home to vote. While these actions continued to inflame the passions of Democrats, the resulting backlash against the Republican-backed orders increased Democratic prospects for election victory and power in the state. If the presidential race was any indication of the fate of abolition, then Delaware was far removed from that goal. With support from the Democrats of Kent and Sussex counties, Delaware became one of the three states carried by Democratic candidate George B. McClellan. From Quaker Anna Ferris came the caustic comment that "it was too much to hope that our benighted lower counties should be so suddenly enlightened." She accurately predicted that the state would remain "chained to Slavery & Democracy for a new term."[65]

Democrats learned a valuable lesson from the boycott of 1863 and thus made no attempt to abstain from the 1864 election. Rather, they avenged their earlier defeat by electing John A. Nicholson over Republican Smithers. In the race for state representatives, Democrats maintained their majorities in both houses with a six-to-three advantage in the senate and a fourteen-to-seven count in the house. In both houses the breakdown followed a strict county division of Democratic Kent and Sussex counties versus Republican New Castle County.[66]

By the end of 1864, Delaware Democrats held majorities in both legislative houses and claimed the loyalties of both United States senators and the single congressional representative. The only high office still held by state Republicans was the governorship. It was to this Democratic-controlled state and legislature that the thirteenth amendment to the United States Constitution was submitted for ratification. The lines of battle quickly fell along the old and unbending intrastate line of demarcation: Republicans and New Castle County supported the amendment, while Democratic Kent and Sussex counties opposed the measure.

After the election of 1864, Democratic dominance proved too much for supporters of the thirteenth amendment. One of the leading supporters, Smithers, lost his seat in the 1864 election; he was serving the closing days of his term when the measure was proposed. Clearly, the outgoing Smithers could not offer the political clout needed for ratification, but judging from his reaction, he seemed unaware of this difficulty. Smithers predicted that Delaware would overwhelmingly support the amendment; even among Democrats, he said, could be found "hundreds, perhaps thousands, who will hail with joy the accomplishment of this great measure of justice, tranquility, and security."[67] Smithers, like Fisher before him, grossly underestimated the Democratic and southern Delaware opposition.

Anna Ferris, usually an astute observer of national and state politics, also completely misjudged Delaware's response on this issue. She felt "less excited" about the national abolition of slavery, for she expected her state to join in the peaceful and routine ratification of the thirteenth amendment.

> Congress has passed by the required majority the amendment to the
> Constitution abolishing Slavery! We all feel thankful, but as the success
> of the measure was certain in the next Congress, if it had not passed in
> this, we are less excited about it than we ought to be—Only Father is
> sufficiently enthusiastic & tells us all, over & over, that it is the greatest
> day we ever saw—I am glad he has lived to feel that he sees the salva-
> tion of his country, & that we all begin to feel that "our eyes have seen
> the coming of the glory of the Lord & to hope that the horrors of the
> war may at last end in the glory of liberty & the blessings of peace."[68]

Her assumption that Delaware would affirm the "glory of liberty" for its
blacks remained a dream until 1901.

With the defeat of Smithers, the only remaining high-ranking Republican who could possibly influence the outcome of the ratification battle
was Governor Cannon. Turning his attention to the amendment, Cannon in his 1865 annual message asked that the state join hands with a
Union "not drifting but marching steadily to Freedom." The state no
longer had a choice, he said; its economic and geographical ties with
the free North, plus the recent abolition of slavery by Maryland and
Missouri, demanded that Delaware follow suit. Of particular concern to
Cannon was the effect of a free Maryland on the still slave state of Delaware. With legal freedom in Maryland, tiny Delaware was completely

> surrounded by free territory inviting on all sides the escape of our
> slaves. Precarious as property in persons of will and free-agency always
> is, that species of property is now rendered doubly insecure. There is
> no law of the land requiring the rendition of fugitives from labor. Once
> escaped to the neighboring border of free territory, the slave is subject
> to no claim of his former master. In addition to this there is now nei-
> ther market nor demand for this species of property. A citizen of Dela-
> ware cannot lawfully either import or export a slave. He who holds a
> slave within the State cannot sell here, because he who does not hold a
> slave does not wish to buy . . . slavery in Delaware does not exist as a
> source of profit; . . . we have all its disadvantages without its advan-
> tages.[69]

But like Smithers, Cannon could not help the Republicans; he died on
1 March 1865, barely two months after delivering his annual message.

The appointment and subsequent election of Democrat Gove Saulsbury to the executive office sealed the fate of the thirteenth amendment. By March 1865 all branches of Delaware's government plus the
state's senators and representative to the United States Congress were
firmly controlled by Democrats, the very party that vehemently opposed

all forms of legislated emancipation. With complete control over state politics, 1865 was not the time for Democrats to change course. Because racial politics had proved very effective, Democrats had no reason to support an amendment guaranteed to end legal slavery and in so doing blunt if not demolish their most potent political weapon.

But that was not how Delaware Democrats phrased their objections. The *Delawarean,* for example, speculated that the amendment would harm all citizens, black and white alike. For blacks, it offered a lower quality of life, the paper said, a withholding of "the provident care of indulgent masters," plus deprivation of "many of the comforts they have heretofore enjoyed." The impact on white Delawareans would be equally destructive, promised the paper, a complete sacrifice of privileges held dear.

> The adoption of this amendment is the accomplishment of one of the steps in the abolition programme. They aim at the equalization of the white and black races. They are now throwing off the mask and avowing openly, in Congress, that the negro must be equal with the white man in all political rights, and the abolition party are marshalling under the motto, "Equality before the law"—which means the law shall make no distinction between whites and blacks. . . . For ourselves, and our party, we protest against the whole policy of the negroists, and shall labor to maintain the supremacy of our own race, and shall submit to equality only when resistance shall be in vain.[70]

Democrats opposed the amendment, said Senator Willard Saulsbury because the white citizens of Delaware were a "staid" and "conservative" people who only wished "to preserve the form and system of government which their [forefathers] established."[71] To maintain the Democratic control of his state's politics, Saulsbury proposed an alternate plan to the United States Senate, one mandating the restoration of slavery throughout the nation, coupled with a ban on congressional-sponsored emancipation.

Contrary to his earlier stand on Lincoln's compensated emancipation plan, Saulsbury now endorsed federal funding of compensation and colonization, but only if the request originated from slaveholders. Under his plan, slaveholders would have the right to travel freely with their slaves throughout the nation without suffering interference from either the federal or state governments. Saulsbury's plan would continue the ban on the external slave trade but completely deny citizenship to all descendants of Africa. Finally, no issue affecting slavery could be altered by the national government without the consent of all the remaining slave states. Saulsbury's proposal was soundly defeated by the United States Senate, with only one other senator supporting his bill.[72]

Like Senator Saulsbury, Governor Gove Saulsbury opposed the thirteenth amendment. His opposition was not based on the economic impact of emancipation, for he freely acknowledged that even with universal emancipation "no very serious disadvantage can result either to the agricultural labor" of the state or "to the slaves themselves, who can readily find employment in the occupations to which they are accustomed." The political ramifications of universal emancipation, however, greatly concerned the governor and the other Delaware Democrats. Republicans, he predicted, would next "demand for the negro the right of suffrage, and seek to place him, politically at least, upon an equal with the white man." But extension of the franchise to free blacks would, without doubt, seriously challenge Democratic control of Delaware politics; this Saulsbury sought to avoid at all costs. Concluding his assessment of the thirteenth amendment, Saulsbury claimed to

> have no hesitation in saying that I believe its [the black race's] true position is that of a subordinate race, and as in legislation in this respect, classes, and not individuals, are to be regarded, it is my calm, deliberate and settled conviction that the members of that race should continue to be excluded from a participation with our own race in political rights and privileges. . . . I advise, therefore, that there should be no relaxation in legislative action in this respect in this State. Ours is a government of white men, for the benefit of white men, and while we should ever act generously and kindly toward this, and all inferior and dependent races, duty to ourselves and our posterity, as well as proper regard for them, forbids that we should admit them to a participation of equal political rights. In this country, at least, white men should be considered as constituting the governing class, the negro race as a class to be governed. . . . I claim for my own race the right to govern, and I recommend to you, in whom is vested the legislative power of the State, to see to it that this right shall be fully asserted, guarded and maintained.[73]

Democratic-controlled Delaware guarded and maintained this right and privilege until the twentieth century.

Delaware's final word on ratification of the thirteenth amendment came from the state senate. Before the formal vote the senate appointed a three-member bipartisan committee, one from each county, to recommend an appropriate response. But even this committee of only three members failed to reach a consensus: two separate reports were submitted, one from Senator John P. Belville of New Castle County in favor of ratification and another opposing the thirteenth amendment from senators John H. Bewley and James Ponder of Kent and Sussex counties.

The majority report denounced the amendment as "violative of the reserved rights of the several States" and claimed that the measure would certainly "form an insuperable barrier to the restoration of the seceded States to the Federal Union." On 8 February 1865, by a partisan vote of six to two, with the two dissenting votes coming from New Castle County senators, the Delaware senate accepted this majority report, thus rejecting ratification of the thirteenth amendment to the United States Constitution.[74]

# Epilogue

IN FEBRUARY 1901 the Delaware legislature unanimously ratified "certain amendments to the Constitution of the United States."[1] Conspicuously missing from the minutes of the session was any direct identification of these amendments by the legislature. Only by delving into Delaware's history does it become apparent that what the legislature so casually alluded to as "certain amendments" was actually a reference to the ratification of the three Civil War amendments, the Thirteenth, Fourteenth, and Fifteenth. It was a most surprising ending to Delaware's century-long fierce opposition to legislated abolition. After decades of contesting the legality of slavery, the Delaware legislature ended the debate not with a bang, as one might expect, but with a whimper. Quietly and in a move that was uncharacteristic of the Delaware slavery stalemate, northern, southern, Republican, and Democratic Delaware joined hands to ratify unanimously what the legislature euphemistically described as those "certain amendments to the Constitution of the United States."

Three-quarters of a century before the Civil War, Delaware earned the nickname the "First State" for being the first among the thirteen states to ratify the new national Constitution. In 1865 Delaware acquired another "first," a dubious one this time, for it became the first nonseceded state to reject ratification of the amendment offering freedom to people of color. And ironically, because of Delaware's own intransigent behavior, the "First State" to enter a union of states, a union based on liberty, freedom, and the natural rights of mankind, also became the last of the nonseceded states to ratify universal emancipation for its black population.

Not until February 1901 did Delaware redeem its honor by ratifying the amendments that offered freedom and citizenship to all blacks and promised the franchise to qualified black males. Delaware's belated ratification of these amendments ensued not from a moral stance but out of political considerations. After decades of political struggle, Delaware Republicans finally gained complete control of state government by the beginning of the twentieth century. However, because Republican control of state politics was in its infancy, only by using the black vote could the Republican party maintain its tenuous hold on state politics. It was within this context that the Republicans proposed the ratification of the Civil War amendments.

The different political climate prevailing in Delaware at the turn of the century assured ratification of the amendments. First, the 1900 election brought the Republicans, the party that had chosen out of political expediency to extend the franchise to black males, into power in both its traditional base of New Castle County but also in Kent and Sussex counties. Granting franchise rights to blacks would secure this new power base for the Republicans. Second, the party that successfully fought to run Delaware as a "government of white men for the benefit of white men," the Democrats, no longer had the political clout to delay or defeat ratification of the Civil War amendments.

The exclusion of Delaware blacks from the electorate dated back to the beginning of Delaware as a state. The state's first constitution, passed in 1776, restricted the franchise to white males. The ban on black voting remained in force from the Revolutionary era through the end of the Civil War to the delight of Delaware Democrats. But Democratic hopes of permanently excluding blacks from the franchise received a rude shock in 1870. The national ratification of the fifteenth amendment in that year, again over Democratic Delaware's objections, seriously jeopardized the Democrats' political interests, for it threatened to place the vote in the hands of qualified black males. Had the state of Delaware fully complied with the provisions of the Fifteenth Amendment, a possible 4,500 black men could have been added to the voting rolls.[2] Because elections in Delaware were often decided by very slim margins, the prospect of over 4,000 black males voting pleased the party that expected to receive the black vote, the Republicans, and terrified their political opponents, the Democrats.

Alarmed by the turn of events, Delaware Democrats devised various ingenious and often illegal means to disqualify prospective black male voters. Democrats used their control of state politics to defeat the intent of the Fifteenth Amendment. They appointed tax collectors who were Democratic in sentiment; these Democratic tax collectors effectively removed blacks from the voting rolls by refusing to collect taxes from prospective black voters, by claiming that resident black voters had moved out of state, and by declaring many living black male voters to be dead. So pervasive did these practices become that in March 1872 Republicans with the help of the United States attorney general investigated and filed charges under the 1870 enforcement act against several corrupt Democratic tax collectors.[3]

Although only one tax collector was convicted, the negative publicity associated with the case may have tempered the actions of enthusiastic Democratic tax collectors long enough to allow the Republicans in 1872 to elect their first representative to Congress since the Civil War. However, this Republican win also revealed the effects of renewed divisions within Democratic ranks, and the use of federal troops to monitor Delaware elections in that year may have also curbed voter fraud.[4] Aside from the Republican victory in the congressional race, control of state politics firmly remained in the Democratic camp.

Faced with the Republican determination to challenge the tactics employed by the Democratic tax collectors, Democratic leaders soon devised other less obvious but equally effective means to disfranchise black voters. The most potent was the introduction of the poll tax as a qualifier in state elections. The Democratic-sponsored 1873 assessment and collection laws made citizens responsible for not only paying their own taxes but ensuring that their names were properly recorded on the tax rolls. Names of delinquent taxpayers would be removed and kept off the voting lists for approximately two years.[5] Although the law applied to all voters, it affected black voters the most, for their poverty and the corrupt practices of Democratic tax collectors disfranchised many of them. Indeed, the poll tax effectively kept blacks out of Delaware politics until near the end of the nineteenth century.

Republican fortunes began to change during the 1880s when millionaire John Edward Charles O'Sullivan Addicks decided to run for political office. As a newcomer, Addicks had no loyal political following, but he wanted to become a senator and was blessed with the money to influence politics. Addicks used the same poll tax tactic that the Democrats had so effectively employed, but turned inside out. Unlike Democrats, he sought not to keep the black vote away but to deliver it at election time. To this end Addicks paid the appropriate poll taxes for black voters, ensured that the payment was properly recorded by the tax collectors, and in many instances bribed blacks (up to $50 per voter) to vote, for the Republicans of course.[6] Addicks played this political money game throughout the state. Ultimately, he enhanced the Republican strength in New Castle County, created Republican footholds in Kent and Sussex counties, and prepared the political landscape for a future Republican majority.

Addicks never realized his dream of a Senate seat, but he very successfully beat the Democrats at their own political game. Partly because of Addicks's money—he spent over $3 million—but also because of political infighting among the Democrats, the Republicans in 1888 won a majority in the state legislature, the first time since the Civil War. However, the party failed to capitalize on this victory, as it also divided into those Republicans for Addicks and those against him. The division within Republican ranks allowed the Democrats to return a majority in 1896. The following year when the state convention met to consider a new constitution, the Democratic-controlled convention—reacting most certainly to Addicks's successful manipulation of the poll tax guidelines—chose to abandon the use of the poll tax in state elections, replacing it with residency and literacy requirements.[7] Although a potent political weapon, using literacy, at the turn of the century, to disqualify black male voters proved less effective than the poll tax.

In spite of Democratic scheming, the Republicans bridged their differences in time to win the election of 1900. This election marked the beginning of a Republican ascendancy in Delaware politics, with the party now claiming the governorship as well as majorities in both houses of the legislature. It was to bolster this new and tenuous power base, and to prevent a future Democratic victory, that the Republican-controlled legislature courted the black vote by ratifying the Thirteenth, Fourteenth, and Fifteenth amendments. The leading sponsor of the bill for ratifying these Civil War amendments, James Frank Allee, had served as the chief lieutenant of Addicks, who had campaigned for but also purchased the black vote for the Delaware Republicans.[8] The Quaker and abolitionist background of the new governor of Delaware, Republican John Hunn, may have also helped to pave the way for ratification.

Unlike the earlier ratification battles, the proposal in 1901 aroused little legislative debate or rancor. Indeed, the legislature seemed so uncomfortable with, or perhaps embarrassed by, its past actions that it kept the proceedings very short, only briefly mentioning the unanimous approval of "certain amendments to the Constitution of the United States." Understandably, Republicans favored ratification, for it provided the means to political power. Democrats who had for so long upheld the belief in maintaining "a government of white men for the benefit of white men" no longer had the majority to prevent ratification. Perhaps,

sensing a fait accompli, the minority Democrats chose to acquiesce quietly in the ratification of the Civil War amendments. Thus, in February
1901 the senate and house of the "First State," with the concurrence
of the governor, ratified those unnamed "certain amendments to the
Constitution of the United States."

# Notes

DSA    Delaware State Archives, Dover

HSD    Historical Society of Delaware, Wilmington

HSP    Historical Society of Pennsylvania, Philadelphia

LPPN   Legislative Papers, Petitions, Negroes and Slavery, DSA

MDCM   Minutes of Duck Creek Monthly Meeting of Friends, HSP

NYCD   *Documents Relative to the Colonial History of the State of New York*,
       15 vols. (Albany, 1856–87)

PAS    Pennsylvania Abolition Society

SMIP   Slavery Material, Indentures, Petitions for Freedom, 1701–
       99, box 5, DSA

| | |
|---|---|
| *Apprentices and Indentures* | Apprentices, Indentures, Kent County Court of Quarter Sessions Owners' Petitions to Sell Slaves or Indentured Servants, DSA |
| *Manumissions* | Kent County Recorder of Deeds, Manumissions, 1780–1865, DSA |

INTRODUCTION

1. John A. Munroe, "The Negro in Delaware," *South Atlantic Quarterly* 56 (1957): 428–44.

2. Gov. Gove Saulsbury to the Joint Session of the Delaware Legislature, *Journal of the Senate of the State of Delaware*, 13 June 1865.

3. C. Vann Woodward, *The Strange Career of Jim Crow*, 3d rev. ed. (New York, 1974); J. Morgan Kousser, *The Shaping of Southern Politics: Suffrage Restriction and the Establishment of the One Party System, 1880–1910* (New Haven, 1974).

4. Winthrop D. Jordan, *White over Black: American Attitudes toward the Negro, 1550–1812* (Chapel Hill, N. C., 1968), p. 324; Max Farrand, ed., *The Records of the Federal Convention of 1787*, 3d ed., 4 vols. (New Haven, 1966), 2: 9–10.

5. William K. Scarborough, ed., *The Diary of Edmund Ruffin*, 3 vols. (Baton Rouge, La., 1972), 1: 630.

6. *Senate Journal*, 8 Feb. 1865.

7. Scarborough, *Diary of Edmund Ruffin*, 3:747, 787–88. Delaware was the first of the nonseceding states to reject the thirteenth amendment

but not the only state; New Jersey and Kentucky also opposed the amendment.

## 1. THE DUTCH, SWEDES, ENGLISH, AND SLAVERY

1. C. T. Odhner, "The Founding of New Sweden, 1637–1642," *Pennsylvania Magazine of History and Biography* 3 (1879): 277; J. Thomas Scharf, *History of Delaware*, 2 vols. (Philadelphia, 1888), 1:38 n.1.

2. C. A. Weslager, *Dutch Explorers, Traders, and Settlers in Delaware Valley, 1609–1664* (Philadelphia, 1961), pp. 25–42.

3. Ibid., pp. 25–42; NYCD 1:39, 65.

4. NYCD 1:39; Oliver A. Rink, "Company Management or Private Trade: The Two Patroonship Plans for New Netherland," *New York History* 59 (1978): 5–26.

5. Thomas J. Condon, *New York Beginnings: The Commercial Origins of New Netherland* (New York, 1968), pp. 145–51; John B. Linn and William H. Egle, eds., *Pennsylvania Archives*, 2d ser. (Harrisburg, Pa., 1890), 5:86; Rink, "Company Management or Private Trade."

6. C. A. Weslager, *The Swedes and Dutch at New Castle* (Wilmington, Del., 1987), pp. 22–24; Rink, "Company Management or Private Trade."

7. Carol Hoffecker, *Delaware, a Bicentennial History* (New York, 1977), pp. 12–13.

8. Amandus Johnson, *The Swedish Settlements on the Delaware*, 2 vols. (New York, 1911), 1:195, 2:710; Joseph J. Mickley, "Some Account of William Usselinx and Peter Minuit, Two Individuals Who Were Instrumental in Establishing the First Permanent Colony in Delaware," *Papers of the Historical Society of Delaware* 3 (1881): 22–26; Weslager, *Dutch Explorers*, pp. 135–36, 159–83.

9. Weslager, *Dutch Explorers*, pp. 129–83.

10. *Pennsylvania Archives*, 2d ser., 5:56–57; Weslager, *Dutch Explorers*, pp. 129–58.

11. *Pennsylvania Archives*, 2d ser., 16:234; Samuel Hazard, *Annals of Pennsylvania from the Discovery of the Delaware, 1609–1682* (New York, 1970) p. 49; Weslager, *Dutch Explorers*, pp. 58–60.

12. NYCD 1:146; Condon, *New York Beginnings*, p. 77.

13. Condon, *New York Beginnings*, pp. 105–8; P. C. Emmer, "The Dutch and the Making of the Second Atlantic System," in *Slavery and the Rise of the Atlantic System*, ed. Barbara L. Solow (Cambridge, Mass., 1991), pp. 75–96.

14. *Pennsylvania Archives*, 2d ser., 5:88, 95.

15. John A. Munroe, *Colonial Delaware: A History* (New York, 1978), pp. 42–57.

16. Weslager, *Swedes and Dutch at New Castle*, pp. 157–62.

17. *Pennsylvania Archives*, 2d ser., 5:496–98; John A. Munroe, *History of Delaware* (Newark, Del., 1993), p. 28.

18. Joyce D. Goodfriend, "Burghers and Blacks: The Evolution of a Slave Society at New Amsterdam," *New York History* 59 (1978): 125–44.

19. Philip D. Curtin, *The Atlantic Slave Trade: A Census* (Madison, Wis., 1969), pp. 84–85; Condon, *New York Beginnings*, pp. 62–64; Goodfriend, "Burghers and Blacks"; Johannes Postma, "The Dispersal of African Slaves in the West by Dutch Slave Traders, 1630–1803," in *The Atlantic Slave Trade: Effects on Economies, Societies, and Peoples in Africa, the Americas, and Europe*, ed. Joseph E. Inikori and Stanley Engerman (Durham, N.C., 1992).

20. Goodfriend, "Burghers and Blacks"; Curtin, *Atlantic Slave Trade*, p. 84.

21. Goodfriend, "Burghers and Blacks."

22. Ibid.; *Pennsylvania Archives*, 2d ser., 5:95.

23. E. B. O'Callaghan, ed., *Voyage of the Slavers St. John and Arms of Amsterdam, 1659, 1663* (Albany, 1867), pp. 183–84, 193–94; Goodfriend, "Burghers and Blacks."

24. Hazard, *Annals of Pennsylvania*, p. 331; NYCD 12:364.

25. NYCD 2:213–14.

26. Ibid., p. 214.

27. O'Callaghan, *Voyage of the Slavers*, pp. 198–201, 222.

28. Munroe, *Colonial Delaware*, pp. 72–78.

29. Ibid., pp. 59–78, 90.

30. Hazard, *Annals of Pennsylvania*, p. 374.

31. Ibid., pp. 407–9; Munroe, *Colonial Delaware*, pp. 69–71.

32. *Pennsylvania Archives*, 2d ser., 5:671; Hazard, *Annals of Pennsylvania*, pp. 414–16; Munroe, *Colonial Delaware*, pp. 71–78.

33. Richard S. Dunn and Mary Maples Dunn, eds., *The Papers of William Penn*, 5 vols. (Philadelphia, 1981–86), 2:323–24, 343.

34. Ronald Bailey, "The Slave(ry) Trade and the Development of Capitalism in the United States: The Textile Industry in New England," in Inikori and Engerman, *Atlantic Slave Trade*, pp. 205–46; Richard Nelson Bean, "The British Trans-Atlantic Slave Trade, 1650–1775" (Ph.D diss., Univ. of Washington, 1975), pp. 40–42; Curtin, *Atlantic Slave Trade*, pp. 127–62.

35. Darold D. Wax, "Black Immigrants: The Slave Trade in Colonial Maryland," *Maryland Historical Magazine* 73 (1978): 30–43; James A. Rawley, *The Transatlantic Slave Trade: A History* (New York, 1981), pp. 149–56; Hazard, *Annals of Pennsylvania*, pp. 455–56.

36. C. H. B. Turner, *Some Records of Sussex County, Delaware* (Philadelphia, 1909), pp. 75–76; Darold D. Wax, "Negro Imports into Pennsylvania, 1720–1766," *Pennsylvania History* 32 (1965): 258.

37. Munroe, *History of Delaware*, pp. 53–57; Munroe, *Colonial Delaware*, pp. 149–67; *Pennsylvania Archives*, 2d ser., 2:676.

38. Munroe, *Colonial Delaware*, pp. 137–67; Munroe, *History of Delaware*, pp. 53–57.

39. U.S. Bureau of the Census, *Historical Statistics of the United States, Colonial Times to 1970* (Washington, D.C., 1975), 2:1168.

40. Weslager, *Swedes and Dutch at New Castle*, pp. 183–85; Charles T. Gehring, trans. and ed., *Delaware Papers (Dutch Period): A Collection of Documents Pertaining to the Regulation of Affairs on the South River of New Netherland, 1648–1664* (Baltimore, 1981), p. 243.

41. Weslager, *Dutch Explorers*, p. 243.

42. NYCD 3:345; Weslager, *Dutch Explorers*, p. 244.

43. NYCD 2:213–14; O'Callaghan, *Voyage of the Slavers*, pp. 198–201.

44. *Pennsylvania Archives*, 2d ser., 5:602; Hazard, *Annals of Pennsylvania*, p. 372.

45. *Pennsylvania Archives*, 2d ser., 5:578; Hazard, *Annals of Pennsylvania*, p. 366; Weslager, *Dutch Explorers*, p. 238.

46. Munroe, *Colonial Delaware*, pp. 62–63; Weslager, *Dutch Explorers*, p. 244.

47. Weslager, *Dutch Explorers*, pp. 174–75; Christopher Ward, *Dutch and Swedes on the Delaware, 1609–1664* (Philadelphia, 1930), pp. 92–116, 270–72.

48. Percy W. Bidwell and John I. Falconer, *History of Agriculture in the Northern United States, 1620–1860* (New York, 1941), p. 15; Munroe, *Colonial Delaware*, p. 24.

49. Wayne D. Rasmussen, ed. *Agriculture in the United States: A Documentary History* (New York, 1975), pp. 119–20.

50. Gehring, *New York Historical Manuscripts: Dutch*, p. 75; Munroe, *Colonial Delaware*, pp. 44–45.

51. Weslager, *Dutch Explorers*, p. 242.

52. Paul G. E. Clemens, *The Atlantic Economy and Colonial Maryland's Eastern Shore: From Tobacco to Grain* (Ithaca, N.Y., 1980), pp. 20–35; Lewis C. Gray, *History of Agriculture in the Southern United States*, 2 vols. (Gloucester, Mass., 1958), 2:615–17; Munroe, *Colonial Delaware*, p. 94.

53. Barbara J. Fields, *Slavery and Freedom on the Middle Ground: Maryland during the Nineteenth Century* (New Haven, 1985), pp. 4–6; Allan Kulikoff, *Tobacco and Slaves: The Development of Southern Cultures in the Chesapeake, 1680–1800* (Chapel Hill, N.C., 1986), pp. 99–104, 118–57.

54. Hazard, *Annals of Pennsylvania*, p. 468; Leon De Valinger, Jr., ed., *Court Records of Kent County, Delaware, 1680–1705* (Millwood, N.Y., 1959), pp. 6, 16, 71.

55. Avery O. Craven, *Soil Exhaustion as a Factor in the Agricultural History of Virginia and Maryland, 1606–1860* (Urbana, Ill., 1926), pp. 11–71; Kulikoff, *Tobacco and Slaves*, pp. 78–117; Gloria Main, *Tobacco Colony: Life in Early Maryland, 1650–1720* (Princeton, N.J., 1982), pp. 9–139; Russell R. Menard, "The Tobacco Industry in the Chesapeake Colonies, 1617–1730: An Interpretation" *Research in Economic History* 5 (1980): 109–28.

56. Main, *Tobacco Colony*, pp. 31–37; J. Thomas Scharf, *History of Maryland: From the Earliest Period to the Present Day*, 3 vols. (Hatboro, 1967), 2:46–47.

57. Quoted in Craven, *Soil Exhaustion in Virginia and Maryland,* p. 31.

58. Clemens, *Atlantic Economy,* pp. 51–57; David W. Galenson, *White Servitude in Colonial America: An Economic Analysis* (Cambridge, 1981); Kulikoff, *Tobacco and Slaves,* pp. 37–43; Main, *Tobacco Colony,* pp. 24–27, 100–103; Menard, "Tobacco Industry in the Chesapeake Colonies," pp. 121–22, Russell R. Menard, "From Servants to Slaves: The Transformation of the Chesapeake Labor System," *Southern Studies* 16 (1977): 355–90.

59. Whittington B. Johnson, "The Origin and Nature of African Slavery in Seventeenth Century Maryland," *Maryland Historical Magazine* 73 (1978): 242; Munroe, *Colonial Delaware,* pp. 185–86.

60. Kulikoff, *Tobacco and Slaves,* pp. 317–34; U.S. Bureau of the Census, Manuscript Returns for Delaware, 1810, 1860.

61. Gary B. Nash, "Slaves and Slaveowners in Colonial Philadelphia," *William and Mary Quarterly* 30 (1973): 226–52; Nash, "Forging Freedom: The Emancipation Experience in the Northern Seaport Cities 1775–1820," in *Slavery and Freedom in the Age of the American Revolution,* ed. Ira Berlin and Ronald Hoffman (Charlottesville, Va., 1983), pp. 3–6; Richard C. Wade, *Slavery in the Cities: The South, 1820–1860* (New York, 1964), p. 3; U.S. Bureau of the Census, Manuscript Returns for Delaware, 1800–1860; Hoffecker, *Delaware,* pp. 112–13; John A. Munroe, *Federalist Delaware, 1775–1815* (New Brunswick, N.J., 1954), p. 148.

62. U.S. Bureau of the Census, Manuscript Returns for Delaware, 1800, 1840.

63. A. Leon Higginbotham, Jr., *In the Matter of Color: Race and the American Legal Process, the Colonial Period* (New York, 1978), pp. 80–81, 148–50, 305–10; Jordan, *White over Black,* pp. 102–10.

64. Higginbotham, *In the Matter of Color,* pp. 100–114; William R. Riddell, "The Slave in Early New York," *Journal of Negro History* 13 (1928): 53–86.

65. Higginbotham, *In the Matter of Color,* pp. 270–71.

66. Quoted in ibid., p. 271.

67. Ibid., pp. 280–82.

68. "An Act for the Trial of Negroes" (1726), *Laws of the State of Delaware, 1700–1792* (New Castle, Del., 1797), 1:102–4.

69. Ibid., pp. 105–9.

### 2. THE MAKING OF VOLUNTARY EMANCIPATION, 1740–1865

1. *Laws of the State of Delaware* 1:210–16.

2. Ibid., 1:435–37, passed Oct. 1767.

3. Ibid., 2:884–88, passed Feb. 1787.

4. Ibid., pp. 941–44, passed Feb. 1789.

5. Ibid., pp. 1093–95, passed June 1793.

6. Ibid., pp. 1321–25, passed Jan. 1797.

7. Hugh Barbour and J. William Frost, *The Quakers* (New York, 1988),

pp. 119–36; Jean R. Soderlund, *Quakers and Slavery: A Divided Spirit* (Princeton, N.J., 1985), pp. 15–31.

8. J. William Frost, *Quaker Origins of Antislavery* (Norwood, Pa., 1980), pp. 66–67.

9. Barbour and Frost, *Quakers*, pp. 120–21.

10. Jack D. Marietta, *The Reformation of American Quakerism, 1748–1783* (Philadelphia, 1984), pp. 111–21.

11. Ibid.; Soderlund, *Quakers and Slavery*, pp. 87–111.

12. Frost, *Quaker Origins of Antislavery*, pp. 182–86.

13. Soderlund, *Quakers and Slavery*, pp. 87–111.

14. Warner Mifflin, *The Defense of Warner Mifflin against Aspersions Cast on Him on Account of His Endeavours to Promote Righteousness, Mercy, and Peace, among Mankind* (Philadelphia, 1796), HSP; Hilda Justice, *Life and Ancestry of Warner Mifflin, Friend, Philanthropist, Patriot* (Philadelphia, 1905).

15. MDCM, vol. 1, 24 Aug. 1771, 28 March 1772, vol. 2, 24 Nov., Dec. 1781.

16. Ibid., vol. 1, 22 July 1775, 22 Sept. 1781.

17. Ibid., 24 July 1779.

18. DCMS, deeds by John Dickinson, July 1779, Mary Turley, March 1792, Elizabeth Molleston, Feb. 1781.

19. MDCM, vol. 1, Oct. 1776.

20. Ibid., 28 Jan., 26 Oct. 1775, 22 June 1776, 24 July 1779.

21. Ibid., Oct. 1776, 23 Aug. 1777, 24 April 1779.

22. Ibid., 25 April 1778, DCMS, deed by Charles and Elizabeth Hilliard, April 1778.

23. DCMS, deed by Henry and Margaret Newell, 18 Jan. 1779; MDCM, 23 Jan., 24 April 1779.

24. DCMS, deeds by Thomas and Elizabeth Bowman, 27 May 1777, 16 Dec. 1779, Jonathan Neal, 22 Jan. 1777.

25. Frost, *Quaker Origins of Antislavery*, pp. 182–83.

26. DCMS, deeds by John Flynn, Jan. 1781, Warner Mifflin, 22 Oct. 1774.

27. Ibid., deeds by the Manlove family, 17 Dec. 1779, Catherine Ennals, May 1779.

28. Ibid., deeds by Joshua Fisher, 19 April 1776. The Duck Creek Monthly appended a note to Fisher's manumission deeds: "The following manumissions were executed by a Friend, a Merchant of the City of Philadelphia for Slaves whom he heretofore sold in this our Government & late redeemed by Consideration to their Masters paid and the Slaves manumitted, continuing still to dwell among us, it was thought proper that their Manumission be admitted to Record among the Manumissions of this Meeting."

29. LPPN, petition dated 28 Dec. 1785; MDCM, vol. 2, 24 Feb. 1787.

30. SMIP, 18 Aug. 1787; 16 Sept. 1788.

31. Ibid., undated petition by Mariah Cole; Mariah Cole v. Sylvia Sipple,

May 1795, Kent County Court of Common Pleas Appearance Docket, May 1788–1807, DSA.

32. Delaware *Journal of the House of Representatives of the State of Delaware*, 9 Jan. 1801; LPPN, 22 Jan. 1810.

33. LPPN, 1788, 1789; *House Journal*, 20, 22, 27, 30, 31 Jan., 3 Feb. 1789; *Laws of the State of Delaware* 2:941–44, passed Feb. 1789.

34. *House Journal*, 24 Jan. 1797.

35. LPPN, 1801.

36. Ibid., 1786, 1791, 1793.

37. Mifflin to John Parrish, May 6, 1792, Cox, Parrish, Wharton Papers, 8:37, HSP.

38. Garrett to William Lloyd Garrison, 5 Dec. 1850, to Samuel May, Jr., 24 Nov. 1863, James A. McGowan, *Station Master on the Underground Railroad: The Life and Letters of Thomas Garrett* (Moylan, Pa., 1977), pp. 48–69, 111, 151–52.

39. Garrett to Garrison, 5 Dec. 1850, ibid., p. 111.

40. Ibid., p. 127.

41. Garrett to Eliza Wigham, 27 Dec. 1856, ibid., p. 136.

42. Ibid., pp. 79, 131, 151.

43. Garrett to Garrison, 11 Nov. 1854, to May, 24 Nov. 1863, ibid., pp. 113, 151.

44. Garrett to Still, 23 Jan. 1864, ibid., p. 108.

45. 5 April 1870, Thomas Garrett Collection, Friends Historical Library, Swarthmore.

46. Lewis V. Baldwin, *"Invisible" Strands in African Methodism: A History of the African Union Methodist Protest and Union American Methodist Episcopal Churches, 1805–1980* (Metuchen, N.J., 1983), pp. 11–16; Donald G. Mathews, *Slavery and Methodism: A Chapter in American Morality, 1780–1845* (Princeton, N.J., 1965), pp. 3–6.

47. Mathews, *Slavery and Methodism*, pp. 6–10.

48. Ibid., pp. 10–29.

49. William Henry Williams, *The Garden of American Methodism: The Delmarva Peninsula, 1769–1820* (Wilmington, Del., 1984), pp. 161–65.

50. DASO, 18 July 1801.

51. Manumissions, deeds by Joseph Emmall, 20 Oct. 1787, William Armor, 31 Jan. 1800.

52. LPPN, 1817.

53. DASO, 28 April 1804.

54. Monte A. Calvert, "The Abolition Society of Delaware, 1801–1807," *Delaware History* 10 (1962): 295–301.

55. Ibid.; Thomas Collins to Benjamin Franklin, 16 April 1788, PAS Papers, Correspondence, Incoming, 1788, HSP; LPPN, 1788; ACPA, 1, Minutes of the 1795 Convention.

56. LPPN, 1788; ACPA, Minutes of Jan. 1795, and Jan. 1796.

57. Entry of 2 May 1794, PAS, General Meeting Minutes, 1787–97, HSP; petition dated 16 Dec. 1799, Slavery and Abolition Petitions, Delaware folder 1, HSP; Minutes of ACPA, May 1797.

58. Calvert, "Abolition Society of Delaware"; Minutes of ACPA, June 1801.

59. LPPN, 1801.

60. DASO, 18 July 1801.

61. Ibid.

62. Minutes of ACPA, June 1801.

63. DASM, 4, 16 Aug., 16 Dec. 1806.

64. Ibid., 23 Dec. 1802, 20 June 1803.

65. Minutes of ACPA, Aug. 1817.

66. Ibid., Oct. 1823.

67. See Berlin and Hoffman, *Slavery and Freedom in the Age of the American Revolution;* Robin Blackburn, *The Overthrow of Colonial Slavery, 1776–1848* (London, 1988), pp. 109–30; David Brion Davis, *The Problem of Slavery in the Age of Revolution, 1770–1823* (Ithaca, N.Y., 1975); Duncan J. MacLeod, *Slavery, Race, and the American Revolution* (London, 1974); Gary B. Nash, *Race and Revolution* (Madison, Wis., 1991); Arthur Zilversmit, *The First Emancipation: The Abolition of Slavery in the North* (Chicago, 1967).

68. *Delaware Gazette,* 5 Sept. 1789.

69. Ibid., 12, 19 Sept., 7 Oct. 1789.

70. Ibid., 26 Sept., 7, 24 Oct. 1789.

71. Ibid., 23 Sept. 1789.

72. Ibid., 24 Oct. 1789.

73. Davis, *Problem of Slavery in the Age of Revolution,* pp. 262–73.

74. *Delaware Gazette,* 26, 30 Sept. 1789.

75. Manumissions, deeds by Anna White, 18 March 1790, Sarah Brown, 10 July 1780, Benjamin Yoe, 1 Nov. 1789, James Scotton, 27 Dec. 1799, Richard Cooper, 28 June 1816.

76. Q-16, deed by America Rogers, 1803; Manumissions, deeds by Thomas Marim, March 1827, Elizabeth Orrell, 12 Feb. 1849, Thomas Parker, 1812.

77. Allen v. Negro Sarah et al., in Samuel M. Harrington, *Reports of the Cases Argued and Adjudged in the Superior Court of Errors and Appeals of the State of Delaware,* 5 vols. (Dover Del., 1837), 2:434–40.

78. Harrington, *Reports* 3:551–53; SMIP, May 1792, Dec. 1794.

79. SMIP, 18 April 1851.

80. Menard, "Tobacco Industry in the Chesapeake Colonies."

81. See Clemens, *Atlantic Economy and Colonial Maryland's Eastern Shore;* Carville V. Earle, "A Staple Interpretation of Slavery and Free Labor," *Geographical Review* 68 (1978): 51–65; Kulikoff, *Tobacco and Slaves;* Edward C. Papenfuse, "Planter Behavior and Economic Opportunity in a Staple Economy," *Agricultural History* 46 (1972): 306.

82. Clemens, *Atlantic Economy,* pp. 168–205.

83. R. O. Bausman and J. A. Munroe, eds., "James Tilton's Notes of the Agriculture of Delaware in 1788," *Agricultural History* 20 (1946): 180–83; Christopher D. Ebeling, Manuscript History of Delaware, HSP, pp. 47–49.

84. Bausman and Munroe, "James Tilton's Notes."

85. *Delaware Gazette,* 15 May 1790, 31 March, 19 Dec. 1826.

86. Earle, "Staple Interpretation of Slavery and Free Labor."

87. Fields, *Slavery and Freedom on the Middle Ground,* pp. 1–22.

88. SMIP, 24 Dec. 1794, 3 May 1796; Negro Isaac v. Ferguson, in Helen T. Catterall, *Judicial Cases concerning American Slavery and the Negro,* 5 vols. (Washington, D.C., 1956), 4:217.

89. Apprentices and Indentures, petition by Richard Cooper, May 1800.

90. Ibid., petitions by Richard Lockwood, May 1811, John White, Aug. 1811.

91. Ibid., 1 June 1825.

### 3. AT THE MARGIN OF FREEDOM

1. Munroe, *History of Delaware,* pp. 53–57.

2. U.S. Bureau of the Census, Manuscript Returns for Delaware, 1800, 1810.

3. H. Clay Reed, "Lincoln's Compensated Emancipation Plan and Its Relations to Delaware," *Delaware Notes* 7 (1931): 31.

4. Williams, *Garden of American Methodism,* pp. 161–65.

5. Ibid., pp. 42–49.

6. Munroe, *Colonial Delaware,* pp. 189–90; Williams, *Garden of American Methodism,* pp. 163–65.

7. John A. Munroe, "The Philadelawareans: A Study in the Relations between Philadelphia and Delaware in the Late Eighteenth Century," *Pennsylvania Magazine of History and Biography* 69 (1945): 128–49.

8. Munroe, *Colonial Delaware,* p. 187.

9. DCMS, deed by John Dickinson, July 1775; *House Journal,* 29 Oct. 1782; Munroe, *History of Delaware,* p. 98.

10. Munroe, *Colonial Delaware,* pp. 182–92.

11. LPPN, petition from citizens of Sussex County, 1837.

12. Jerry Shields, *The Infamous Patty Cannon in History and Legend* (Dover, Del., 1990); *Delaware Gazette,* 17 Feb. 1826, 10, 17 April 1829.

13. *Laws of the State of Delaware* 2:1093–95 passed June 1793.

14. The State v. Rachel Scott, 1826, Slavery Material, Court Orders to Sell Slaves, 1798–1829, Court of Quarter Sessions, DSA.

15. LPPN, petition of grand jurors of New Castle County, 17 Dec. 1816, read in House of Representatives, 7 Jan. 1817.

16. *Laws of the State of Delaware* 9:400–401, passed Feb. 1841.

17. Comment by Thomas Rodney, 8 Dec. 1797, Brown Collection, HSD.

18. P-15, deed by Spencer Lacey, 5 Dec. 1791; probate of John Fleetwood, 24 Dec. 1794, Sussex County Probate vol. A71, DSA.

19. P-15, deed by Isaac Moore, 6 March 1788; Q-16, deeds by Solomon Moore, 13 Nov. 1797, William Moore, 1797.

20. Manumissions, deed by William Armor, 1 Jan. 1800.

21. Will of Joseph Cannon, Sussex County Probate vol. A63, 1845–46, DSA; Q-16, deed by James Pettyjohn, 11 Sept. 1798.

22. Q-16, deeds by Spencer Phillips, May 1799, Sally and Thaddeus Jackson, 1801.

23. P-15, deed by Barkely Townsend, 1796; B-2, deed by John Willbank, 1792.

24. Deed by James Latimer, 19 Aug. 1793, Slaves Manumitted folder 2, HSD.

25. Manumissions, deed by Edmund Lynch, 1791.

26. Ibid., deed by James Scotton, 27 Dec. 1799; Q-16, deed by Adam Black, 9 April 1804.

27. Q-16, deed by James Miller, Dec. 1803.

28. Ibid., deed by John Marsh, 10 Aug. 1797.

29. Ibid., deeds by Rhoad Shankland, 17 Dec. 1799, Cornl. Paynter, 7 Dec. 1804, Anthony Heaveloe, 1801.

30. Ibid., deed by John Hazzard, 8 Sept. 1802.

31. DCMS, Jan. 1776.

32. Ibid., deeds by Warner Mifflin, 22 Oct. 1774, 9 Jan. 1775, John Dickinson, 22 July 1775.

33. Ibid., May 1775, Jan. 1778; MDCM, vol. 1, Oct. 1776, May 1778.

34. MDCM, vol. 1, Oct. 1776; DCMS, April 1778.

35. Munroe, *Colonial Delaware*, pp. 189–92; deed by Richard Bassett, 3 March 1793, PAS Papers, microfilm edition, reel 21, Manumission Book E, HSP.

36. Q-16, deed by Caleb Rodney, 18 Dec. 1800.

37. Ibid., deed by George Armstrong, 1803.

38. Will of Mary Allfree, 1807–08, New Castle County Probate, DSA.

39. B-2, deed by Margaret Gill, 1789; Q-16, deed by Naomi Bruce, 10 March 1801.

40. Q-16, deeds by Adam Short, 19 Feb. 1803, Joseph Collins, 23 Dec. 1803.

41. Ibid., deeds by Sarah Clarke, 29 May 1799, James Clayton, 30 Aug. 1799; Manumissions, deed by Sarah Hoffecker, 19 July 1816.

42. Q-16, deed by John Maull, 1804.

43. Manumissions, deed by Sarah Brown, 10 July 1780; Q-16, deed by Joseph Collins, 23 Dec. 1803.

44. Compiled from P-15 and Q-16 both for Sussex County. Very few of the surviving record of manumission cover New Castle, thus making an assessment of New Castle indentures impossible.

45. P-15, deed by Richard Green, 1794; Manumissions, deed by Reynear Williams, 6 Aug. 1789.

46. Q-16, deed by John Holland, 1804.

47. Manumissions, deed by Hillary Coudwright, 21 Feb. 1813.

48. Ibid., deed by Samuel Warren, 4 Oct. 1812; Q-16, deed by Jacob Wolfe, 4 July 1803.

49. Q-16, deeds by Samuel Davis, 1 Jan. 1799, Joseph Copes, 27 April 1801.

50. Nash, *Forging Freedom,* pp. 60–65.

51. Ibid.

52. Indentures by Samuel Dickerson, Manumission Book A, p. 85, Book B, pp. 80, 85, 86, 93, 95, 101, 1794, PAS Papers, HSP.

53. Apprentices and Indentures, petition of Joseph Buckmaster, 9 Dec. 1822; indenture by Joseph Ricketts, 12 Oct. 1795, Manumission Book D, pt. 2, pp. 493–94, PAS Papers, HSP.

54. Manumissions, deed by John Taylor, 28 Feb. 1788.

55. Q-16, deed by Wingate Jones, 10 Nov. 1802.

56. F-6, deed by Joseph Fernando, 1728; Harold B. Hancock, "Not Quite Men: The Free Negroes in Delaware in the 1830s," *Civil War History* 17 (1971): 321–31; Q-16, deed by James Dickinson, 20 Aug. 1796.

57. Q-16, deeds by Pemberton and Priscilla Carlisle, 1 March 1801, Burton West, 8 Aug. 1800, Thomas Wilson, 19 March 1800.

58. Deed by Abraham Neels, 21 April 1791, Slavery Material to 1866, Miscellaneous, Petitions to Export Slaves, Birth Certificates, Court Trials, Petitions to Sell Slaves, DSA; B-2, deed by Henry Safford, 28 Sept. 1793.

59. SMIP, 3 May 1796.

60. DASM, 20 June, 1 July 1803, 22 Aug., 4 Sept. 1805.

61. *Delaware Gazette,* 15 Aug. 1789.

62. Billy G. Smith and Richard Wojtowicz, *Blacks Who Stole Themselves: Advertisements for Runaways in the Pennsylvania Gazette, 1728–1790* (Philadelphia; 1989), p. 150.

63. *Delaware Gazette,* 29 May 1790.

64. Smith, *Blacks Who Stole Themselves,* p. 137, 24 May 1780.

65. Ibid., pp. 67, 123, 144–45.

66. Ibid., p. 146.

67. Ibid., p. 88.

68. Ibid., pp. 26–27; *Delaware Gazette,* 24 Oct. 1789.

69. Smith, *Blacks Who Stole Themselves,* p. 25.

70. *House Journal,* 5 Jan. 1810.

71. *Laws of the state of Delaware* 4: 337–40 passed 1 Feb. 1810.

72. *Delaware Gazette,* 9 Aug., 9 Sept. 1825.

73. DASM, 21, 24 Sept., 12 Oct., 9 Nov. 1802, 29 April, 20 June 1803.

### 4. ON THE BANK OF THE RIVER JORDAN

1. Isaac Tindal, n. vs. Daniel Hudson, Harrington, *Reports* 2:442.

2. LPPN, 1849.

3. *Laws of the State of Delaware* 2:884–88, passed 4 Feb. 1787, 6:415–17, passed 28 Jan. 1825.

4. Ibid., 6:582, passed 19 Jan. 1826.

5. Ibid., 9:256–57, passed 15 Feb. 1839, 9:400–401, passed 18 Feb. 1841.

6. LPPN, 1786; *House Journal,* 6 June 1786.

7. *House Journal,* 8 Jan. 1807.

8. *Laws of the State of Delaware* 4:108–13, passed 6 Feb. 1807.

9. Ibid., 4:400–404, passed 28 Jan. 1811.

10. LPPN, 1841.

11. *Laws of the State of Delaware* 10:319–20, 414–16, passed 16, 28 Feb. 1849.

12. Ibid., 12:330–34, passed 18 March 1863.

13. Elisha Proctor, Negro v. The State, Harrington, *Reports* 5:387–88.

14. *Laws of the State of Delaware* 4:467–69, passed 4 Feb. 1811.

15. Ibid., 6:450, passed 5 Feb. 1827, 12:81, passed 26 Feb. 1861.

16. James Newton, "Delaware's Reaction to the Nat Turner Rebellion," *Negro History Bulletin* 38 (1974): 328–29; Hancock, "Not Quite Men," pp. 320–31.

17. LPPN, petition dated 4 Oct. 1831.

18. Ibid., petition dated 25 Nov. 1831, and petition from Kent County dated 1832.

19. *House Journal,* 3 Jan. 1832.

20. *Laws of the State of Delaware* 8:208–10, passed 10 Feb. 1832.

21. LPPN, 1853.

22. Ibid., 1833.

23. Ibid., 1849.

24. Ibid., 1853.

25. Ibid., 1816.

26. *Laws of the State of Delaware,* passed 9 Feb. 1816.

27. Carol Wilson, *Freedom at Risk: The Kidnapping of Free Blacks in America, 1780–1865* (Lexington, Ky., 1994), pp. 9–39.

28. Catterall, *Judicial Cases* 4:213–14.

29. DASP, 19 June, 17 July 1802, 4 April 1817.

30. DASM, 22 Aug., 11 Sept. 1805, 4 Aug. 1806.

31. Ibid., 16 Nov. 1803, 29 Nov. 1816, 14 Jan. 1817.

32. DASP, 9 April, 3 July 1818.

33. DASM, 22 Aug. 1805, 23 Dec. 1802, 29 March 1803.

34. ACPA, Report of the Delaware Abolition Society, 1801.

35. DASM, 16 Jan., 9 Nov. 1802; DASP, 16 Jan., 17 April 1802.

36. DASP, 28 Jan. 1804.

37. Ibid., 5 Jan. 1805.

38. Ibid., 27 Jan. 1805.

39. Ibid., 19 Sept. 1807, 16 Jan 1808.

40. Ibid., 21 Jan. 1809.

41. Ibid., 15 April 1809; ACPA, 4 Jan. 1809.

42. LPPN, Memorial of African School Society, 10 Jan. 1815.

43. ACPA, 9 Jan. 1815.

44. LPPN, Memorial of the African School Society, 1815.

45. DASP, 2 May 1817.

46.

LPPN, Memorial of the African School Society, 1824.

47. Ibid., Memorial of the African School Society, 1843.

48. Ibid., petitions from the African School Society and from "32 Citizens of Wilmington," 1847; entry of 15 March 1847, Female African School Society, Minute Book, 1839–53, HSP.

49. McGowan, *Station Master,* p. 128.

50. ACPA, Oct. 1826, Oct. 1827.

51. U.S. Bureau of the Census, Manuscript Returns for Delaware, 1850, 1860. In 1850, 80 out of 187 free black schoolchildren lived in Wilmington, as did 163 out of 250 in 1860.

52. Ibid.

53. Pauline A. Young, "The Negro in Delaware, Past and Present" in *Delaware: A History of the First State,* ed. H. Clay Reed, 2 vols. (New York, 1947), 2:583–88.

### 5. CARRYING THEIR OWN WEIGHT

1. LPPN, petition of citizens of Kent County, 1833, petition of free blacks, 1841.

2. Ibid., petition of free blacks, 1849.

3. Apprentices and Indentures, petitions by John Miller, 14 Aug. 1830, Henry Miller, 3 Jan. 1848, Kitty Manlove, 17 July 1848.

4. Ibid., petitions by George W. Rap, 31 July 1830, Azail Johnson, 2 July 1829.

5. Nash, *Forging Freedom,* pp. 137–43.

6. *Laws of the State of Delaware* 10:414–16, passed 28 Feb. 1849.

7. U.S. Bureau of the Census, Manuscript Returns for Delaware, 1850, 1860.

8. Ibid. The census counted 474 free black laborers in the city of Wilmington in 1850.

9. Sussex County Assessment Lists, Broadkill Hundred, 1844, DSA.

10. Ibid., 1804, 1828, 1836.

11. Harold B. Hancock, "William Yates's Letter of 1837: Slavery and Colored People in Delaware," *Delaware History* 14 (1971): 205–16.

12. Kent County Assessment Lists, Little Creek Hundred, 1804, DSA; Hancock, "William Yates's Letter of 1837."

13. U.S. Bureau of the Census, Manuscript Returns for Delaware, 1850.

14. Ibid., 1850, 1860.

15. Ibid.

16. Ibid.

17. Ibid.

18. LPPN, 1823, 1825; *House Journal*, 9 Jan. 1823, 6, 14 Jan. 1825.

19. LPPN, 1830; *House Journal*, 5, 12 Jan. 1830.

20. Williams, *Garden of American Methodism*, pp. 111–19, 143–46.

21. See E. Franklin Frazier, *The Negro Church in America* (New York, 1974); Charles H. Wesley, *Richard Allen, Apostle of Freedom* (Washington, D.C., 1935); Carol V. George, *Segregated Sabbaths: Richard Allen and the Rise of Independent Black Churches, 1760–1840* (New York, 1973); Nash, *Forging Freedom*, pp. 109–33.

22. Nash, *Forging Freedom*, pp. 67–70, 95–99.

23. Baldwin, *Invisible Strands in African Methodism*, pp. 38–41.

24. Williams, *Garden of American Methodism*, pp. 111–19, 143–46; Baldwin, *Invisible Strands in African Methodism*, pp. 37–69.

25. Williams, *Garden of American Methodism*, p. 116; Lewis V. Baldwin, *The Mark of a Man: Peter Spencer and the African Union Methodist Tradition* (Lanham, Md., 1987), pp. 13–15.

26. John D.C. Hanna, ed., *The Centennial Services of Asbury Methodist Episcopal Church*, (Wilmington, Del., 1889), pp. 172–73; Numbers 33:35–36, 34:2–3; Baldwin, *Mark of a Man*, p. 12.

27. Baldwin, *Mark of a Man*, pp. 13–15.

28. Ibid.; Baldwin, *Invisible Strands in African Methodism*, pp. 41–45.

29. Baldwin, *Mark of a Man*, pp. 16, 75.

30. Williams, *Garden of American Methodism*, p. 116.

31. Baldwin, *Invisible Strands in African Methodism*, pp. 55–61.

32. *Delaware Gazette*, 14 Oct. 1823, 27 Jan. 1824.

33. LPPN, Memorial of the Wilmington Union Colonization Society, 1827; *House Journal*, 11 Jan. 1827.

34. LPPN, petition of sundry persons in relation to the colonization society, 1827; *House Journal*, 11 Jan. 1827.

35. *Delaware Gazette*, 21 Feb. 1826.

36. *House Journal*, 15 Jan. 1827; *Laws of the State of Delaware* 7:87, passed 3 Feb. 1827.

37. Ibid.

38. William Lloyd Garrison, *Thoughts on African Colonization* (New York, 1968), pt. 2, p. 36.

39. Ibid., pp. 36–40.

### 6. "A GOVERNMENT OF WHITE MEN FOR THE BENEFIT OF WHITE MEN"

1. *Senate Journal*, 10 Jan. 1866.

2. Munroe, *Colonial Delaware*, pp. 187–88.

3. *House Journal*, 24 Jan. 1797.

4. Ibid., 21–23 Jan. 1805.

5. Ibid., 15 Jan. 1812.

6. Ibid., 25, 29 Jan., 2, 7 Feb. 1822.

7. Ibid., 7, 10, 22 Jan. 1823; *Senate Journal*, 23 Jan. 1823.

8. *House Journal*, 3, 4, 11 Feb. 1825, 7, 16 Jan., 2, 9 Feb. 1826, 9, 25 Jan., 6 Feb. 1827.

9. Ibid., 24, 25 Jan. 1839; LPPN, petition from the women of Wilmington, 1839.

10. *House Journal*, 22 Jan. 1845, 2, 18, 19, 24 Feb. 1847, 12, 23 Jan. 1849.

11. LPPN, 1803.

12. *House Journal*, 26, 27 Jan. 1803.

13. Ibid., 2 Feb. 1847.

14. Ibid., 18, 19 Feb. 1847.

15. *Senate Journal*, 20 Feb. 1847; *House Journal*, 24 Feb. 1847.

16. *Laws of the State of Delaware* 10:231, passed 25 Feb. 1847; *Delaware Gazette*, 9 March 1849.

17. Harold B. Hancock, *Delaware during the Civil War: A Political History* (Wilmington, Del., 1961), pp. 38–48; *House Journal*, 3 Jan. 1861; *Senate Journal*, 3 Jan. 1861.

18. E. B. Long and Barbara Long, *The Civil War Day by Day: An Almanac, 1861–1865* (New York, 1971), p. 143; John G. Nicolay and John Hay, eds., *Abraham Lincoln: Complete Works*, 2 vols. (New York, 1907), 2:91.

19. Reed, "Lincoln's Compensated Emancipation Plan," pp. 27–78; Hancock, *Delaware during the Civil War*, pp. 106–7; *House Journal*, 5 Feb. 1862.

20. Hancock, *Delaware during the Civil War*, p. 109.

21. *Delaware Gazette*, 6 June 1862.

22. U.S. Bureau of the Census, Manuscript Returns for Delaware, 1850, 1860; Reed, "Lincoln's Compensated Emancipation Plan."

23. Reed, "Lincoln's Compensated Emancipation Plan," pp. 37–39. According to the 1860 census, Short owned three slaves and not eight as reported by Reed.

24. Ibid., pp. 44–45.

25. *Delaware State Journal and Statesman*, 4 Feb. 1862; Reed, "Lincoln's Compensated Emancipation Plan," pp. 39–69.

26. *House Journal*, 5, 6 Feb. 1862.

27. *Delaware Gazette*, 9 Jan. 1863.

28. Ibid., 11 Feb., 17 June 1862.

29. *Congressional Globe*, 11 March 1862.

30. Reed, "Lincoln's Compensated Emancipation Plan," pp. 42–46; *Congressional Globe*, 12 Feb. 1863.

31. *Congressional Globe*, 30 Jan. 1863.

32. Ibid., 11 March, 12 May 1862.

33. *House Journal*, 5, 6 Feb. 1862; *Delaware Gazette*, 13 June 1862.

34. *Delaware State Journal and Statesman*, 7 Feb. 1862.

35. *Congressional Globe,* 11 March, 12 May 1862.

36. Ibid., 9 July 1862.

37. *Delaware Gazette,* 6 June 1862.

38. Ibid., 23 Jan. 1863.

39. *Congressional Globe,* 12 May 1862.

40. *Congressional Globe,* 3 April 1862; *Senate Journal,* 13 June 1865.

41. *Delaware Gazette,* 9, 23 Jan. 1863.

42. Ibid., 6, 13 June 1862; H. Clay Reed, "Lincoln's Compensated Emancipation Plan."

43. *Delaware Gazette,* 13 June 1862.

44. *Congressional Globe,* 3 April 1862.

45. *Delaware Gazette,* 19 Aug. 1862; Reed, "Lincoln's Compensated Emancipation Plan," pp. 50–71.

46. *Congressional Globe,* 11 March 1862.

47. *Delaware Gazette,* 23 Jan. 1863.

48. Hancock, *Delaware during the Civil War,* pp. 1–37; Reed, "Lincoln's Compensated Emancipation Plan."

49. Hancock, *Delaware during the Civil War,* pp. 12–37. The origin of the People's party in Delaware dates to 1858. Membership included former Whigs and Know-Nothings, and its primary base of support was New Castle County. It disbanded after 1860, and the majority of its members drifted to the Republican party.

50. Reed, "Lincoln's Compensated Emancipation Plan"; *House Journal,* 5, 6 Feb. 1862.

51. Reed, "Lincoln's Compensated Emancipation Plan," pp. 27–78.

52. Nicolay and Hay, *Abraham Lincoln* 2:91, 132–36, 204–5; James Ford Rhodes, *History of the Civil War, 1861–1865* (New York, 1930), pp. 149–51.

53. Hancock, *Delaware during the Civil War,* pp. 114–21.

54. *Delawarean,* 6 Sept. 1862; *Delaware Journal,* 22 Aug. 1862; Hancock, *Delaware during the Civil War,* pp. 114–21.

55. Hancock, *Delaware during the Civil War,* pp. 119–28.

56. Ibid., pp. 119–21.

57. *Delaware Gazette,* 15 July 1862.

58. Hancock, *Delaware during the Civil War,* pp. 114–28.

59. Ibid., pp. 122–28.

60. Ibid., pp. 137–38.

61. *House Journal,* 9, 11 Aug. 1864.

62. Ira Berlin et al., eds., *Freedom: A Documentary History of Emancipation, 1861–1867,* ser. 1, vol. 1, *The Destruction of Slavery* (Cambridge, Mass., 1985), pp. 46–48; and *Freedom: A Documentary History of Emancipation, 1861–1867,* ser. 2, *The Black Military Experience* (Cambridge, Mass., 1982), pp. 11–12.

63. Hancock, *Delaware during the Civil War,* p. 140.

64. Ibid., pp. 122–41.

65. Ibid., pp. 146–53; Anna Ferris Diaries, entry of 12 Nov. 1864, Ferris

Collection, Friends Historical Library, Swarthmore; Harold B. Hancock, "The Civil War Diaries of Anna M. Ferris," *Delaware History* 9 (1961): 221–64.

66. Hancock, *Delaware during the Civil War,* pp. 146–53.

67. *Congressional Globe,* 11 Jan. 1865.

68. Ferris Diaries, Jan. 1865; Hancock, "Civil War Diaries of Anna M. Ferris," pp. 257–58.

69. *Senate Journal,* 3 Jan. 1865; *Delaware Gazette,* 6 Jan. 1865.

70. *Delawarean,* 23 Dec. 1865.

71. *Congressional Globe,* 21 Dec. 1865.

72. Ibid., 31 March, 8 April 1864.

73. *Senate Journal,* 13 June 1865, 10 Jan. 1866.

74. Ibid., 8 Feb. 1865.

EPILOGUE

1. *House Journal,* 31 Jan., 6 Feb. 1901; *Senate Journal,* 30, 31 Jan., 5, 6 Feb. 1901.

2. Munroe, *History of Delaware,* p. 150; Harold C. Livesay, "The Reconstruction Era: Delaware Blacks, 1865–1915," in *Readings in Delaware History,* ed. Carol E. Hoffecker (Newark, Del., 1973), pp. 121–32.

3. Munroe, *History of Delaware,* pp. 150–53; Livesay, "Reconstruction Era," pp. 127–28.

4. Livesay, "Reconstruction Era," p. 128.

5. Ibid., pp. 128–29; Munroe, *History of Delaware,* pp. 151–53.

6. Livesay, "Reconstruction Era," pp. 130–31; Munroe, *History of Delaware,* pp. 173–80; Hoffecker, *Delaware,* pp. 187–89.

7. Hoffecker, *Delaware,* pp. 187–89; Munroe, *History of Delaware,* pp. 156–72; Livesay, "Reconstruction Era," pp. 130–31.

8. Henry C. Conrad, *History of the State of Delaware,* 3 vols. (Lancaster, Pa., 1908), 1:249–50.

# Index

## Carter G. Woodson Institute Series in Black Studies

# A House Divided

*Slavery and Emancipation*
*in Delaware, 1635–1865*

*Carter G. Woodson Institute*

*Series in Black Studies*

ARMSTEAD L. ROBINSON

*General Editor*